C++ Data Structures and Algorithms

Learn how to write efficient code to build scalable and robust applications in C++

Wisnu Anggoro

BIRMINGHAM - MUMBAI

C++ Data Structures and Algorithms

Copyright © 2018 Packt Publishing

All rights reserved. No part of this book may be reproduced, stored in a retrieval system, or transmitted in any form or by any means, without the prior written permission of the publisher, except in the case of brief quotations embedded in critical articles or reviews.

Every effort has been made in the preparation of this book to ensure the accuracy of the information presented. However, the information contained in this book is sold without warranty, either express or implied. Neither the author, nor Packt Publishing or its dealers and distributors, will be held liable for any damages caused or alleged to have been caused directly or indirectly by this book.

Packt Publishing has endeavored to provide trademark information about all of the companies and products mentioned in this book by the appropriate use of capitals. However, Packt Publishing cannot guarantee the accuracy of this information.

Commissioning Editor: Richa Tripathi
Acquisition Editor: Chaitanya Nair
Content Development Editor: Lawrence Veigas
Technical Editor: Supriya Thabe
Copy Editor: Safis Editing
Project Coordinator: Prajakta Naik
Proofreader: Safis Editing
Indexer: Aishwarya Gangawane
Graphics: Jisha Chirayil
Production Coordinator: Arvindkumar Gupta

First published: April 2018

Production reference: 1240418

Published by Packt Publishing Ltd.
Livery Place
35 Livery Street
Birmingham
B3 2PB, UK.

ISBN 978-1-78883-521-3

www.packtpub.com

`mapt.io`

Mapt is an online digital library that gives you full access to over 5,000 books and videos, as well as industry leading tools to help you plan your personal development and advance your career. For more information, please visit our website.

Why subscribe?

- Spend less time learning and more time coding with practical eBooks and Videos from over 4,000 industry professionals

- Improve your learning with Skill Plans built especially for you

- Get a free eBook or video every month

- Mapt is fully searchable

- Copy and paste, print, and bookmark content

PacktPub.com

Did you know that Packt offers eBook versions of every book published, with PDF and ePub files available? You can upgrade to the eBook version at `www.PacktPub.com` and as a print book customer, you are entitled to a discount on the eBook copy. Get in touch with us at `service@packtpub.com` for more details.

At `www.PacktPub.com`, you can also read a collection of free technical articles, sign up for a range of free newsletters, and receive exclusive discounts and offers on Packt books and eBooks.

Contributors

About the author

Wisnu Anggoro is a Microsoft Certified Professional in C# programming and an experienced C/C++ developer. He has been programming since junior high school (about 20 years ago) and started developing computer applications using the BASIC language in MS-DOS. He has a lot of experience with smart card, desktop, and web application programming.

He is currently a senior smart card software engineer at CIPTA, an Indonesian company that specializes in the innovation and technology of smart cards.

I would like to thank God, whose blessings have made me who I am today. My wife, Vivin, who has supported me to achieve all my dreams. To my beloved sons, Olav and Oliver, who are very naughty sometimes but never fail to make me happy every day. To my parents for their inspiration.

Also, I would like to show my gratitude to Benediktus Dwi Desiyanto, my mentor and superior at CIPTA, who always helped me develop my skillsets.

About the reviewer

Mark Elston is a software engineer at an automated test equipment firm working primarily in IC and mobile device testing. His 30 years of experience include developing aircraft and missile simulations for the Air Force and Navy, hardware control systems for NASA, and tester operating systems for commercial products. He has also developed several Android applications for fun. His latest passion is delving into the world of functional programming and design.

I would like to thank my wife for her understanding when I had a chapter to finish reviewing. I would also like to thank the Packt team for giving me the opportunity to work with them on this project. It has been enlightening and entertaining. Finally, I would like to thank the author for taking my comments into account. It is a pleasure to be part of a project where your inputs are valued.

Packt is searching for authors like you

If you're interested in becoming an author for Packt, please visit authors.packtpub.com and apply today. We have worked with thousands of developers and tech professionals, just like you, to help them share their insight with the global tech community. You can make a general application, apply for a specific hot topic that we are recruiting an author for, or submit your own idea.

Table of Contents

Preface

Data structures and algorithms are a must-learn for all programmers and software developers. Learning data structures and algorithms can help us solve problems, not only in programming but also in real life. Many people have found algorithms that solve specific problems. When we have a different problem, we can take advantage of the algorithm to solve it by ourselves.

In this book, we will begin by giving you a basic introduction to data structures and algorithms in C++. We will then move on to learn how to store data in linked lists, arrays, stacks, and so on. We will look at some interesting sorting algorithms such as insertion sort, heap sort, merge sort, which are algorithms every developer should be familiar with. We will also dive into searching algorithms, such as linear search, binary search, interpolation and much more.

By the end of this book, you'll be proficient in the use of data structures and algorithms.

Who this book is for

This book is for developers who would like to learn data structures and algorithms in C++. Basic C++ programming knowledge is recommended but not necessary.

What this book covers

Chapter 1, *Learning Data Structures and Algorithms in C++*, introduces basic C++ programming, including fundamental and advanced data types, controlling code flow, the use of an Integrated Development Environment (IDE), and abstract data types, which will be used in developing data structures. We will also analyze an algorithm using asymptotic analysis, including worst-average-best cases and an explanation of Big Theta, Big-O, Big Omega.

Chapter 2, *Storing Data in Lists and Linked Lists*, explains how to build a linear data type to store data, that is, a list. It also will explain how to use the list data type we built earlier to create another data type, which is a linked list. However, before we build a data type in this chapter, we will be introduced to Node, the fundamental data type required to build a list and linked list.

Chapter 3, *Constructing Stacks and Queues*, covers how to create stack, queue, and deque data types, which are also linear data types. We also explain how to use these three types and when we need to use them.

Chapter 4, *Arranging Data Elements Using a Sorting Algorithm*, talks about sorting elements in a data structure. Here, we will learn how to arrange the order of elements using several sorting algorithms; they are bubble sort, selection sort, insertion sort, merge sort, quick sort, counting sort, and radix sort.

Chapter 5, *Finding out an Element Using Searching Algorithm*, walks us through the process of finding an element in a data structure. By giving a value to the algorithm, we can find out whether or not the value is in the data structure. There are seven sorting algorithms we are going to discuss; they are linear, binary, ternary, interpolation, jump, exponential, and sublist search.

Chapter 6, *Dealing with the String Data Types*, discusses how to construct a string data type in C++ programming. Using a string data type, we can construct several words and then do some fun stuff such as anagrams and palindromes. Also, we will learn about binary string, which contains binary digits only, and subsequent string, which is derived from another string. At last in this chapter, we'll discuss using pattern searching to find out a specific short string in a large string.

Chapter 7, *Building a Hierarchical Tree Structure*, introduces the tree data structure, using which we can construct a tree-like data type. Using the tree data structure, we can develop a binary search tree; we can easily search any element in the tree using binary search algorithm. The binary search tree we have built can be also balanced to prevent a skewed tree. Also, in this chapter, we are going to implement a priority queue using a binary heap.

Chapter 8, *Associating a Value to a Key in Hash Table*, explains how to design a hash table, which is a data structure that stores an element based on the hash function. A collision might happen in a hash table data structure, so we also discuss how to handle the collision using separate chaining and open addressing techniques.

Chapter 9, *Implementation of Algorithms in Real Life*, elaborates some algorithm paradigms and implements them in the real world. There are six algorithm paradigms to discuss in this chapter; they are greedy algorithms, Divide and Conquer algorithms, dynamic programming, Brute-force algorithms, randomized algorithms, and backtracking algorithms.

To get the most out of this book

To get through this book and successfully complete all the source code examples, you will need the following specifications:

- Desktop PC or Notebook with Windows, Linux, or macOS
- GNU GCC v5.4.0 or above
- Code Block IDE v17.12 (for Windows and Linux OS) or Code Block IDE v13.12 (for macOS)

Download the example code files

You can download the example code files for this book from your account at www.packtpub.com. If you purchased this book elsewhere, you can visit www.packtpub.com/support and register to have the files emailed directly to you.

You can download the code files by following these steps:

1. Log in or register at www.packtpub.com.
2. Select the **SUPPORT** tab.
3. Click on **Code Downloads & Errata**.
4. Enter the name of the book in the **Search** box and follow the onscreen instructions.

Once the file is downloaded, please make sure that you unzip or extract the folder using the latest version of:

- WinRAR/7-Zip for Windows
- Zipeg/iZip/UnRarX for Mac
- 7-Zip/PeaZip for Linux

The code bundle for the book is also hosted on GitHub at https://github.com/PacktPublishing/CPP-Data-Structures-and-Algorithms. We also have other code bundles from our rich catalog of books and videos available at https://github.com/PacktPublishing/. Check them out!

Download the color images

We also provide a PDF file that has color images of the screenshots/diagrams used in this book. You can download it here: https://www.packtpub.com/sites/default/files/ downloads/CPPDataStructuresandAlgorithms_ColorImages.

Conventions used

There are a number of text conventions used throughout this book.

CodeInText: Indicates code words in text, database table names, folder names, filenames, file extensions, pathnames, dummy URLs, user input, and Twitter handles. Here is an example: "After finishing the wizard, we will have a new project with a main.cpp file."

A block of code is set as follows:

```
// in_out.cpp
#include <iostream>

int main ()
{
  int i;
  std::cout << "Please enter an integer value: ";
  std::cin >> i;
  std::cout << "The value you entered is " << i;
  std::cout << "\n";
  return 0;
}
```

When we wish to draw your attention to a particular part of a code block, the relevant lines or items are set in bold:

```
class Node
{
public:
    T Value;
    Node<T> * Next;

    Node(T value) : Value(value), Next(NULL) {}
};
```

Any command-line input or output is written as follows:

```
g++ simple.cpp
```

Bold: Indicates a new term, an important word, or words that you see onscreen. For example, words in menus or dialog boxes appear in the text like this. Here is an example: "We can create a new project by clicking on the **File** menu, then clicking **New**, and then selecting **Project**."

Warnings or important notes appear like this.

Tips and tricks appear like this.

Get in touch

Feedback from our readers is always welcome.

General feedback: Email `feedback@packtpub.com` and mention the book title in the subject of your message. If you have questions about any aspect of this book, please email us at `questions@packtpub.com`.

Errata: Although we have taken every care to ensure the accuracy of our content, mistakes do happen. If you have found a mistake in this book, we would be grateful if you would report this to us. Please visit `www.packtpub.com/submit-errata`, selecting your book, clicking on the Errata Submission Form link, and entering the details.

Piracy: If you come across any illegal copies of our works in any form on the Internet, we would be grateful if you would provide us with the location address or website name. Please contact us at `copyright@packtpub.com` with a link to the material.

If you are interested in becoming an author: If there is a topic that you have expertise in and you are interested in either writing or contributing to a book, please visit `authors.packtpub.com`.

Reviews

Please leave a review. Once you have read and used this book, why not leave a review on the site that you purchased it from? Potential readers can then see and use your unbiased opinion to make purchase decisions, we at Packt can understand what you think about our products, and our authors can see your feedback on their book. Thank you!

For more information about Packt, please visit packtpub.com.

1
Learning Data Structures and Algorithms in C++

In this first chapter, we are going to build the solid foundations so we can go through the following chapters easily. The topics we are going to discuss in this chapter are:

- Creating, building, and running a simple C++ program
- Constructing an abstract data type to make a user-defined data type
- Leveraging the code with C++ templates and the **Standard Template Library** (**STL**)
- Analyzing the complexity of algorithms to measure the performance of the code

Technical requirements

To follow along with this chapter including the source code, we require the following:

- A desktop PC or Notebook with Windows, Linux, or macOS
- GNU GCC v5.4.0 or above
- Code::Block IDE v17.12 (for Windows and Linux OS) or Code::Block IDE v13.12 (for macOS)
- You will find the code files on GitHub—`https://github.com/PacktPublishing/CPP-Data-Structures-and-Algorithms`

Introduction to basic C++

Before we go through the data structures and algorithms in C++, we need to have a strong, fundamental understanding of the language itself. In this section, we are going to build a simple program, build it, and then run it. We are also going to discuss the fundamental and advanced data types, and before we move on to algorithm analysis, we are going to discuss control flow in this section.

Creating your first code in C++

In C++, the code is executed from the `main()` function first. The function itself is a collection of statements to perform a specific task. As a result of this, a program in C++ has to contain at least one function named `main()`. The following code is the simplest program in C++ that will be successfully compiled and run:

```
int main()
{
    return 0;
}
```

Suppose the preceding code is saved as a `simple.cpp` file. We can compile the code using the g++ compiler by running the following compiling command on the console from the active directory where the `simple.cpp` file is placed:

g++ simple.cpp

If no error message appears, the output file will be generated automatically. If we run the preceding compiling command on a Windows console, we will get a file named `a.exe`. However, if we run the command on Bash shells, such as Linux or macOS, we will get a file named `a.out`.

We can specify the output file name using the `-o` option followed by the desired filename. For instance, the following compiling command will produce the output file named `simple.out`:

g++ simple.cpp -o simple.out

Indeed, when we run the output file (by typing a and then pressing *Enter* on a Windows console or by typing ./a.out and then pressing *Enter* on Bash shell), we won't see anything on the console window. This is because we don't print anything to the console yet. To make our simple.cpp file meaningful, let's refactor the code so that it can receive the input data from the user and then print the data back to the user. The refactored code should look as follows:

```cpp
// in_out.cpp
#include <iostream>

int main ()
{
    int i;
    std::cout << "Please enter an integer value: ";
    std::cin >> i;
    std::cout << "The value you entered is " << i;
    std::cout << "\n";
    return 0;
}
```

As we can see in the preceding code, we appended several lines of code so that the program can print to the console and the user can give an input to the program. Initially, the program displays text that asks the user to input an integer number. After the user types the desired number and presses *Enter*, the program will print that number. We also defined a new variable named i of the int data type. This variable is used to store data in an integer data format (we will talk about variables and data types in the upcoming section).

Suppose we save the preceding code as in_out.cpp; we can compile it using the following command:

```
g++ in_out.cpp
```

If we then run the program, we will get the following output on the console (I chose the number 3 in this example):

```
Please enter an integer value: 3
The value you entered is 3
```

Now, we know that to print text to the console, we use the `std::cout` command, and to give some inputs to the program, we use the `std::cin` command. In the `in_out.cpp` file, we also see `#include <iostream>` at the beginning of the file. It's used to tell the compiler where to find the implementation of the `std::cout` and `std::cin` commands since their implementation is stated in the `iostream` header file.

And at the very beginning of the file, we can see that the line begins with double slashes (`//`). This means that the line won't be considered as code, so the compiler will ignore it. It's used to comment or mark an action in the code so that other programmers can understand our code.

Enhancing code development experience with IDE

So far, we have been able to create a C++ code, compile the code, and run the code. However, it will be boring if we have to compile the code using the Command Prompt and then execute the code afterwards. To ease our development process, we will use an **integrated development environment** (**IDE**) so that we can compile and run the code with just a click. You can use any C++ IDE available on the market, either paid or free. However, I personally chose Code::Blocks IDE since it's free, open source, and cross-platform so it can run on Windows, Linux, and macOS machines. You can find the information about this IDE, such as how to download, install, and use it on its official website at `http://www.codeblocks.org/`.

Actually, we can automate the compiling process using a toolchain such as Make or CMake. However, this needs further explanation, and since this book is intended to discuss data structures and algorithms, the toolchain explanation will increase the total pages of the book, and so we will not discuss this here. In this case, the use of IDE is the best solution to automate the compiling process since it actually accesses the toolchain as well.

After installing Code::Blocks IDE, we can create a new project by clicking on the **File** menu, then clicking **New**, and then selecting **Project**. A new window will appear and we can select the desired project type. For most examples in this book, we will use the **Console Application** as the project type. Press the **Go** button to continue.

On the upcoming window, we can specify the language, which is C++, and then define the project name and destination location (I named the project `FirstApp`). After finishing the wizard, we will have a new project with a `main.cpp` file containing the following code:

```
#include <iostream>

using namespace std;

int main()
{
    cout << "Hello world!" << endl;
    return 0;
}
```

Now, we can compile and run the preceding code by just clicking the **Build and run** option under the **Build** menu. The following console window will appear:

In the preceding screenshot, we see the console using `namespace std` in the line after the `#include <iostream>` line. The use of this line of code is to tell the compiler that the code uses a `namespace` named `std`. As a result, we don't need to specify the `std::` in every invocation of the `cin` and `cout` commands. The code should be simpler than before.

Defining the variables using fundamental data types

In the previous sample codes, we dealt with the variable (a placeholder is used to store a data element) so that we can manipulate the data in the variable for various operations. In C++, we have to define a variable to be of a specific data type so it can only store the specific type of variable that was defined previously. Here is a list of the fundamental data types in C++. We used some of these data types in the previous example:

- Boolean data type (`bool`), which is used to store two pieces of conditional data only—`true` or `false`

- Character data type (`char`, `wchar_t`, `char16_t`, and `char32_t`), which is used to store a single ASCII character
- Floating point data type (`float`, `double`, and `long double`), which is used to store a number with a decimal
- Integer data type (`short`, `int`, `long`, and `long long`), which is used to store a whole number
- No data (`void`), which is basically a keyword to use as a placeholder where you would normally put a data type to represent *no data*

There are two ways to create a variable—by defining it or by initializing it. Defining a variable will create a variable without deciding upon its initial value. The initializing variable will create a variable and store an initial value in it. Here is the code snippet for how we can define variables:

```
int iVar;
char32_t cVar;
long long llVar;
bool boVar;
```

And here is the sample code snippet of how initializing variables works:

```
int iVar = 100;
char32_t cVar = 'a';
long long llVar = 9223372036854775805;
bool boVar = true;
```

The preceding code snippet is the way we initialize the variables using the **copy initialization** technique. In this technique, we assign a value to the variable using an equals sign symbol (=). Another technique we can use to initialize a variable is the **direct initialization** technique. In this technique, we use parenthesis to assign a value to the variable. The following code snippet uses this technique to initialize the variables:

```
int iVar(100);
char32_t cVar('a');
long long llVar(9223372036854775805);
bool boVar(true);
```

Besides copy initialization and direct initialization techniques, we can use uniform initialization by utilizing curly braces. The following code snippet uses the so-called **brace-initialization** technique to initialize the variables:

```
int iVar{100};
char32_t cVar{'a'};
long long llVar{9223372036854775805};
bool boVar{true};
```

We cannot define a variable with a `void` data type such as void `vVar` because when we define a variable, we have to decide what data type we are choosing so that we can store the data in the variable. If we define a variable as `void`, it means that we don't plan to store anything in the variable.

Controlling the flow of the code

As we discussed earlier, the C++ program is run from the `main()` function by executing each statement one by one from the beginning to the end. However, we can change this path using flow control statements. There are several flow control statements in C++, but we are only going to discuss some of them, since these are the ones that are going to be used often in algorithm design.

Conditional statement

One of the things that can make the flow of a program change is a conditional statement. By using this statement, only the line in the `true` condition will be run. We can use the `if` and `else` keywords to apply this statement.

Let's modify our previous `in_out.cpp` code so that it uses the conditional statement. The program will only decide whether the input number is greater than `100` or not. The code should be as follows:

```
// If.cbp
#include <iostream>

using namespace std;

int main ()
{
    int i;
    cout << "Please enter an integer value: ";
    cin >> i;
```

```
    cout << "The value you entered is ";

    if(i > 100)
        cout << "greater than 100.";
    else
        cout << "equals or less than 100.";

    cout << endl;
    return 0;
}
```

As we can see, we have a pair of the `if` and `else` keywords that will decide whether the input number is greater than `100` or not. By examining the preceding code, only one statement will be executed inside the conditional statement, either the statement under the `if` keyword or the statement under the `else` keyword.

If we build and run the preceding code, we will see the following console window:

From the preceding console window, we can see that the line `std::cout << "equals or less than 100.";` is not executed at all since we have input a number that is greater than `100`.

Also, in the `if...else` condition, we can have more than two conditional statements. We can refactor the preceding code so that it has more than two conditional statements, as follows:

```
// If_ElseIf.cbp
#include <iostream>

using namespace std;

int main ()
{
    int i;
    cout << "Please enter an integer value: ";
    cin >> i;
    cout << "The value you entered is ";

    if(i > 100)
```

```
        cout << "greater than 100.";
    else if(i < 100)
        cout << "less than 100.";
    else
        cout << "equals to 100";

    cout << endl;
    return 0;
}
```

Another conditional statement keyword is `switch`. Before we discuss this keyword, let's create a simple calculator program that can add two numbers. It should also be capable of performing the subtract, multiply, and divide operations. We will use the `if...else` keyword first. The code should be as follows:

```
// If_ElseIf_2.cbp
#include <iostream>

using namespace std;

int main ()
{
  int i, a, b;

  cout << "Operation Mode: " << endl;
  cout << "1. Addition" << endl;
  cout << "2. Subtraction" << endl;
  cout << "3. Multiplication" << endl;
  cout << "4. Division" << endl;
  cout << "Please enter the operation mode: ";
  cin >> i;

  cout << "Please enter the first number: ";
  cin >> a;
  cout << "Please enter the second number: ";
  cin >> b;

  cout << "The result of ";

  if(i == 1)
      cout << a << " + " << b << " is " << a + b;
  else if(i == 2)
      cout << a << " - " << b << " is " << a - b;
  else if(i == 3)
      cout << a << " * " << b << " is " << a * b;
  else if(i == 4)
      cout << a << " / " << b << " is " << a / b;
```

```
    cout << endl;
    return 0;
}
```

As we can see in the preceding code, we have four options that we have to choose from. We use the `if...else` conditional statement for this purpose. The output of the preceding code should be as follows:

```
Terminal
Operation Mode:
1. Addition
2. Subtraction
3. Multiplication
4. Division
Please enter the operation mode: 2
Please enter the first number: 12
Please enter the second number: 4
The result of 12 - 4 is 8

Process returned 0 (0x0)   execution time : 10.009 s
Press ENTER to continue.
```

However, we can use the `switch` keyword as well. The code should be as follows after being refactored:

```cpp
// Switch.cbp
#include <iostream>

using namespace std;

int main ()
{
    int i, a, b;

    cout << "Operation Mode: " << endl;
    cout << "1. Addition" << endl;
    cout << "2. Subtraction" << endl;
    cout << "3. Multiplication" << endl;
    cout << "4. Division" << endl;
    cout << "Please enter the operation mode: ";
    cin >> i;

    cout << "Please enter the first number: ";
    cin >> a;
    cout << "Please enter the second number: ";
    cin >> b;

    cout << "The result of ";
```

```
switch(i)
{
  case 1:
      cout << a << " + " << b << " is " << a + b;
      break;
  case 2:
      cout << a << " - " << b << " is " << a - b;
      break;
  case 3:
      cout << a << " * " << b << " is " << a * b;
      break;
  case 4:
      cout << a << " / " << b << " is " << a / b;
      break;
}

cout << endl;
return 0;
}
```

And if we run the preceding code, we will get the same output compared with the `If_ElseIf_2.cbp` code.

Loop statement

There are several loop statements in C++, and they are `for`, `while`, and `do...while`. The `for` loop is usually used when we know how many iterations we want, whereas `while` and `do...while` will iterate until the desired condition is met.

Suppose we are going to generate ten random numbers between 0 to 100; the `for` loop is the best solution for it since we know how many numbers we need to generate. For this purpose, we can create the following code:

```
// For.cbp
#include <iostream>
#include <cstdlib>
#include <ctime>

using namespace std;

int GenerateRandomNumber(int min, int max)
{
    // static used for efficiency,
    // so we only calculate this value once
    static const double fraction =
```

```
                  1.0 / (static_cast<double>(RAND_MAX) + 1.0);

          // evenly distribute the random number
          // across our range
          return min + static_cast<int>(
              (max - min + 1) * (rand() * fraction));
      }

      int main()
      {
          // set initial seed value to system clock
          srand(static_cast<unsigned int>(time(0)));

          // loop ten times
          for (int i=0; i < 10; ++i)
          {
              cout << GenerateRandomNumber(0, 100) << " ";
          }
          cout << "\n";

          return 0;
      }
```

From the preceding code, we create another function besides `main()`, that is, `GenerateRandomNumber()`. The code will invoke the function ten times using the `for` loop, as we can see in the preceding code. The output we will get should be as follows:

```
Terminal
62 57 7 21 90 11 40 37 70 8

Process returned 0 (0x0)    execution time : 0.034 s
Press ENTER to continue.
```

Back to the others loop statements which we discussed earlier, which are `while` and `do...while` loop. They are quite similar based on their behavior. The difference is when we use the `while` loop, there is a chance the statement inside the loop scope is not run, whereas the statement in the loop scope must be run at least once in the `do...while` loop.

Now, let's create a simple game using those loop statements. The computer will generate a number between 1 to 100, and then the user has to guess what number has been generated by the computer. The program will give a hint to the user just after she or he inputs the guessed number. It will tell the user whether the number is greater than the computer's number or lower than it. If the guessed number matches with the computer's number, the game is over. The code should be as follows:

```cpp
// While.cbp
#include <iostream>
#include <cstdlib>
#include <ctime>

using namespace std;

int GenerateRandomNumber(int min, int max)
{
    // static used for efficiency,
    // so we only calculate this value once
    static const double fraction =
        1.0 / (static_cast<double>(RAND_MAX) + 1.0);

    // evenly distribute the random number
    // across our range
    return min + static_cast<int>(
        (max - min + 1) * (rand() * fraction));
}

int main()
{
    // set initial seed value to system clock
    srand(static_cast<unsigned int>(time(0)));

    // Computer generate random number
    // between 1 to 100
    int computerNumber = GenerateRandomNumber(1, 100);

    // User inputs a guessed number
    int userNumber;
    cout << "Please enter a number between 1 to 100: ";
    cin >> userNumber;

    // Run the WHILE loop
    while(userNumber != computerNumber)
    {
        cout << userNumber << " is ";
        if(userNumber > computerNumber)
            cout << "greater";
```

```
            else
                cout << "lower";
            cout << " than computer's number" << endl;
            cout << "Choose another number: ";
            cin >> userNumber;
        }

        cout << "Yeeaayy.. You've got the number." << endl;
        return 0;
    }
```

From the preceding code, we can see that we have two variables, `computerNumber` and `userNumber`, handling the number that will be compared. There will be a probability that `computerNumber` is equal to `userNumber`. If this happens, the statement inside the `while` loop scope won't be executed at all. The flow of the preceding program can be seen in the following output console screenshot:

We have successfully implemented the `while` loop in the preceding code. Although the `while` loop is similar to the `do...while` loop, as we discussed earlier, we cannot refactor the preceding code by just replacing the `while` loop with the `do...while` loop. However, we can create another game as our example in implementing the `do...while` loop. However, now the user has to choose a number and then the program will guess it. The code should be as follows:

```
// Do-While.cbp
#include <iostream>
#include <cstdlib>
#include <ctime>
```

```cpp
using namespace std;

int GenerateRandomNumber(int min, int max)
{
    // static used for efficiency,
    // so we only calculate this value once
    static const double fraction =
        1.0 / (static_cast<double>(RAND_MAX) + 1.0);

    // evenly distribute the random number
    // across our range
    return min + static_cast<int>(
        (max - min + 1) * (rand() * fraction));
}

int main()
{
    // set initial seed value to system clock
    srand(static_cast<unsigned int>(time(0)));

    char userChar;

    int iMin = 1;
    int iMax = 100;
    int iGuess;

    // Menu display
    cout << "Choose a number between 1 to 100, ";
    cout << "and I'll guess your number." << endl;
    cout << "Press L and ENTER if my guessed number is lower than
     yours";
    cout << endl;
    cout << "Press G and ENTER if my guessed number is greater than
     yours";
    cout << endl;
    cout << "Press Y and ENTER if I've successfully guessed your
     number!";
    cout << endl << endl;

    // Run the DO-WHILE loop
    do
    {
        iGuess = GenerateRandomNumber(iMin, iMax);
        cout << "I guess your number is " << iGuess << endl;
        cout << "What do you think? ";
        cin >> userChar;
        if(userChar == 'L' || userChar == 'l')
            iMin = iGuess + 1;
```

```
        else if(userChar == 'G' || userChar == 'g')
            iMax = iGuess - 1;

    }
    while(userChar != 'Y' && userChar != 'y');

    cout << "Yeeaayy.. I've got your number." << endl;
    return 0;
}
```

As we can see in the preceding code, the program has to guess the user's number at least once, and if it's lucky, the guessed number matches with the user's number, so that we use the `do...while` loop here. When we build and run the code, we will have an output similar to the following screenshot:

In the preceding screenshot, I chose number 56. The program then guessed 81. Since the number is greater than my number, the program guessed another number, which is 28. It then guessed another number based on the hint from me until it found the correct number. The program will leave the `do...while` loop if the user presses y, as we can see in the preceding code.

Leveraging the variable capability using advanced data types

We have discussed the fundamental data type in the previous section. This data type is used in defining or initializing a variable to ensure that the variable can store the selected data type. However, there are other data types that can be used to define a variable. They are **enum** (**enumeration**) and struct.

Enumeration is a data type that has several possible values and they are defined as the constant which is called **enumerators**. It is used to create a collection of constants. Suppose we want to develop a card game using C++. As we know, a deck of playing cards contains 52 cards, which consists of four suits (Clubs, Diamonds, Hearts, and Spades) with 13 elements in each suit. We can notate the card deck as follows:

```
enum CardSuits
{
    Club,
    Diamond,
    Heart,
    Spade
};

enum CardElements
{
    Ace,
    Two,
    Three,
    Four,
    Five,
    Six,
    Seven,
    Eight,
    Nine,
    Ten,
    Jack,
    Queen,
    King
};
```

If we want to apply the preceding enum data types (CardSuits and CardElements), we can use the following variable initialization:

```
CardSuits suit = Club;
CardElements element = Ace;
```

Actually, enums always contain integer constants. The string we put in the enum element is the constant name only. The first element holds a value of 0, except we define another value explicitly. The next elements are in an incremental number from the first element. So, for our preceding CardSuits enum, Club is equal to 0, and the Diamond, Heart, and Spade are 1, 2, and 3, respectively.

Now, let's create a program that will generate a random card. We can borrow the GenerateRandomNumber() function from our previous code. The following is the complete code for this purpose:

```cpp
// Enum.cbp
#include <iostream>
#include <cstdlib>
#include <ctime>

using namespace std;

enum CardSuits
{
    Club,
    Diamond,
    Heart,
    Spade
};

enum CardElements
{
    Ace,
    Two,
    Three,
    Four,
    Five,
    Six,
    Seven,
    Eight,
    Nine,
    Ten,
    Jack,
    Queen,
    King
};

string GetSuitString(CardSuits suit)
{
    string s;
```

```
    switch(suit)
    {
        case Club:
            s = "Club";
            break;
        case Diamond:
            s = "Diamond";
            break;
        case Heart:
            s = "Heart";
            break;
        case Spade:
            s = "Spade";
            break;
    }

    return s;
}

string GetElementString(CardElements element)
{
    string e;

    switch(element)
    {
        case Ace:
            e = "Ace";
            break;
        case Two:
            e = "Two";
            break;
        case Three:
            e = "Three";
            break;
        case Four:
            e = "Four";
            break;
        case Five:
            e = "Five";
            break;
        case Six:
            e = "Six";
            break;
        case Seven:
            e = "Seven";
            break;
        case Eight:
            e = "Eight";
```

```
            break;
        case Nine:
            e = "Nine";
            break;
        case Ten:
            e = "Ten";
            break;
        case Jack:
            e = "Jack";
            break;
        case Queen:
            e = "Queen";
            break;
        case King:
            e = "King";
            break;
    }

    return e;
}

int GenerateRandomNumber(int min, int max)
{
    // static used for efficiency,
    // so we only calculate this value once
    static const double fraction =
        1.0 / (static_cast<double>(RAND_MAX) + 1.0);

    // evenly distribute the random number
    // across our range
    return min + static_cast<int>(
        (max - min + 1) * (rand() * fraction));
}

int main()
{
    // set initial seed value to system clock
    srand(static_cast<unsigned int>(time(0)));

    // generate random suit and element card
    int iSuit = GenerateRandomNumber(0, 3);
    int iElement = GenerateRandomNumber(0, 12);

    CardSuits suit = static_cast<CardSuits>(
        iSuit);
    CardElements element = static_cast<CardElements>(
        iElement);
```

```
cout << "Your card is ";
cout << GetElementString(element);
cout << " of " << GetSuitString(suit) << endl;

return 0;
}
```

From the preceding code, we can see that we can access the `enum` data by using an integer value. However, we have to cast the `int` value so that it can fit the `enum` data by using `static_cast<>`, which is shown as follows:

```
int iSuit = GenerateRandomNumber(0, 3);
int iElement = GenerateRandomNumber(0, 12);

CardSuits suit = static_cast<CardSuits>(iSuit);
CardElements element = static_cast<CardElements>(iElement);
```

If we build and run the code, we will get the following console output:

```
Terminal
Your card is Ten of Diamond

Process returned 0 (0x0)    execution time : 0.011 s
Press ENTER to continue.
```

Another advanced data type we have in C++ is *structs*. It is an aggregate data type which groups multiple individual variables together. From the preceding code, we have the `suit` and `element` variables that can be grouped as follows:

```
struct Cards
{
    CardSuits suit;
    CardElements element;
};
```

If we add the preceding `struct` to our preceding `Enum.cbp` code, we just need to refactor the `main()` function as follows:

```
int main()
{
    // set initial seed value to system clock
    srand(static_cast<unsigned int>(time(0)));

    Cards card;
    card.suit = static_cast<CardSuits>(
        GenerateRandomNumber(0, 3));
```

```
card.element = static_cast<CardElements>(
    GenerateRandomNumber(0, 12));

cout << "Your card is ";
cout << GetElementString(card.element);
cout << " of " << GetSuitString(card.suit) << endl;

return 0;
}
```

If we run the preceding code (you can find the code as `Struct.cbp` in the repository), we will get the same output as `Enum.cbp`.

Developing abstract data types

An **abstract data type** (ADT) is a type that consists of a collection of data and associated operations for manipulating the data. The ADT will only mention the list of operations that can be performed but not the implementation. The implementation itself is hidden, which is why it's called **abstract**.

Imagine we have a DVD player we usually use in our pleasure time. The player has a remote control, too. The remote control has various menu buttons such as ejecting the disc, playing or stopping the video, increasing or decreasing volume, and so forth. Similar to the ADT, we don't have any idea how the player increases the volume when we press the increasing button (similar to the operation in ADT). We just call the increasing operation and then the player does it for us; we do not need to know the implementation of that operation.

Regarding the process flow, we need to take into account the ADT's implement abstraction, information hiding, and encapsulation techniques. The explanation of these three techniques is as follows:

- **Abstraction** is hiding the implementation details of the operations that are available in the ADT
- **Information hiding** is hiding the data which is being affected by that implementation
- **Encapsulation** is grouping all similar data and functions into a group

Applying C++ classes to build user-defined ADTs

Classes are containers for variables and the operations (methods) that will affect the variables. As we discussed earlier, as ADTs implement encapsulation techniques for grouping all similar data and functions into a group, the classes can also be applied to group them. A class has three access control sections for wrapping the data and methods, and they are:

- **Public**: Data and methods can be accessed by any user of the class
- **Protected**: Data and methods can only be accessed by class methods, derived classes, and friends
- **Private**: Data and methods can only be accessed by class methods and friends

Let's go back to the definition of abstraction and information hiding in the previous section. We can implement abstraction by using `protected` or `private` keywords to hide the methods from outside the class and implement the information hiding by using a `protected` or `private` keyword to hide the data from outside the class.

Now, let's build a simple class named `Animal`, as shown in the following code snippet:

```
class Animal
{
private:
    string m_name;

public:
    void GiveName(string name)
    {
        m_name = name;
    }

    string GetName()
    {
        return m_name;
    }
};
```

As we can see in the preceding code snippet, we cannot access the m_name variable directly since we assigned it as `private`. However, we have two `public` methods to access the variable from the inside class. The `GiveName()` methods will modify the m_name value, and the `GetName()` methods will return the m_name value. The following is the code to consume the `Animal` class:

```cpp
// Simple_Class.cbp
#include <iostream>

using namespace std;

class Animal
{
private:
    string m_name;

public:
    void GiveName(string name)
    {
        m_name = name;
    }

    string GetName()
    {
        return m_name;
    }
};

int main()
{
    Animal dog = Animal();
    dog.GiveName("dog");

    cout << "Hi, I'm a " << dog.GetName() << endl;

    return 0;
}
```

In the preceding code, we created a variable named `dog` of the type `Animal`. Since then, the `dog` has the ability that `Animal` has, such as invoking the `GiveName()` and `GetName()` methods. The following is the window we should see if we build and run the code:

```
⊗⊖⊡  Terminal
Hi, I'm a dog

Process returned 0 (0x0)    execution time : 0.012 s
Press ENTER to continue.
```

Now, we can say that `Animal` ADT has two functions, and they are `GiveName(string name)` and `GetName()`.

After discussing simple class, you might see that there's a similarity between structs and classes. They both actually have similar behaviors. The differences are, however, that structs have the default `public` members, while classes have the default `private` members. I personally recommend using structs as data structures only (they don't have any methods in them) and using classes to build the ADTs.

As we can see in the preceding code, we assign the variable to the instance of the `Animal` class by using its constructor, which is shown as follows:

```
Animal dog = Animal();
```

However, we can initialize a class data member by using a class constructor. The constructor name is the same as the class name. Let's refactor our preceding `Animal` class so it has a constructor. The refactored code should be as follows:

```cpp
// Constructor.cbp
#include <iostream>

using namespace std;

class Animal
{
private:
    string m_name;

public:
    Animal(string name)  : m_name(name)
    {

    }

    string GetName()
    {
        return m_name;
    }
};
```

```
int main()
{
    Animal dog = Animal("dog");

    cout << "Hi, I'm a " << dog.GetName() << endl;

    return 0;
}
```

As we can see in the preceding code, when we define the dog variable, we also initialize the m_name private variable of the class. We don't need the GiveName() method anymore to assign the private variable. Indeed, we will get the same output again if we build and run the preceding code.

In the preceding code, we assign dog as the Animal data type. However, we can also derive a new class based on the base class. By deriving from the base class, the derived class will also have the behavior that the base class has. Let's refactor the Animal class again. We will add a virtual method named MakeSound(). The virtual method is a method that has no implementation yet, and only has the definition (also known as the **interface**). The derived class has to add the implementation to the virtual method using the override keyword, or else the compiler will complain. After we have a new Animal class, we will make a class named Dog that derives from the Animal class. The code should be as follows:

```
// Derived_Class.cbp
#include <iostream>

using namespace std;

class Animal
{
private:
    string m_name;

public:
    Animal(string name) : m_name(name)
    {

    }

    // The interface that has to be implemented
    // in derived class
    virtual string MakeSound() = 0;

    string GetName()
    {
```

```cpp
            return m_name;
        }
};

class Dog : public Animal
{
public:
    // Forward the constructor arguments
    Dog(string name) : Animal(name) {}

    // here we implement the interface
    string MakeSound() override
    {
        return "woof-woof!";
    }
};

int main()
{
    Dog dog = Dog("Bulldog");

    cout << dog.GetName() << " is barking: ";
    cout << dog.MakeSound() << endl;

    return 0;
}
```

Now, we have two classes, the `Animal` class (as the base class) and the `Dog` class (as the derived class). As shown in the preceding code, the `Dog` class has to implement the `MakeSound()` method since it has been defined as a virtual method in the `Animal` class. The instance of the `Dog` class can also invoke the `GetName()` method, even though it's not implemented inside the `Dog` class since the derived class derives all base class behavior. If we run the preceding code, we will see the following console window:

```
Terminal
Bulldog is barking: woof-woof!

Process returned 0 (0x0)    execution time : 0.013 s
Press ENTER to continue.
```

Again, we can say that the `Dog` ADT has two functions, and they are the `GetName()` and `MakeSound()` functions.

Another necessary requirement of ADT is that it has to be able to control all copy operations to avoid dynamic memory aliasing problems caused by shallow copying (some members of the copy may reference the same objects as the original). For this purpose, we can use assignment operator overloading. As the sample, we will refactor the Dog class so it now has the copy assignment operator. The code should be as follows:

```cpp
// Assignment_Operator_Overload.cbp
#include <iostream>

using namespace std;

class Animal
{
protected:
    string m_name;

public:
    Animal(string name) : m_name(name)
    {

    }

    // The interface that has to be implemented
    // in derived class
    virtual string MakeSound() = 0;

    string GetName()
    {
        return m_name;
    }
};

class Dog : public Animal
{
public:
    // Forward the constructor arguments
    Dog(string name) : Animal(name) {}

    // Copy assignment operator overloading
    void operator = (const Dog &D)
    {
        m_name = D.m_name;
    }

    // here we implement the interface
    string MakeSound() override
    {
```

```
            return "woof-woof!";
        }
};

int main()
{
    Dog dog = Dog("Bulldog");
    cout << dog.GetName() << " is barking: ";
    cout << dog.MakeSound() << endl;

    Dog dog2 = dog;
    cout << dog2.GetName() << " is barking: ";
    cout << dog2.MakeSound() << endl;

    return 0;
}
```

We have added a `copy assignment` operator which is overloading in the `Dog` class. However, since we tried to access the `m_name` variable in the base class from the derived class, we need to make `m_name protected` instead of `private`. In the `main()` method, when we copy `dog` to `dog2` in `Dog dog2 = dog;`, we can ensure that it's not a shallow copy.

Playing with templates

Now, let's play with the templates. The templates are the features that allow the functions and classes to operate with generic types. It makes a function or class work on many different data types without having to be rewritten for each one. Using the template, we can build various data types, which we will discuss later in this book.

Function templates

Suppose we have another class that is derived from the `Animal` class, for instance, `Cat`. We are going to make a function that will invoke the `GetName()` and `MakeSound()` methods for both the `Dog` and `Cat` instances. Without creating two separated functions, we can use the template, which is shown as follows:

```
// Function_Templates.cbp
#include <iostream>

using namespace std;

class Animal
```

```cpp
{
protected:
    string m_name;

public:
    Animal(string name) : m_name(name)
    {

    }

    // The interface that has to be implemented
    // in derived class
    virtual string MakeSound() = 0;

    string GetName()
    {
        return m_name;
    }
};

class Dog : public Animal
{
public:
    // Forward the constructor arguments
    Dog(string name) : Animal(name) {}

    // Copy assignment operator overloading
    void operator = (const Dog &D)
    {
        m_name = D.m_name;
    }

    // here we implement the interface
    string MakeSound() override
    {
        return "woof-woof!";
    }
};

class Cat : public Animal
{
public:
    // Forward the constructor arguments
    Cat(string name) : Animal(name) {}

    // Copy assignment operator overloading
    void operator = (const Cat &D)
    {
```

```
            m_name = D.m_name;
        }

        // here we implement the interface
        string MakeSound() override
        {
            return "meow-meow!";
        }
};

template<typename T>
void GetNameAndMakeSound(T& theAnimal)
{
    cout << theAnimal.GetName() << " goes ";
    cout << theAnimal.MakeSound() << endl;
}

int main()
{
    Dog dog = Dog("Bulldog");
    GetNameAndMakeSound(dog);

    Cat cat = Cat("Persian Cat");
    GetNameAndMakeSound(cat);

    return 0;
}
```

From the preceding code, we can see that we can pass both the Dog and Cat data types to the GetNameAndMakeSound() function since we have defined the <typename T> template before the function definition. The typename is a keyword in C++, which is used to write a template. The **keyword** is used for specifying that a symbol in a template definition or declaration is a type (in the preceding example, the symbol is T). As a result, the function becomes generic and can accept various data types, and if we build and run the preceding code, we will be shown the following console window:

```
⊗⊖⊕  Terminal
Bulldog goes woof-woof!
Persian Cat goes meow-meow!

Process returned 0 (0x0)    execution time : 0.009 s
Press ENTER to continue.
```

Please ensure that the data type we pass to the generic function has the ability to do all the operation invoking from the generic function. However, the compiler will compile if the data type we pass does not have the expected operation. In the preceding function template example, we need to pass a data type that is an instance of the `Animal` class, so we can pass either instance of the `Animal` class or an instance of a derived class of the `Animal` class.

Class templates

Similar to the function template, the class template is used to build a generic class that can accept various data types. Let's refactor the preceding `Function_Template.cbp` code by adding a new class template. The code should be as follows:

```cpp
// Class_Templates.cbp
#include <iostream>

using namespace std;

class Animal
{
protected:
    string m_name;

public:
    Animal(string name) : m_name(name)
    {

    }

    // The interface that has to be implemented
    // in derived class
    virtual string MakeSound() = 0;

    string GetName()
    {
        return m_name;
    }
};

class Dog : public Animal
{
public:
    // Forward the constructor arguments
    Dog(string name) : Animal(name) {}

    // Copy assignment operator overloading
```

```cpp
    void operator = (const Dog &D)
    {
         m_name = D.m_name;
    }

    // here we implement the interface
    string MakeSound() override
    {
         return "woof-woof!";
    }
};

class Cat : public Animal
{
public:
    // Forward the constructor arguments
    Cat(string name) : Animal(name) {}

    // Copy assignment operator overloading
    void operator = (const Cat &D)
    {
         m_name = D.m_name;
    }

    // here we implement the interface
    string MakeSound() override
    {
         return "meow-meow!";
    }

};

template<typename T>
void GetNameAndMakeSound(T& theAnimal)
{
    cout << theAnimal.GetName() << " goes ";
    cout << theAnimal.MakeSound() << endl;
}

template <typename T>
class AnimalTemplate
{
private:
    T m_animal;

public:
    AnimalTemplate(T animal) : m_animal(animal) {}
```

```
            void GetNameAndMakeSound()
            {
                cout << m_animal.GetName() << " goes ";
                cout << m_animal.MakeSound() << endl;
            }
    };

    int main()
    {
        Dog dog = Dog("Bulldog");
        AnimalTemplate<Dog> dogTemplate(dog);
        dogTemplate.GetNameAndMakeSound();

        Cat cat = Cat("Persian Cat");
        AnimalTemplate<Cat> catTemplate(cat);
        catTemplate.GetNameAndMakeSound();

        return 0;
    }
```

As we can see in the preceding code, we have a new class named `AnimalTemplate`. It's a template class and it can be used by any data type. However, we have to define the data type in the angle bracket, as we can see in the preceding code, when we use the instances `dogTemplate` and `catTemplate`. If we build and run the code, we will get the same output as we did for the `Function_Template.cbp` code.

Standard Template Library

C++ programming has another powerful feature regarding the use of template classes, which is the Standard Template Library. It's a set of class templates to provide all functions that are commonly used in manipulating various data structures. There are four components that build the STL, and they are algorithms, containers, iterators, and functions. Now, let's look at these components further.

Algorithms are used on ranges of elements, such as sorting and searching. The sorting algorithm is used to arrange the elements, both in ascending and descending order. The searching algorithm is used to look for a specific value from the ranges of elements.

Containers are used to store objects and data. The common container that is widely used is vector. The vector is similar to an array, except it has the ability to resize itself automatically when an element is inserted or deleted.

Iterators are used to work upon a sequence of values. Each container has its own iterator. For instance, there are `begin()`, `end()`, `rbegin()`, and `rend()` functions in the vector container.

Functions are used to overload the existing function. The instance of this component is called a **functor**, or **function object**. The functor is defined as a pointer of a function where we can parameterize the existing function.

We are not building any code in this section since we just need to know that the STL is a powerful library in C++ and that it exists, fortunately. We are going to discuss the STL deeper in the following chapters while we construct data structures.

Analyzing the algorithm

To create a good algorithm, we have to ensure that we have got the best performance from the algorithm. In this section, we are going to discuss the ways we can analyze the time complexity of basic functions.

Asymptotic analysis

Let's start with asymptotic analysis to find out the time complexity of the algorithms. This analysis omits the constants and the least significant parts. Suppose we have a function that will print a number from 0 to n. The following is the code for the function:

```
void Looping(int n)
{
    int i = 0;

    while(i < n)
    {
        cout << i << endl;
        i = i + 1;
    }
}
```

Now, let's calculate the time complexity of the preceding algorithm by counting each instruction of the function. We start with the first statement:

```
int i = 0;
```

The preceding statement is only executed once in the function, so its value is 1. The following is the code snippet of the rest statements in the `Looping()` function:

```
while (i < n)
{
    cout << i << endl;
    i = i + 1;
}
```

The comparison in the `while` loop is valued at 1. For simplicity, we can say that the value of the two statements inside the `while` loop scope is 3 since it needs 1 to print the `i` variable, and 2 for assignment (=) and addition (+).

However, how much of the preceding code snippet is executed depends on the value of `n`, so it will be `(1 + 3)` * `n` or 4n. The total instruction that has to be executed for the preceding `Looping()` function is `1 + 4n`. Therefore, the complexity of the preceding `Looping()` function is:

```
Time Complexity(n) = 4n + 1
```

And here is the curve that represents its complexity:

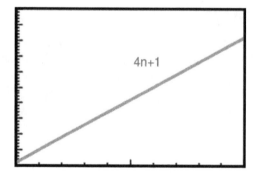

In all curve graphs that will be represented in this book, the *x* axis represents *Input Size (n)* and the *y* axis represents *Execution Time*.

As we can see in the preceding graph, the curve is linear. However, since the time complexity also depends on the other parameters, such as hardware specification, we may have another complexity for the preceding `Looping()` function if we run the function on faster hardware. Let's say the time complexity becomes **2n + 0.5**, so that the curve will be as follow:

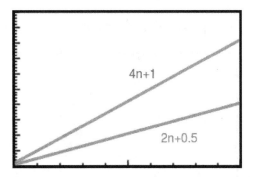

As we can see, the curve is still linear for the two complexities. For this reason, we can omit a constant and the least significant parts in asymptotic analysis, so we can say that the preceding complexity is n, as found in the following notation:

```
Time Complexity(n) = n
```

Let's move on to another function. If we have the nested `while` loop, we will have another complexity, as we can see in the following code:

```
void Pairing(int n)
{
    int i = 0;

    while(i < n)
    {
        int j = 0;

        while(j < n)
        {
            cout << i << ", " << j << endl;
            j = j + 1;
        }
        i = i + 1;
    }
}
```

Based on the preceding `Looping()` function, we can say that the complexity of the inner `while` loop of the preceding `Pairing()` function is `4n + 1`. We then calculate the outer `while` loop so it becomes `1 + (n * (1 + (4n + 1) + 2)`, which equals `1 + 3n + 4n²`. Therefore, the complexity of the preceding code is:

```
Time Complexity(n) = 4n² + 3n + 1
```

The curve for the preceding complexity will be as follows:

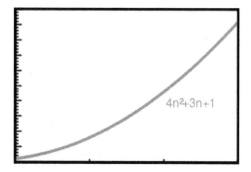

And if we run the preceding code in the slower hardware, the complexity might become twice as slow. The notation should be as follows:

```
Time Complexity(n) = 8n² + 6n + 2
```

And the curve of the preceding notation should be as follows:

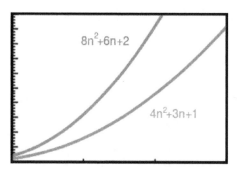

As shown previously, since the asymptotic analysis omits the constants and the least significant parts, the complexity notation will be as follows:

```
Time Complexity(n) = n2
```

Worst, average, and best cases

In the previous section, we were able to define time complexity for our code using an asymptotic algorithm. In this section, we are going to determine a case of the implementation of an algorithm. There are three cases when implementing time complexity in an algorithm; they are worst, average, and best cases. Before we go through them, let's look at the following Search() function implementation:

```
int Search(int arr[], int arrSize, int x)
{
    // Iterate through arr elements
    for (int i = 0; i < arrSize; ++i)
    {
        // If x is found
        // returns index of x
        if (arr[i] == x)
            return i;
    }

    // If x is not found
    // returns -1
    return -1;
}
```

As we can see in the preceding Search() function, it will find an index of target element (x) from an arr array containing arrSize elements. Suppose we have the array {42, 55, 39, 71, 20, 18, 6, 84}. Here are the cases we will find:

- **Worst case analysis** is a calculation of the upper bound on the running time of the algorithm. In the Search() function, the upper bound can be an element that does not appear in the arr, for instance, 60, so it has to iterate through all elements of arr and still cannot find the element.
- **Average case analysis** is a calculation of all possible inputs on the running time of algorithm, including an element that is not present in the arr array.
- **Best case analysis** is a calculation of the lower bound on the running time of the algorithm. In the Search() function, the lower bound is the first element of the arr array, which is 42. When we search for element 42, the function will only iterate through the arr array once, so the arrSize doesn't matter.

Big Theta, Big-O, and Big Omega

After discussing asymptotic analysis and the three cases in algorithms, let's discuss asymptotic notation to represent the time complexity of an algorithm. There are three asymptotic notations that are mostly used in an algorithm; they are Big Theta, Big-O, and Big Omega.

The Big Theta notation (θ) is a notation that bounds a function from above and below, like we saw previously in asymptotic analysis, which also omits a constant from a notation.

Suppose we have a function with time complexity 4n + 1. Since it's a linear function, we can notate it like in the following code:

```
f(n) = 4n + 1
```

Now, suppose we have a function, g(n), where f(n) is the Big-Theta of g(n) if the value, f(n), is always between c1*g(n) (lower bound) and c2*g(n) (upper bound). Since f(n) has a constant of 4 in the *n* variable, we will take a random lower bound which is lower than 4, that is 3, and an upper bound which is greater than 4, that is 5. Please see the following curve for reference:

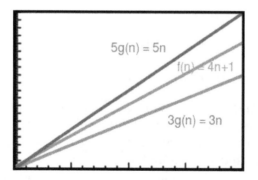

From the f(n) time complexity, we can get the asymptotic complexity n, so then we have g(n) = n, which is based on the asymptotic complexity of 4n + 1. Now, we can decide the upper bound and lower bound for g(n) = n. Let's pick 3 for the lower bound and 5 for the upper bound. Now, we can manipulate the g(n) = n function as follows:

```
3.g(n) = 3.n
5.g(n) = 5.n
```

Big-O notation (*O*) is a notation that bounds a function from above only using the upper bound of an algorithm. From the previous notation, f(n) = 4n + 1, we can say that the time complexity of the f(n) is O(n). If we are going to use Big Theta notation, we can say that the worst case time complexity of f(n) is θ(n) and the best case time complexity of f(n) is θ(1).

Big Omega notation is contrary to Big-O notation. It uses the lower bound to analyze time complexity. In other words, it uses the best case in Big Theta notation. For the f(n) notation, we can say that the time complexity is Ω(1).

Recursive method

In the previous code sample, we calculated the complexity of the iterative method. Now, let's do this with the recursive method. Suppose we need to calculate the factorial of a certain number, for instance 6, which will produce 6 * 5 * 4 * 3 * 2 * 1 = 720. For this purpose, we can use the recursive method, which is shown in the following code snippet:

```
int Factorial(int n)
{
    if(n == 1)
        return 1;

    return n * Factorial(n - 1);
}
```

For the preceding function, we can calculate the complexity similarly to how we did for the iterative method, which is f(n) = n since it depends on how much data is being processed (which is n). We can use a constant, for instance c, to calculate the lower bound and the upper bound.

Amortized analysis

In the previous section, we just discussed the single input, n, for calculating the complexity. However, sometimes we will deal with more than just one input. Please look at the following SumOfDivision() function implementation:

```
int SumOfDivision(
    int nArr[], int n, int mArr[], int m)
{
    int total = 0;
```

```
for(int i = 0; i < n; ++i)
{
    for(int j = 0; j < m; ++j)
    {
        total += (nArr[i] * mArr[j]);
    }
}

return total;
}
```

And that's where amortized analysis comes in. Amortized analysis calculates the complexity of performing the operation for varying inputs, for instance, when we insert some elements into several arrays. Now, the complexity doesn't only depend on the n input only, but also the m input. The complexity can be as follows:

```
Time Complexity(n, m) = n · m
```

We are going to discuss these analysis methods in more detail in the following chapters.

Summary

This chapter provided us with an introduction to basic C++ (simple program, IDE, flow control) and all data types (fundamental and advanced data types, including template and STL) that we will use to construct the data structures in the following chapters. We also discussed a basic complexity analysis, and we will dig into this deeper in the upcoming chapters.

Next, we are going to create our first data structures, that is, linked list, and we are going to perform some operations on the data structure.

QA section

- What is the first function in C++ which is executed for the first time?
- Please list the fundamental data types in C++!
- What can we use to control the flow of code?
- What is the difference between enums and structs?
- What are the abstraction, information hiding, and encapsulation techniques? Please explain!

- What is the keyword to create a template in C++?
- What is the difference between the function template and the class template?
- What is the difference between Big Theta, Big-O, and Big Omega?

Further reading

You can also refer to the following links:

- `http://www.learncpp.com/`
- `https://www.geeksforgeeks.org/analysis-of-algorithms-set-1-asymptotic-analysis/`
- `https://www.geeksforgeeks.org/analysis-of-algorithms-set-2-asymptotic-analysis/`
- `https://www.geeksforgeeks.org/analysis-of-algorithms-set-3asymptotic-notations/`

Storing Data in Lists and Linked Lists

2

In the previous chapter, we discussed basic C++ programming, so that now we can build a program and run it. We also tried to find out the complexity of the code flow using algorithm analysis. In this chapter, we are going to learn about building the list and linked list data structures and find out the complexity of each data structure. To understand all of the concepts in these data structures, these are the topics we are going to discuss:

- Understanding the array data type and how to use it
- Building the list data structure using the array data type
- Understanding the concept of node and node chaining
- Building `SinglyLinkedList` and `DoublyLinkedList` using node chaining
- Applying the Standard Template Library to implement the list and linked list

Technical requirements

To follow along with this chapter including the source code, we require the following:

- A desktop PC or Notebook with Windows, Linux, or macOS
- GNU GCC v5.4.0 or above
- Code::Block IDE v17.12 (for Windows and Linux OS) or Code::Block IDE v13.12 (for macOS)
- You will find the code files on GitHub at `https://github.com/PacktPublishing/CPP-Data-Structures-and-Algorithms`

Getting closer to an array

An **array** is a series of elements with the same data type that is placed in contiguous memory locations. This means that the memory allocation is assigned in consecutive memory blocks. Since it implements contiguous memory locations, the elements of the array can be individually accessed by the index. Let's take a look at the following array illustration:

Memory Address	0x0400	0x0401	0x0402	0x0403	0x0404
Content	21	47	87	35	92
Index	0	1	2	3	4

As we can see in the preceding illustration, we have an array containing five elements. Since the array uses zero-based indexing, the index starts from **0**. This index is used to access the element value and to also replace the element value. The memory address stated in the illustration is for example purposes only. In reality, the memory address might be different. However, it illustrates that the memory allocation is contiguous.

Now, if we want to create the preceding array in C++, here is the code:

```cpp
// Project: Array.cbp
// File    : Array.cpp

#include <iostream>

using namespace std;

int main()
{
    // Initialize an array
    int arr[] = { 21, 47, 87, 35, 92 };

    // Access each element
    cout << "Array elements: ";
    for(int i = 0; i < sizeof(arr)/sizeof(*arr); ++i)
        cout << arr[i] << " ";
    cout << endl;

    // Manipulate several elements
    arr[2] = 30;
```

```
        arr[3] = 64;

        // Access each element again
        cout << "Array elements: ";
        for(int i = 0; i < sizeof(arr)/sizeof(*arr); ++i)
            cout << arr[i] << " ";
        cout << endl;

        return 0;
    }
```

From the preceding code, we see that initializing an array is simple, and this is done by defining the array data type, the array's name followed by a couple of square brackets (`[]`), and the element's value. In the preceding code, our array's name is `arr`. We can access each element by using the index. In the code, we print each element by iterating each element and accessing the element value using `arr[i]`. We also manipulate the value of indexes 2 and 3 by using `arr[2] = 30` and `arr[3] = 64`. If we build and run the code, we will get the following result:

```
⊗ ⊜ ⊕   Terminal
Array elements: 21 47 87 35 92
Array elements: 21 47 30 64 92

Process returned 0 (0x0)     execution time : 0.004 s
Press ENTER to continue.
```

As we can see in the preceding screenshot, we've got what we expected since we have successfully initialized an array, accessed each element, and manipulated the element's value.

> The array data type doesn't have a built-in method to find out how many elements the array has. Even though we already know that the number of elements is five, we use `sizeof(arr)/sizeof(*arr)` to figure out the number of elements. It's the best practice in array manipulation because, sometimes, we don't know how many elements the array has. However, this only works when the `sizeof(arr)/sizeof(*arr)` construct is in the same scope as the definition of the array. If, for example, we try this from a function that receives the array as a parameter, this will fail.

There's an interesting fact about arrays—we can access the array's element using a pointer. As you may know, a pointer is a variable that holds the address instead of the value. And, since we discussed earlier that each element in the array has its own address, we can access each array's element using its address.

To use a pointer as an array, we need to initialize it to hold an array, as shown in the following example:

```
int * ptr = new int[5] { 21, 47, 87, 35, 92 };
```

After the preceding initialization, we have a pointer named `ptr` that points to the first element of an array containing five elements. However, the `ptr` variable holds the first array's element address at the start. To access the next address, we can increment the `ptr` variable (`ptr++`) so that it will point to the next element. To get the value of the currently selected address, we can use a wildcard symbol before the pointer name (`*ptr`); see the following two lines of code:

```
cout << *ptr << endl;
cout << ptr << endl;
```

The former statement in the preceding code snippet will print out the value that the pointer points to, and the latter will print the address that the pointer holds. Interestingly, since we initialize the `ptr` pointer as an array, we can access the value of each element and the address as well by its index. Please take a look at the following code snippet:

```
cout << ptr[i] << endl;
cout << &ptr[i] << endl;
```

In the preceding code snippet, the former line will print the value of the selected element and the latter will print the address of the selected element (since we added the apostrophe symbol before the pointer name—`&ptr[i]`). Now, let's wrap them all to create a code, as follows:

```
// Project: Array_As_Pointer.cbp
// File    : Array_As_Pointer.cpp

#include <iostream>

using namespace std;

int main()
{
    // Initialize the array length
    int arrLength = 5;
```

```cpp
// Initialize a pointer
// to hold an array
int * ptr = new int[arrLength] { 21, 47, 87, 35, 92 };

// Display each element value
// by incrementing the pointer (ptr++)
cout << "Using pointer increment" << endl;
cout << "Value\tAddress" << endl;
while(*ptr)
{
    cout << *ptr << "\t";
    cout << ptr << endl;
    ptr++;
}

// Since we have moved forward the pointer five times
// we need to move it back
ptr = ptr - 5;

// Display each element value
// by accessing pointer index (ptr[])
cout << "Using pointer index" << endl;
cout << "Value\tAddress" << endl;
for(int i = 0; i < arrLength; ++i)
{
    cout << ptr[i] << "\t";
    cout << &ptr[i] << endl;
}

return 0;
}
```

And if we build and run the preceding code, we will get the following output:

```
Terminal
Using pointer increment
Value    Address
21       0x2043c20
47       0x2043c24
87       0x2043c28
35       0x2043c2c
92       0x2043c30

Using pointer index
Value    Address
21       0x2043c20
47       0x2043c24
87       0x2043c28
35       0x2043c2c
92       0x2043c30

Process returned 0 (0x0)   execution time : 0.002 s
Press ENTER to continue.
```

As we can see in the preceding screenshot, we can access each element of the pointer array by Using pointer increment and Using pointer index. However, if we use pointer increment, we have to remember that after increasing the pointer, it will no longer hold the address of the array. The solution is that we need to decrement the pointer again, like we did in the preceding code.

The array we discussed is also called a **one-dimensional** array. We can also initialize a multidimensional array, for instance a 3 x 5 array, by using the following code:
```
int multiArray[][] = new int[3][5];
```

The other implementation of the multi-dimensional array is similar to the one-dimensional array.

Building a List ADT

A **list** is a sequence of items with similar data types, where the order of the item's position matters. There are several common operations that are available in a List ADT, and they are:

- Get(i), which will return the value of selected index, i. If the i index is out of bounds, it will simply return -1.

- `Insert(i, v)`, which will insert the v value at the position of index i.
- `Search(v)`, which will return the index of the first occurrence of v (if the v value doesn't exist, the return value is -1).
- `Remove(i)`, which will remove the item in the i index.

 For simplicity, we are going to build a List ADT that accepts `int` data only, from zero (0) and higher.

Now, by using the array data type we discussed earlier, let's build a new ADT named `List` which contains the preceding operations. We need two variables to hold the list of items (`m_items`) and the number of items in the list (`m_count`). We will make them `private` so that it cannot be accessed from the outside class. All four operations described previously will be also implemented in this class. In addition, we need a constructor, a destructor, and a method to let us know the number of items that the `List` class has, which is named `Count()`. Based on this requirement, the `List.h` file will contain the following code:

```
// Project: List.cbp
// File : List.h
#ifndef LIST_H
#define LIST_H

#include <iostream>

class List
{
    private:
        int m_count;
        int * m_items;

    public:
        List();
        ~List();
        int Get(int index);
        void Insert(int index, int val);
        int Search(int val);
        void Remove(int index);
        int Count();
};
#endif // LIST_H
```

Fetching an item in the List

Let's implement the Get() method. It simply returns the value of the selected index. However, we need to ensure that the index passed to the method is not out of bounds. The implementation should be as follows:

```
int List::Get(int index)
{
    // Check if the index is out of bound
    if(index < 0 || index > m_count)
        return -1;

    return m_items[index];
}
```

As we can see in the preceding code, the complexity of the Get() method is O(1) since it doesn't depend on the number of the List elements.

Inserting an item into the List ADT

For the Insert() method, we need to increase the capacity of the m_items variable each time we insert a new item. After that, we need to iterate each item of the old m_items variable and then assign them to the new m_items variable. We also need to ensure where we put the new item stated by the index variable passed by the user. The implementation should be as follows:

```
void List::Insert(int index, int val)
{
    // Check if the index is out of bound
    if(index < 0 || index > m_count)
        return;

    // Copy the current array
    int * oldArray = m_items;

    // Increase the array length
    m_count++;

    // Initialize a new array
    m_items = new int[m_count];

    // Fill the new array with inserted data
    for(int i=0, j=0; i < m_count; ++i)
    {
```

```
        if(index == i)
        {
            m_items[i] = val;
        }
        else
        {
            m_items[i] = oldArray[j];
            ++j;
        }
    }

    // Remove copied array
    delete [] oldArray;
}
```

As we can see in the preceding code, we need to counter variables i and j to assign an old array to new array. Since it will iterate all elements of List items, the number of items matters. The complexity will be O(N), where is N in the number of the List elements.

Finding out the index of a selected item in the List ADT

The Search() method will also iterate each items' list until it finds the matched value. The return value of this method will be the index of List. It will return -1 if no result is found. The implementation should be as follows:

```
int List::Search(int val)
{
    // Looping through the array elements
    // return the array index if value is found
    for(int i=0; i < m_count; ++i)
    {
        if(m_items[i] == val)
        {
            return i;
        }
    }

    return -1;
}
```

As you can guess, the complexity of this method will be O(n) for the average and worst case scenarios, since it will iterate through all list elements. However, in the best case, it can be O(1) if val is found at the first position.

Removing an item from the List ADT

The Remove() method will iterate all List elements, and then assign the new array to hold new List elements. It will skip the selected index to remove the item. The implementation should be as follows:

```
void List::Remove(int index)
{
    // Check if the index is out of bound
    if(index < 0 || index > m_count)
        return;

    // Copy the current array
    int * oldArray = m_items;

    // Decrease the array length
    m_count--;

    // Initialize a new array
    m_items = new int[m_count];

    // Fill the new array
    // and remove the selected index
    for(int i=0, j=0; i < m_count; ++i, ++j)
    {
        if(index == j)
        {
            ++j;
        }

        m_items[i] = oldArray[j];
    }

    // Remove copied array
    delete [] oldArray;
}
```

Similar to the Insert() method, the complexity of the Remove() method is O(N), even if the user removes the first position.

Consuming a List ADT

Now, let's consume our new `List` data type. We will initialize a new `List` and give some items to it. We will then insert several items again and find out if it works. Then, we will remove an item that we previously searched for, and then search for the item again to ensure it has now gone. Here is the code that we can find in the `main.cpp` file of the `List.cbp` project:

```cpp
// Project: List.cbp
// File : main.cpp
#include "List.h"

using namespace std;

int main()
{
    // Initialize a List
    List list = List();

    // Add several items to the List
    list.Insert(0, 21);
    list.Insert(1, 47);
    list.Insert(2, 87);
    list.Insert(3, 35);
    list.Insert(4, 92);

    // Print current List
    cout << "List elements:" << endl;
    for(int i = 0; i < list.Count(); ++i)
    {
        cout << list.Get(i) << " ";
    }
    cout << endl << endl;

    // Insert several items in the middle of the List
    list.Insert(2, 25);
    list.Insert(2, 71);

    // Print the List again
    cout << "New List elements:" << endl;
    for(int i = 0; i < list.Count(); ++i)
    {
        cout << list.Get(i) << " ";
    }
    cout << endl << endl;
```

```
// Search value 71
cout << "Search element 71" << endl;
int result = list.Search(71);
if(result == -1)
    cout << "71 is not found";
else
    cout << "71 is found at index " << result;
cout << endl << endl;

// Remove index 2
cout << "Remove element at index 2" << endl;
list.Remove(2);
cout << endl;

// Print the List again
cout << "New List elements:" << endl;
for(int i = 0; i < list.Count(); ++i)
{
    cout << list.Get(i) << " ";
}
cout << endl << endl;

// Search value 71 again
cout << "Search element 71 again" << endl;
result = list.Search(71);
if(result == -1)
    cout << "71 is not found";
else
    cout << "71 is found at index " << result;
cout << endl;

return 0;
}
```

Fortunately, our `List` data type works well and we can apply all the operations that `List` should have. If we build and run the `List.cbp` project, we will get the following output:

```
List elements:
21 47 87 35 92

New List elements:
21 47 71 25 87 35 92

Search element 71
71 is found at index 2

Remove element at index 2

New List elements:
21 47 25 87 35 92

Search element 71 again
71 is not found

Process returned 0 (0x0)    execution time : 0.003 s
Press ENTER to continue.
```

Introduction to node

The **node** is the basic building block of many data structures which we will discuss in this book. Node has two functions. Its first function is that it holds a piece of data, also known as the **Value** of node. The second function is its connectivity between another node and itself, using an object reference pointer, also known as the **Next** pointer. Based on this explanation, we can create a Node data type in C++, as follows:

```cpp
class Node
{
public:
    int Value;
    Node * Next;
};
```

We will also use the following diagram to represent a single node:

Value	Next

Now, let's create three single nodes using our new `Node` data type. The nodes will contain the values 7, 14, and 21 for each node. The code should be as follows:

```
Node * node1 = new Node;
node1->Value = 7;

Node * node2 = new Node;
node2->Value = 14;

Node * node3 = new Node;
node3->Value = 21;
```

Note that, since we don't initialize the `Next` pointer for all nodes, it will be automatically filled with the null pointer (`NULL`). The illustration will be as follows:

It's time to connect the preceding three nodes so that it becomes a node chain. We will set the `Next` pointer of `node1` to the `node2` object, set the `Next` pointer of `node2` to the `node3` object, and keep the `Next` pointer of `node3` remaining `NULL` to indicate that it's the end of the chain. The code will be as follows:

```
node1->Next = node2;
node2->Next = node3;
```

By executing the preceding code snippet, the illustration of the preceding three nodes will be as follows:

To prove that our code is working, we can add a `PrintNode()` function to print the node chain. The following is the complete code for creating a `Node` data type, initializing the data type, creating a node chain, and printing the chain:

```
// Project: Node_Chain.cbp
// File : main.cpp
#include <iostream>

using namespace std;

class Node
```

```cpp
{
public:
    int Value;
    Node * Next;
};

void PrintNode(Node * node)
{
    // It will print the initial node
    // until it finds NULL for the Next pointer
    // that indicate the end of the node chain
    while(node != NULL)
    {
        cout << node->Value << " -> ";
        node = node->Next;
    }

    cout << "NULL" << endl;
}

int main()
{
    // +------+------+
    // |   7  | NULL |
    // +------+------+
    Node * node1 = new Node;
    node1->Value = 7;

    // +------+------+
    // |  14  | NULL |
    // +------+------+
    Node * node2 = new Node;
    node2->Value = 14;

    // +------+------+
    // |  21  | NULL |
    // +------+------+
    Node * node3 = new Node;
    node3->Value = 21;

    // +------+------+   +------+------+   +------+------+
    // |   7  |   +---->|  14  | NULL |   |  21  | NULL |
    // +------+------+   +------+------+   +------+------+
    node1->Next = node2;

    // +------+------+   +------+------+   +------+------+
    // |   7  |   +---->|  14  |   +---->|  21  | NULL |
    // +------+------+   +------+------+   +------+------+
```

```
        node2->Next = node3;

        // Print the node
        PrintNode(node1);

        return 0;
    }
```

As we can see in the preceding code, we have a `PrintNode()` function to iterate the input node until the `Next` pointer of the selected node is `NULL`. And since we will use the `PrintNode()` function to prove that the node chain is working by running the preceding code, we will get the following output:

```
⊗ ⊖ ⊡  Terminal
7 -> 14 -> 21 -> NULL

Process returned 0 (0x0)   execution time : 0.003 s
Press ENTER to continue.
```

Indeed, we get what we expected—our node chaining is working and we have a new data type named `Node`. However, a problem will occur since we can only store the `int` data type to the `Value` property of the `Node` data type. Should we create a new `Node` data type if we want to deal with other data types, such as `float`, `bool`, or `char`? Fortunately, the answer is *no*. If we recall our discussion about *Playing with Templates* in `Chapter 1`, *Learning Data Structures and Algorithms in C++*, we can refactor the preceding `Node` data type to handle not only the `int` data type, but also all various data types available in the C++ language. The `Node` class will now look as follows:

```
template <typename T>
class Node
{
public:
    T Value;
    Node<T> * Next;

    Node(T value) : Value(value), Next(NULL) {}
};
```

As we can see from the preceding code snippet, we added a constructor to the data type. The initialization of the instance of the class can be simplified as follows:

```
Node<float> * node1 = new Node<float>(4.93);
Node<float> * node2 = new Node<float>(6.45);
Node<float> * node3 = new Node<float>(8.17);
```

We can see that, now we just need a one line instruction to create a single node since it has a constructor. The rest of the operation is the same as the previous full code in `Node_Chain.cbp`. The full code for this `Node` template class should be as follows:

```cpp
// Project: Node_Chain_Template.cbp
// File : main.cpp
#include <iostream>

using namespace std;

template <typename T>
class Node
{
public:
    T Value;
    Node<T> * Next;

    Node(T value) : Value(value){}
};

template<typename T>
void PrintNode(Node<T> * node)
{
    // It will print the initial node
    // until it finds NULL for the Next pointer
    // that indicate the end of the Node Chain
    while(node != NULL)
    {
        cout << node->Value << " -> ";
        node = node->Next;
    }

    cout << "NULL" << endl;
}

int main()
{
    // +------+------+
    // | 4.93 | NULL |
    // +------+------+
    Node<float> * node1 = new Node<float>(4.93);

    // +------+------+
    // | 6.45 | NULL |
    // +------+------+
    Node<float> * node2 = new Node<float>(6.45);
```

```
// +------+------+
// | 8.17 | NULL |
// +------+------+
Node<float> * node3 = new Node<float>(8.17);

// +------+------+    +------+------+    +------+------+
// | 4.93 |    +---->| 6.45 | NULL |    | 8.17 | NULL |
// +------+------+    +------+------+    +------+------+
node1->Next = node2;

// +------+------+    +------+------+    +------+------+
// | 4.93 |    +---->| 6.45 |    +---->| 8.17 | NULL |
// +------+------+    +------+------+    +------+------+
node2->Next = node3;

// Print the node
PrintNode(node1);

return 0;
}
```

Also, we need to refactor the `PrintNode()` function to become a function template—which we have discussed in Chapter 1, *Learning Data Structures and Algorithms in C++* since we will pass a class template to it. Again, we will get a similar output when we run the preceding code comparing it to the `Node_Chain.cbp` project, as follows:

```
Terminal
4.93 -> 6.45 -> 8.17 -> NULL

Process returned 0 (0x0)   execution time : 0.008 s
Press ENTER to continue.
```

Now, using our new `Node<T>` data type, let's move on to creating the linked list.

Building a Singly Linked List ADT

The **Singly Linked List** (also known as the **linked list**) is a sequence of items linked with each other. It's actually a chaining of nodes, where each node contains the item's value and the next pointer. In other words, each item in the linked list has a link to its next item in the sequence. The thing that differs between the linked list and the node chain is that the linked list has a Head and a Tail pointer. The Head informs the first item and the Tail informs the last item in the linked list. Similar to the List ADT, we discussed earlier, the linked list has Get(), Insert(), Search(), and Remove() operations, where all of the operations have the same functionality compared to List. However, since we now have Head and Tail pointers, we will also create others operations, and these are InsertHead(), InsertTail(), RemoveHead(), and RemoveTail(). The declaration of the LinkedList class should be as follows:

```cpp
template <typename T>
class LinkedList
{
private:
    int m_count;

public:
    // The first node in the list
    // or null if empty
    Node<T> * Head;

    // The last node in the list
    // or null if empty
    Node<T> * Tail;

    // Constructor
    LinkedList();

    // Get() operation
    Node<T> * Get(int index);

    // Insert() operation
    void InsertHead(T val);
    void InsertTail(T val);
    void Insert(int index, T val);

    // Search() operation
    int Search(T val);

    // Remove() operation
    void RemoveHead();
```

```
        void RemoveTail();
        void Remove(int index);

        // Additional operation
        int Count();
        void PrintList();
};
```

As you can see in the preceding declaration code, we have the `Count()` operation, which has the same functionality as the `List`, which is used to inform us about the number of items in the `LinkedList` class. There is also the `PrintList()` operation to make it easier to print the content of the `LinkedList` class.

Fetching an item in the LinkedList class

The first operation we are going to discuss is `Get()`. It will return the `Node` of the selected index, however, it will return `NULL` if the selected index is out of bounds. The implementation of the `Get()` method should be as follows:

```
template <typename T>
Node<T> * LinkedList<T>::Get(int index)
{
    // Check if the index is out of bound
    if(index < 0 || index > m_count)
        return NULL;

    // Start from the Head
    Node<T> * node = Head;

    // Iterate through the linked list elements
    // until it finds the selected index
    for(int i = 0; i < index; ++i)
    {
        node = node->Next;
    }

    // Simply return the node result
    return node;
}
```

As we can see, the complexity of the Get() operation is O(N) since it has to iterate through the N elements that the LinkedList class has. However, in the best case, the complexity can be O(1) if the selected index is 0. Unfortunately, as we discussed earlier, the complexity is always O(1) in the List ADT, no matter which index is selected.

Inserting an item in the LinkedList class

Let's move on to the Insert() operation for the LinkedList class. There are four cases for this operation, and they are:

1. The new item is inserted at the beginning of the linked list, which is index = 0, so that it becomes the new Head.
2. The new item is added to an empty linked list. If the linked list has only one element, both Head and Tail will point to the only element.
3. The new item is inserted into the last of the linked list, which is index = N, so it becomes the new Tail.
4. The new item is inserted in the other position of the linked list, where index = 1 to N-1.

Now, let's create the implementation for inserting an operation. For cases **1** and **2**, we can solve these problems by creating an InsertHead() operation. The implementation of this operation is simple and efficient, as we can see in the following code:

```
template <typename T>
void LinkedList<T>::InsertHead(T val)
{
    // Create a new Node
    Node<T> * node = new Node<T>(val);

    // The current Head will no longer become a Head
    // so the Next pointer of the new Node will
    // point to the current Head
    node->Next = Head;

    // The new Node now become the Head
    Head = node;

    // If the linked list is empty
    // The Tail is also the Head
    if(m_count == 0)
        Tail = Head;
```

```
        // One element is added
        m_count++;
    }
```

Based on the preceding code, the InsertHead() operation will create a new Node and then assign it to the new Head. If the linked list is empty before applying this operation, the new Node will also become a new Tail. For this, the complexity of this operation is O(1), regardless of the number of the linked list element.

For case **3** in the inserting operation, we can implement the InsertTail() operation. This operation is also simple and efficient. We just need to create a new Node and then assign it to the new Tail. The Next pointer of the previous Tail will point to this new Tail. The code for this operation should be as follows:

```
template <typename T>
void LinkedList<T>::InsertTail(T val)
{
    // If the linked list is empty,
    // just simply invoke InsertHead()
    if(m_count == 0)
    {
        InsertHead(val);
        return;
    }

    // Create a new Node
    Node<T> * node = new Node<T>(val);

    // The current Tail will no longer become a Tail
    // so the Next pointer of the current Tail will
    // point to the new node
    Tail->Next = node;

    // The new Node now become the Tail
    Tail = node;

    // One element is added
    m_count++;
}
```

Please note that we might run the InsertTail() operation when the linked list has no element. If this occurs, case **2** will happen and we can simply invoke the InsertHead() method. The complexity of the InsertTail() operation is O(1), regardless of the number of the linked list element. It will even invoke the InsertHead() operation since the InsertHead() operation's complexity is also O(1).

Now, for case **4**, we need to traverse the elements of the linked list to find the two elements where we want to insert the new element between them. We will call them `prevNode` and `nextNode`. After we find them, we then create a new node, point the `Next` pointer of `prevNode` to the new node, and then point the `Next` pointer of the new node to the `nextNode`. The implementation of the `Insert()` operation should be as follows:

```cpp
template <typename T>
void LinkedList<T>::Insert(int index, T val)
{
    // Check if the index is out of bound
    if(index < 0 || index > m_count)
        return;

    // If inserting a new Head
    if(index == 0)
    {
        InsertHead(val);
        return;
    }
    // If inserting a new Tail
    else if(index == m_count)
    {
        InsertTail(val);
        return;
    }

    // Start to find previous node
    // from the Head
    Node<T> * prevNode = Head;

    // Traverse the elements until
    // the selected index is found
    for(int i = 0; i < index - 1; ++i)
    {
        prevNode = prevNode->Next;
    }

    // Create the next node which is
    // the element after previous node
    Node<T> * nextNode = prevNode->Next;

    // Create a new node
    Node<T> * node = new Node<T>(val);

    // Insert this new node between
    // the previous node and the next node
    node->Next = nextNode;
```

```
        prevNode->Next = node;

        // One element is added
        m_count++;
    }
```

Since we need to traverse the `List` element, the complexity of this `Insert()` operation is `O(N)`. However, in the best case, the complexity is `O(1)` since we might insert a `Head` or a `Tail` using this operation.

Getting the index of the selected item in the LinkedList

To find out the position of the selected value, we need to traverse the `List` elements. Once the selected value is matched with the value of the current position, the method just needs to return its current position index. The implementation of the `Search()` operation should be as follows:

```
template <typename T>
int LinkedList<T>::Search(T val)
{
    // If LinkedList is empty,
    // just return NOT_FOUND
    if(m_count == 0)
        return -1;

    // Need to count the index
    int index = 0;

    // Traverse from the Head node
    Node<T> * node = Head;

    // Traverse until the selected value
    // is matched with the value
    // of the current position,
    while(node->Value != val)
    {
        index++;
        node = node->Next;

        // This will happen
        // if the selected value
        // is not found
        if(node == NULL)
```

```
        {
            return -1;
        }
    }

    return index;
}
```

Again, since we need to traverse the `List` element, the complexity of this operation will be `O(N)`. However, the selected value may be found in the first position so that the complexity will be `O(1)` in the best case.

Removing an item from the LinkedList ADT

Similar to the inserting operation, the removing operation also has several cases, and they are:

1. The removed item is in the `Head`, which is `index = 0`
2. The removed item is in the `Tail`, which is `index = N-1`
3. The removed item is in the other position of the linked list, where `index = 1 to N-2`

For case **1**, the implementation is straightforward. We just need to point the `Head` pointer to the node which is pointed by the `Next` pointer of the current `Head` (in other words, the second element) and delete the first element of the linked list. Please see the following code:

```
template <typename T>
void LinkedList<T>::RemoveHead()
{
    // Do nothing if list is empty
    if(m_count == 0)
        return;

    // Save the current Head
    // to a new node
    Node<T> * node = Head;

    // Point the Head Pointer
    // to the element next to the current Head
    Head = Head->Next;

    // Now it's safe to remove
    // the first element
    delete node;
```

```
    // One element is removed
    m_count--;
}
```

As we can see in the preceding code, regardless of the number of the linked list element, the complexity of the `RemoveHead()` operation is `O(1)`.

For the `RemoveTail()` operation, we have to traverse all list elements so that we have two last nodes, which are in indexes `N-1` and `N-2`. Then, we set the `Next` pointer of the `N-2` node to point to `NULL`. After that, we can safely remove the last node. Since this operation must traverse all list elements, the complexity will be `O(N)`. The implementation of this operation should be as follows:

```
template <typename T>
void LinkedList<T>::RemoveTail()
{
    // Do nothing if list is empty
    if(m_count == 0)
        return;

    // If List element is only one
    // just simply call RemoveHead()
    if(m_count == 1)
    {
        RemoveHead();
        return;
    }

    // Start to find previous node
    // from the Head
    Node<T> * prevNode = Head;

    // This is the candidate of
    // removed items which is
    // the element next to the prevNode
    Node<T> * node = Head->Next;

    // Traverse the elements until
    // the last element
    while(node->Next != NULL)
    {
        prevNode = prevNode->Next;
        node = node->Next;
    }

    // the prevNode now becomes the Tail
    // so the Next pointer of the prevNode
```

```
    // point to NULL
    prevNode->Next = NULL;
    Tail = prevNode;

    // Now it's safe to remove
    // the last element
    delete node;

    // One element is removed
    m_count--;
}
```

The last operation is the `Remove()` operation, which will remove the list element in-between the first and the last element. In this operation, we need to traverse the list element until the selected index is reached. Similar to the `Insert()` operation, we need to find the element before and after the selected index. After we find them, we can link them together and then we can safely remove the element in the selected index. The code will be as follows:

```
template <typename T>
void LinkedList<T>::Remove(int index)
{
    // Do nothing if list is empty
    if(m_count == 0)
        return;

    // Do nothing if index is out of bound
    if(index < 0 || index >= m_count)
        return;

    // If removing the current Head
    if(index == 0)
    {
        RemoveHead();
        return;
    }
    // If removing the current Tail
    else if(index == m_count - 1)
    {
        RemoveTail();
        return;
    }

    // Start to traverse the list
    // from the Head
    Node<T> * prevNode = Head;
```

```
        // Find the element before
        // the selected index
        for(int i = 0; i < index - 1; ++i)
        {
            prevNode = prevNode->Next;
        }

        // The removed element is after
        // the prevNode
        Node<T> * node = prevNode->Next;

        // The nextNode will be the neighbor of
        // prevNode if the node is removed
        Node<T> * nextNode = node->Next;

        // Link the prevNode to nextNode
        prevNode->Next = nextNode;

        // It's now safe to remove
        // the selected index element
        delete node;

        // One element is removed
        m_count--;
    }
```

As we can see in the preceding code, we will invoke the `RemoveHead()` operation if the index = 0 and will invoke the `RemoveTail()` operation if the index = m_count - 1. It's now clear that in the best case (when the `RemoveHead()` is invoked), the complexity is `O(1)`, and in the worst case (when the `RemoveTail()` is invoked), the complexity is `O(N)`.

Consuming the LinkedList ADT

Now, it's time to consume our new `LinkedList` data type in our code. We can use all of the operations of the data type. We will try to initialize a new `LinkedList`, add several items, and then invoke the `Get()`, `Insert()`, `Search()`, and `Remove()` operations. Don't worry about invoking these operations in a specific order; as long as we have instantiated the `LinkedList` object, everything will work since we have restricted the out of bound index problem. Without further ado, here's the code:

```
// Project: Singly_Linked_List.cbp
// File : main.cpp
#include <iostream>
#include "Node.h"
```

```cpp
#include "LinkedList.h"

using namespace std;

int main()
{
    // NULL
    LinkedList<int> linkedList = LinkedList<int>();

    // 43->NULL
    linkedList.InsertHead(43);

    // 76->43->NULL
    linkedList.InsertHead(76);

    // 76->43->15->NULL
    linkedList.InsertTail(15);

    // 76->43->15->44->NULL
    linkedList.InsertTail(44);

    // Print the list element
    cout << "First Printed:" << endl;
    linkedList.PrintList();
    cout << endl;

    // 76->43->15->44->100->NULL
    linkedList.Insert(4, 100);

    // 76->43->15->48->44->100->NULL
    linkedList.Insert(3, 48);

    // 22->76->43->15->48->44->100->NULL
    linkedList.Insert(0, 22);

    // Print the list element
    cout << "Second Printed:" << endl;
    linkedList.PrintList();
    cout << endl;

    // Get value of the second index
    // It should be 43
    cout << "Get value of the second index:" << endl;
    Node<int> * get = linkedList.Get(2);
    if(get != NULL)
        cout << get->Value;
    else
        cout << "not found";
```

```cpp
    cout << endl << endl;

    // Find the position of value 15
    // It must be 3
    cout << "The position of value 15:" << endl;
    int srch = linkedList.Search(15);
    cout << srch << endl << endl;

    // Remove first element
    cout << "Remove the first element:" << endl;
    linkedList.Remove(0);
    // 76->43->15->48->44->100->NULL
    linkedList.PrintList();
    cout << endl;

    // Remove fifth element
    cout << "Remove the fifth element:" << endl;
    linkedList.Remove(4);
    // 76->43->15->48->100->NULL
    linkedList.PrintList();
    cout << endl;

    // Remove tenth element
    cout << "Remove the tenth element:" << endl;
    linkedList.Remove(9);
    // Nothing happen
    // 76->43->15->48->100->NULL
    linkedList.PrintList();
    cout << endl;

    return 0;
}
```

There are commenting lines before each code line to indicate the expected result. To display the List element, we use the PrintList() method with the following implementation:

```cpp
template <typename T>
void LinkedList<T>::PrintList()
{
    Node<T> * node = Head;

    while(node != NULL)
    {
        std::cout << node->Value << " -> ";
        node = node->Next;
    }
```

```
        std::cout << "NULL" << std::endl;
    }
```

And if we build and run the preceding `Singly_Linked_List.cbp` project, we will see the following window in our monitor:

```
⊗ ⊜ ⊡   Terminal
First Printed:
76 -> 43 -> 15 -> 44 -> NULL

Second Printed:
22 -> 76 -> 43 -> 15 -> 48 -> 44 -> 100 -> NULL

Get value of the second index:
43

The position of value 15:
3

Remove the first element:
76 -> 43 -> 15 -> 48 -> 44 -> 100 -> NULL

Remove the fifth element:
76 -> 43 -> 15 -> 48 -> 100 -> NULL

Remove the tenth element:
76 -> 43 -> 15 -> 48 -> 100 -> NULL


Process returned 0 (0x0)   execution time : 0.006 s
Press ENTER to continue.
```

Building the Doubly Linked List ADT

The **Doubly Linked List** is almost the same as the Singly Linked List, except the Node used by Doubly Linked List has a Previous pointer instead of only having the Next pointer. The existence of the Previous pointer will make the Doubly Linked List possible to move backwards from Tail to Head. As a result, we can reduce the complexity of the RemoveTail() operation to O(1) instead of O(N), like we have in the Singly Linked List data type. We are going to discuss this further later in this section. As of now, let's prepare the new Node data type.

Refactoring the Node<T> data type

Before we build a Doubly Linked List, we need to add a `Previous` pointer to the existing `Node` data type. To avoid any confusion, we will create a new data type named `DoublyNode` with the following declaration:

```
template <typename T>
class DoublyNode
{
    public:
        T Value;
        DoublyNode<T> * Previous;
        DoublyNode<T> * Next;

        DoublyNode(T value);
};
```

The only difference between `Node<T>` and `DoublyNode<T>` is the existence of the `Previous` pointer (as well as the data type name absolutely). By using this new `DoublyNode` data type, we are going to refactor the preceding `LinkedList` ADT into the `DoublyLinkedList` ADT.

Refactoring several operations in the LinkedList ADT

Since the Doubly Linked List is similar to Singly Linked List, we can refactor our existing `LinkedList` ADT to build a new `DoublyLinkedList` ADT since they have the same available operations but with different implementations. However, the implementation of the `Get()` and `Search()` operations is the same for these two ADTs because the traversal process for each element will still move in forwarding, so we won't discuss it anymore. And since `DoublyLinkedList` can move backwards, we will make a new operation named `PrintListBackward()` to leverage our `DoublyLinkedList` data type. To make this clear, here is the declaration of the `DoublyLinkedList<T>` data type:

```
template <typename T>
class DoublyLinkedList
{
    private:
        int m_count;

    public:
        // The first node in the list
```

```
                         // or null if empty
                         DoublyNode<T> * Head;

                         // The last node in the list
                         // or null if empty
                         DoublyNode<T> * Tail;

                         // Constructor
                         DoublyLinkedList();

                         // Get() operation
                         DoublyNode<T> * Get(int index);

                         // Insert() operation
                         void InsertHead(T val);
                         void InsertTail(T val);
                         void Insert(int index, T val);

                         // Search() operation
                         int Search(T val);

                         // Remove() operation
                         void RemoveHead();
                         void RemoveTail();
                         void Remove(int index);

                         // Additional operation
                         int Count();
                         void PrintList();
                         void PrintListBackward();
                 };
```

Removing an element

As we discussed earlier, in the DoublyLinkedList, we can have O(1) for the complexity of the RemoveTail() operation. This can happen now since we have the Previous pointer in each element. To do so, we just need to pick the current Tail node and then assign the previous node of the current Tail as the new Tail. After that, we can safely remove the last element. The implementation of the RemoveTail() operation will be as follows:

```
                 template <typename T>
                 void DoublyLinkedList<T>::RemoveTail()
                 {
                     // Do nothing if list is empty
                     if(m_count == 0)
```

```
        return;

    // If List element is only one
    // just simply call RemoveHead()
    if(m_count == 1)
    {
        RemoveHead();
        return;
    }

    // Save the current Tail
    // to a new node
    DoublyNode<T> * node = Tail;

    // Point the Tail Pointer
    // to the element before the current Tail
    Tail = Tail->Previous;

    // Set the new Next pointer of the new Tail
    // to NULL since we are going to delete
    // the last element
    Tail->Next = NULL;

    // Now it's safe to remove
    // the last element
    delete node;

    // One element is removed
    m_count--;
}
```

For the RemoveHead() operation, the Previous pointer of the new Head must point to NULL, so we can refactor the RemoveHead() operation as follows:

```
template <typename T>
void DoublyLinkedList<T>::RemoveHead()
{
    // Do nothing if list is empty
    if(m_count == 0)
        return;

    // Save the current Head
    // to a new node
    DoublyNode<T> * node = Head;

    // Point the Head Pointer
    // to the element next to the current Head
```

```
        Head = Head->Next;

        // Now it's safe to remove
        // the first element
        delete node;

        // If there's still any element in the list,
        // the previous pointer of the Head
        // should point to NULL
        if(Head != NULL)
            Head->Previous = NULL;

        // One element is removed
        m_count--;
    }
```

And still, the complexity of the RemoveHead() operation is O(1).

For the Remove() operation, when we link the two nodes between the removed node, we also need to point to the Previous pointer of the right element to the left element. The implementation will be as follows:

```
    template <typename T>
    void DoublyLinkedList<T>::Remove(int index)
    {
        // Do nothing if list is empty
        if(m_count == 0)
            return;

        // Do nothing if index is out of bound
        if(index < 0 || index >= m_count)
            return;

        // If removing the current Head
        if(index == 0)
        {
            RemoveHead();
            return;
        }
        // If removing the current Tail
        else if(index == m_count - 1)
        {
            RemoveTail();
            return;
        }

        // Start to traverse the list
```

```
    // from the Head
    DoublyNode<T> * prevNode = Head;

    // Find the element before
    // the selected index
    for(int i = 0; i < index - 1; ++i)
    {
        prevNode = prevNode->Next;
    }

    // The removed element is after
    // the prevNode
    DoublyNode<T> * node = prevNode->Next;

    // The nextNode will be the neighbor of
    // prevNode if the node is removed
    DoublyNode<T> * nextNode = node->Next;

    // Link the prevNode to nextNode
    prevNode->Next = nextNode;
    nextNode->Previous = prevNode;

    // It's now safe to remove
    // the selected index element
    delete node;

    // One element is removed
    m_count--;
}
```

The complexity of this operation is the same as the `Remove()` operation of the `LinkedList` data type; `O(1)` in the best case and `O(N)` in the worst case.

Inserting an element

Due to the existence of the `Previous` pointer, we also need to refactor the inserting operation in the `LinkedList` data type. For the `InsertHead()` operation, the `Previous` pointer of the former `Head` must point to the new `Head`, so that we can have the new `InsertHead()` operation as follows:

```
template <typename T>
void DoublyLinkedList<T>::InsertHead(T val)
{
    // Create a new Node
    DoublyNode<T> * node = new DoublyNode<T>(val);
```

```
// The current Head will no longer become a Head
// so the Next pointer of the new Node will
// point to the current Head
node->Next = Head;

// If the current Head is exist,
// the Previous pointer of the current Head
// should point to the node
if(Head != NULL)
    Head->Previous = node;

// The new Node now become the Head
Head = node;

// If the linked list is empty
// The Tail is also the Head
if(m_count == 0)
    Tail = Head;

// One element is added
m_count++;
}
```

The complexity of this `InsertHead()` operation is still `O(1)`.

For the `InsertTail()` operation, we need to point the `Previous` pointer of the new `Tail` to the node before it. The implementation of the `InsertTail()` operation will be as follows:

```
template <typename T>
void DoublyLinkedList<T>::InsertTail(T val)
{
    // If the linked list is empty,
    // just simply invoke InsertHead()
    if(m_count == 0)
    {
        InsertHead(val);
        return;
    }

    // Create a new Node
    DoublyNode<T> * node = new DoublyNode<T>(val);

    // The current Tail will no longer become a Tail
    // so the Next pointer of the current Tail will
    // point to the new node
    Tail->Next = node;
```

```
        // Also, the previous pointer of the new node
        // should point to the current Tail
        node->Previous = Tail;

        // The new Node now become the Tail
        Tail = node;

        // One element is added
        m_count++;
    }
```

The complexity of this InsertTail() operation is still O(1).

For the Insert() operation, we need to point the Previous pointer of the node after the new element to this new element. Also, the Previous pointer of the new node points to the node before this new node. The implementation of this operation will be as follows:

```
template <typename T>
void DoublyLinkedList<T>::Insert(int index, T val)
{
    // Check if the index is out of bound
    if(index < 0 || index > m_count)
        return;

    // If inserting a new Head
    if(index == 0)
    {
        InsertHead(val);
        return;
    }
    // If inserting a new Tail
    else if(index == m_count)
    {
        InsertTail(val);
        return;
    }

    // Start to find previous node
    // from the Head
    DoublyNode<T> * prevNode = Head;

    // Traverse the elements until
    // the selected index is found
    for(int i = 0; i < index - 1; ++i)
    {
        prevNode = prevNode->Next;
    }
```

```
    // Create the next node which is
    // the element after previous node
    DoublyNode<T> * nextNode = prevNode->Next;

    // Create a new node
    DoublyNode<T> * node = new DoublyNode<T>(val);

    // Insert this new node between
    // the previous node and the next node
    node->Next = nextNode;
    node->Previous = prevNode;
    prevNode->Next = node;
    nextNode->Previous = node;

    // One element is added
    m_count++;
}
```

The complexity of this operation is still the same as the `Insert()` operation of the `LinkedList` data type; `O(1)` in the best case and `O(N)` in the worst case.

Consuming the DoublyLinkedList ADT

Since the `LinkedList<T>` and `DoublyLinkedList<T>` data types have the exact same operations, we can use the code in the `main()` function of the `main.cpp` file in the `Singly_Linked_List.cbp` project to consume the `DoublyLinkedList` data type. The code works like a charm when I try it, and produces the exact same output as the output of the `Singly_Linked_List.cbp` project. However, since we now have a `PrintListBackward()` method, here is the code to apply to the backward movement in the `DoublyLinkedList` data type:

```
// Project: Doubly_Linked_List.cbp
// File : main.cpp
#include <iostream>
#include "DoublyNode.h"
#include "DoublyLinkedList.h"

using namespace std;

int main()
{
    // NULL
    DoublyLinkedList<int> linkedList = DoublyLinkedList<int>();
```

```
// it will be printed backwardly
// 43->NULL
linkedList.InsertHead(43);

// 43->76->NULL
linkedList.InsertHead(76);

// 15->43->76->NULL
linkedList.InsertTail(15);

// 44->15->43->76->NULL
linkedList.InsertTail(44);

// Print the list element
cout << "First Printed:" << endl;
linkedList.PrintListBackward();
cout << endl;

// 100->44->15->43->76->NULL
linkedList.Insert(4, 100);

// 100->44->48->15->43->76->NULL
linkedList.Insert(3, 48);

// 100->44->48->15->43->76->22->NULL
linkedList.Insert(0, 22);

// Print the list element
cout << "Second Printed:" << endl;
linkedList.PrintListBackward();
cout << endl;

return 0;
}
```

And if we build and run the preceding code, it will be displayed in the following window:

Applying List and LinkedList using STL

C++ has three data types which we can use to store specific items such as List, SinglyLinkedList, and DoublyLinkedList. std::vector can be used as List, std::forward_list can be used as SinglyLinkedList, and std::list can be used as DoublyLinkedList. They both have fetching, inserting, searching, and removing operations. However, the method names they have are different with our developed data type, and we are going to discuss this in this section. In this section, we are going to discuss std::vector and std::list only, since std::forward_list is similar to std::list.

std::vector

A **vector**, which is like an array, is a container to store a bunch of items contiguously. However, the vector can double its size automatically if we insert a new item when its capacity has been reached. Also, vectors have many member functions that arrays don't have, and provide iterators that act like pointers but aren't.

Don't forget to include the vector header at the beginning of code file if we are going to use the std::vector data type. To create a new vector object, we can initialize it as follows:

```
// Initialize a vector
vector<int> vectorlist = { 35, 41, 94 };
```

The preceding code will create a new vector containing three elements. However, we can initialize an empty vector and insert the vector using the push_back() method as follows:

```
// Initialize a vector
vector<int> vectorList;
vectorList.push_back(35);
vectorList.push_back(41);
vectorList.push_back(94);
```

To get the item of the specific index, we can use the at() method or we can use the square bracket ([]), as we can see in the following code snippet:

```
// Get item's value based on the index
int i = vectorList.at(1);
int j = vectorList[0];
```

However, it is better to always use the at() method instead of the [] operator when we want to access the specific element by its index in a vector instance. This is because, when we accidentally access the out of range position, the at() method will throw an out_of_range exception. Otherwise, the [] operator will give an undefined behavior.

Another data type that is used when applying a vector is an iterator. This is a pointer that is used to point to a specific position of the vector. Suppose we are going to insert a new item in the vector. We need to initialize the iterator first before we execute the insert() method, as we can see in the following code snippet:

```
// Initialize an iterator
vector<int>::iterator itr;
```

To insert a new item in the first position of the vector, we set the iterator to the beginning of the vector and then pass it to the insert() method as follows:

```
// Insert an item to the first position
itr = vectorList.begin();
vectorList.insert(itr, 58);
```

We can also insert a new item to the last position of the vector by setting the iterator to the end of the vector and then passing it to the insert() method as follows:

```
// Insert an item to the last position
itr = vectorList.end();
vectorList.insert(itr, 37);
```

The `end()` iterator is a past-the-end reference. In other words, trying to get the value of `*(vectorList.end())` will throw an exception.

And, to insert a new item into the middle of the vector, we can set the iterator to point to the beginning of vector, and then we increase the iterator to the desired index. The following is the code snippet that will insert a new item in the fourth position:

```
// Insert an item to the 4th position
itr = vectorList.begin();
vectorList.insert(itr + 3, 67);
```

Since the vector is also the zero-indexing array, the fourth element is laid in the `index = 3`.

To search for the desired element, we can use the `find()` method provided by the vector. However, to use this method, we need to include an algorithm header at the beginning of the code file. This method needs three arguments—the first position pointer (iterator), the last position pointer (iterator), and the value we are going to find. The method will return the position of the found item as the iterator. However, if no elements match, the function returns the last position iterator. The code snippet to search for an item in the vector is as follows:

```
// Search 41 element
// It should be found
itr = find (vectorList.begin(), vectorList.end(), 41);
if (itr != vectorList.end())
    cout << "Element found in vectorList: " << *itr;
else
    cout << "Element not found in vectorList";
cout << endl << endl;
```

The last operation we need is to remove an item from the desired index. We can use the `erase()` method provided by the vector. To use this method, we also need to include the algorithm header. Similar to the `insert()` method, we need to find out the beginning of the vector first by using an iterator. We can then increment the iterator by as many as the index positions we are going to remove. If we run the second element of the vector, the code should be as follows:

```
// Remove the 2nd element
itr = vectorList.begin();
vectorList.erase (itr + 1);
```

For the complete source code of this vector discussion, you can find on the code repository of this book under the `Vector` folder inside the `Chapter02` folder.

std::list

C++ has a built-in template class that implements the Doubly Linked List. Since then, it also contains all of the operations that the `DoublyLinkedList` data type has. Don't forget to include the `list` header at the beginning of code file if we are going to use the `std::list` data type. The usage of the iterator is also the same as the `vector` data type. We will refactor our code in the `main.cpp` file of the `Doubly_Linked_List.cbp` project so that we can use the `list` data type. The code should be as follows:

```cpp
int main()
{
    // Initialize a linked list
    list<int> linkedList;

    // 43->NULL
    linkedList.push_front(43);

    // 76->43->NULL
    linkedList.push_front(76);

    // 76->43->15->NULL
    linkedList.push_back(15);

    // 76->43->15->44->NULL
    linkedList.push_back(44);

    // Print the list element
    cout << "First Printed:" << endl;
    PrintLinkedList(linkedList);
    cout << endl;

    // 76->43->15->44->100->NULL
    list<int>::iterator itr = GetIterator(linkedList.begin(), 4);
    linkedList.insert(itr, 100);

    // 76->43->15->48->44->100->NULL
    itr = GetIterator(linkedList.begin(), 3);
    linkedList.insert(itr, 48);
```

```cpp
// 22->76->43->15->48->44->100->NULL
linkedList.insert(linkedList.begin(), 22);

// Print the list element
cout << "Second Printed:" << endl;
PrintLinkedList(linkedList);
cout << endl;

// Get value of the second index
// It should be 43
cout << "Get value of the second index:" << endl;
itr = GetIterator(linkedList.begin(), 2);
if(itr != linkedList.end())
    cout << *itr;
else
    cout << "not found";
cout << endl << endl;

// Find the position of value 15
// It should be found
itr = find (linkedList.begin(), linkedList.end(), 15);
if (itr != linkedList.end())
    cout << "Element found in linkedList: " << *itr;
else
    cout << "Element not found in linkedList";
cout << endl << endl;

// Remove first element
cout << "Remove the first element:" << endl;
itr = linkedList.begin();
linkedList.erase (itr);
// 76->43->15->48->44->100->NULL
PrintLinkedList(linkedList);
cout << endl;

// Remove fifth element
cout << "Remove the fifth element:" << endl;
itr = GetIterator(linkedList.begin(), 4);
linkedList.erase (itr);
// 76->43->15->48->100->NULL
PrintLinkedList(linkedList);
cout << endl;

return 0;
}
```

As we can see in the preceding code snippet, we need a method named `GetIterator()` since the iterator of the `list` data type is not a random access iterator, and so we need to increment it as many times as the desired index. The implementation of this method is as follows:

```
list<int>::iterator GetIterator(list<int>::iterator it, int x)
{
    for(int i = 0; i < x; ++i, ++it);
    return it;
}
```

To print out the elements of the `list`, we use the following method implementation:

```
void PrintLinkedList(const list<int>& llist)
{
    for (auto l : llist)
    {
        std::cout << l << " -> ";
    }
    cout << "NULL" << endl;
}
```

And, if we build and run the `Std_List.cbp` project, we will get the following output:

```
Terminal
First Printed:
76 -> 43 -> 15 -> 44 -> NULL

Second Printed:
22 -> 76 -> 43 -> 15 -> 48 -> 44 -> 100 -> NULL

Get value of the second index:
43

Element found in linkedList: 15

Remove the first element:
76 -> 43 -> 15 -> 48 -> 44 -> 100 -> NULL

Remove the fifth element:
76 -> 43 -> 15 -> 48 -> 100 -> NULL


Process returned 0 (0x0)   execution time : 0.016 s
Press ENTER to continue.
```

Summary

We have successfully built our own data structures in C++ and have found out the time complexity of each data structure. As we have discussed, each data structure has its own strengths and drawbacks. For instance, by using `List`, we can access the last element faster than `LinkedList`. However, in the `List`, removing the first element will take even more time, since we remove the first element since it needs to re-struct the array inside the `List`.

In the next chapter, we are going to learn how to build other data structures based on the data structures we have discussed in this chapter. These are stack, queue, and dequeue.

QA section

- What does zero-based indexing mean in an array?
- How do we find out how many elements an array has?
- What does a pointer in C++ do?
- Suppose we have a pointer named `ptr`. How do we get the value of the address that the `ptr` points to?
- Specify four common operations in List ADT.
- A node has two functions, please specify.
- What is the difference between a Singly Linked List and a Doubly Linked List?
- What is the STL function that we can use for list and linked list in C++?

Further reading

For a complete summary of time complexity for each data structure that we have discussed in this chapter, please take a look the following table:

Data Structure	Operation	Time Complexity	
		Best Case	Worst Case
List	Get()	O(1)	O(1)
	Insert()	O(N)	O(N)
	Search()	O(1)	O(N)
	Remove()	O(N)	O(N)
Singly Linked List	Get()	O(1)	O(N)
	Insert()	O(1)	O(N)
	Search()	O(1)	O(N)
	Remove()	O(1)	O(N)
Doubly Linked List	Get()	O(1)	O(N)
	Insert()	O(1)	O(N)
	Search()	O(1)	O(N)
	Remove()	O(1)	O(N)

Other reading sources you may find useful:

- https://www.geeksforgeeks.org/list-cpp-stl/
- http://www.cplusplus.com/reference/list/list/
- http://www.cplusplus.com/reference/vector/vector/

3
Constructing Stacks and Queues

In the previous chapter, we discussed several linear data types, which were list, linked list, and Doubly Linked List. In this chapter, we are going to discuss other linear data types, and those are stack, queue, and dequeue. The following are the topics we are going to discuss regarding these three data types:

- Building a Stack ADT and then fetching, pushing, and popping elements in this ADT
- Building a Queue ADT and then fetching, enqueuing, and dequeuing elements in this ADT
- Building a Dequeue ADT and then fetching, enqueuing, and dequeuing elements in this ADT

Technical requirements

To follow along with this chapter, as well as the source code, we require the following:

- A desktop PC or Notebook with Windows, Linux, or macOS
- GNU GCC v5.4.0 or above
- Code::Block IDE v17.12 (for Windows and Linux OS) or Code::Block IDE v13.12 (for macOS)
- You will find the code files on GitHub at `https://github.com/PacktPublishing/CPP-Data-Structures-and-Algorithms`

Building a Stack ADT

A `stack` data type is a list with some restriction in the list's operations. It can only perform the operations from one side, called the *top*. There are three basic operations in the `Stack` data type, and they are `Top()`, `Push()`, and `Pop()`. The `Top()` operation is used to fetch the value of the top position item only, the `Push()` operation will insert the new item in the top position, and the `Pop()` operation will remove the item in the top position. The stack is also known as a **Last In First Out** (**LIFO**) data type. To support these three operations, we will add one operation to the stack, which is `IsEmpty()`, to indicate whether the stack has elements or not. Please take a look at the following stack diagram:

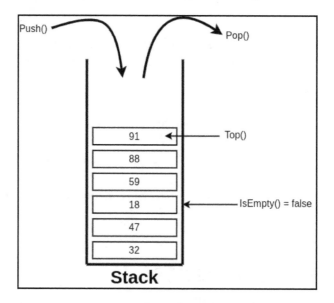

As we can see in the preceding **Stack** diagram, we have storage containing a bunch of numbers. However, the only opened side is the top side so that we can only put and take the number from that side. We can also take a peek at the topmost number from the top side.

In real life, we can imagine that the stack implementation is like when we wear many bangles on our hand. We put on the bangles one by one on our hand only from one side. While taking off the bangles, the last bangle we wear is the first bangle we can remove. Due to this, this is the only time we have access to wearing and removing the bangles.

Now, let's declare the `Stack` class in C++. We are going to use our preceding `LinkedList` data type to build a `Stack` data type. Similar to the `LinkedList` data type, we need an `m_count` private variable to hold the number of items in the `Stack` has. We also need another private variable to hold the top node so that the `Top()` operation can easily find the value of the top item from this variable. The variable name will be `m_top`. The following is the declaration of the `Stack` data type that we can find in the `Stack.h` file:

```
template <typename T>
class Stack
{
private:
    int m_count;
    Node<T> * m_top;

public:
    Stack();
    bool IsEmpty();
    T Top();
    void Push(T val);
    void Pop();
};
```

As we can see in the preceding code snippet, and as we discussed earlier, we have another method named `IsEmpty()`. It's used to ensure that `Stack` has at least one item before we invoke the `Top()` and `Pop()` operations, otherwise we will face a run-time error.

Fetching the item's value in the Stack ADT

In the `Stack` data type, we can only get the value of the top node. Thus, the `Top()` operation will show the value of the `m_top` node. The implementation of this operation is simple, as we can see in the following code snippet:

```
template <typename T>
T Stack<T>::Top()
{
    // Just return the value
    // of m_top node
    return m_top->Value;
}
```

As we can see, the operation just returns the value of `m_top` so that, no matter how many items there are in `Stack`, the complexity of this operation is *O(1)* for both the best case and worst case scenario. And don't forget to invoke the `IsEmpty()` method prior to the invocation of the `Top()` operation. We should not invoke the `Top()` operation if there's no item in `Stack` since it can cause a run-time error. The `IsEmpty()` method itself simply returns FALSE if there's at least one item in `Stack`; otherwise it returns TRUE. The implementation of `IsEmpty()` gives us an *O(1)* complexity and should be as follows:

```
template <typename T>
bool Stack<T>::IsEmpty()
{
    // return TRUE if there are no items
    // otherwise, return FALSE
    return m_count <= 0;
}
```

Pushing the items of the Stack ADT

As we discussed earlier, we can only add a new item from the top position of the stack. Since the `top` variable in the `Stack` is similar to `Head` variable in the `LinkedList`, we can utilize the implementation of `InsertHead()` in the `LinkedList` data type to be implemented in the `Push()` operation in the `Stack` data type. The implementation of the `Push()` operation should be as follows:

```
template <typename T>
void Stack<T>::Push(T val)
{
    // Create a new Node
    Node<T> * node = new Node<T>(val);

    // The Next pointer of this new node
    // will point to current m_top node
    node->Next = m_top;

    // The new Node now becomes the m_top node
    m_top = node;

    // One item is added
    m_count++;
}
```

The preceding code snippet is similar to the implementation of the InsertHead() operation in the LinkedList data type, except it doesn't have a Tail node. We just need to create a new node, then link that to the current top node by setting the Next pointer of the new node to the current top node. Obviously, the complexity of the Push() operation is *O(1)*.

Popping the items from the Stack ADT

Again, removing an item in the Stack data type is similar to the RemoveHead() operation in the LinkedList since we can only access the top node. We simply remove the first node and make the m_top variable handle the second node. The implementation of the Pop() operation should be as follows:

```
template <typename T>
void Stack<T>::Pop()
{
    // Do nothing if Stack is empty
    if(IsEmpty())
        return;

    // Prepare the current m_top
    // to remove
    Node<T> * node = m_top;

    // The new m_top node will be
    // the Next pointer of the current m_top node
    m_top = m_top->Next;

    // Now it's safe to remove
    // the first element
    delete node;

    // One item is removed
    m_count--;
}
```

Since the Pop() operation in the Stack data type adapts the RemoveHead() operation in LinkedList, they both have the exact same time complexity, which is *O(1)* for best and worst case scenario .

Consuming a Stack ADT

Now, it's time to play with our new Stack data type. We are going to create our preceding diagram using the Push() operation, and then print the content of the Stack class using the Pop() operation. To ensure that the stack is not empty, we are going to use the IsEmpty() operation and we'll use the Top() operation to get the topmost element to print the value. The code should be as follows:

```cpp
// Project: Stack.cbp
// File : main.cpp
#include <iostream>
#include "Stack.h"

using namespace std;

int main()
{
    // NULL
    Stack<int> stackInt = Stack<int>();

    // Store several numbers to the stack
    stackInt.Push(32);
    stackInt.Push(47);
    stackInt.Push(18);
    stackInt.Push(59);
    stackInt.Push(88);
    stackInt.Push(91);

    // list the element of stack
    while(!stackInt.IsEmpty())
    {
        // Get the top element
        cout << stackInt.Top() << " - ";

        // Remove the top element
        stackInt.Pop();
    }
    cout << "END" << endl;

    return 0;
}
```

Based on the preceding code, the first number we store in the stack—32, in this case—will be at the bottom position of the stack. When we call the Pop() operation, the last stored number will be removed first. The following output will be displayed if we build and run the preceding code:

```
⊗ ⊖ ⊡  Terminal
91 - 88 - 59 - 18 - 47 - 32 - END

Process returned 0 (0x0)    execution time : 0.002 s
Press ENTER to continue.
```

As we can see in the preceding output, the last number we put into the stack is the first number we get when we invoke the Pop() operation.

Another example of Stack ADT implementation

Another implementation of the stack is when the programming language checks the parenthesis expression's validity. For instance, in C++, we need to scope the bunch of lines using curly braces ({ }); or, when initializing an array, we need a square bracket ([ ]) to define the length of the array. It needs to ensure that the open curly brace has the closed curly brace, or the open square bracket has the close square bracket. Let's see the following possibility for the parenthesis expression:

```
{ ( ) [ { } ] }
{ ( [ ) } ]
{ ( ) } [
```

There are three lines in the preceding parenthesis expression for possibilities. In the first line, we can see that each opened parenthesis has its own closed parenthesis. It's also matched for each opened parenthesis to find out the closed parenthesis. The proof that it is a valid parenthesis expression is as follows:

In the second section, each opened parenthesis also has its closed parenthesis. However, the first opened square bracket must find the closed square bracket before it finds the other closed parentheses. In other words, the second line is an invalid parenthesis expression. The proof is as follows:

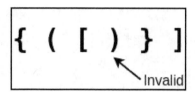

In the last line, we can see that there's an opened squared bracket without the closed square bracket. In this case, the stack will leave one element in the storage so that the parentheses expression is invalid. The proof is as follows:

Applying the `Stack` data type we built previously, let's design code to check the validity of the parenthesis expression. Every time the code retrieves the opened parenthesis, it just needs to store the opened parenthesis in the stack using the `Push()` operation. When the closed parenthesis comes, it needs to check whether the stack is empty. If so, the expression must be invalid since there is no opened parenthesis to be closed. Then, we retrieve the top element using the `Top()` operation. If the value is not matched with the closed parenthesis, it must be invalid as well. In contrast, if the parenthesis is matched, it just needs to remove the top element by using the `Pop()` operation. Until the expression has been scanned, we can decide whether the expression is valid if there's no element left in the stack. The code for this scenario is as follows:

```
bool IsValid (char expression[])
{
    int n = strlen(expression);

    Stack<char> stackChar = Stack<char>();

    for (int i = 0; i < n; ++i)
    {
        // If input is opened parenthesis
        // just store it in the stack
        if(expression[i] == '{')
```

```
    {
        stackChar.Push('{');
    }
    else if(expression[i] == '[')
    {
        stackChar.Push('[');
    }
    else if(expression[i] == '(')
    {
        stackChar.Push('(');
    }
    // Check when the input
    // is closed parenthesis
    else if (
        expression[i] == '}' ||
        expression[i] == ']' ||
        expression[i] == ')')
    {
        // If the stack is empty
        // or the last parenthesis is different
        // than the one we are closed,
        // then the expression is wrong
        if(expression[i] == '}' &&
            (stackChar.IsEmpty() || stackChar.Top() != '{'))
            return false;
        else if(expression[i] == ']' &&
            (stackChar.IsEmpty() || stackChar.Top() != '['))
            return false;
        else if(expression[i] == ')' &&
            (stackChar.IsEmpty() || stackChar.Top() != '('))
            return false;
        else
            stackChar.Pop();
    }
}

// If the stack is empty,
// the expression is valid
// otherwise it's invalid
if (stackChar.IsEmpty())
    return true; //
else
    return false;
}
```

Then, we can invoke the preceding `IsValid()` method using the following code snippet:

```cpp
int main()
{
    // Prepare array for storing
    // the expression
    char expr[1000];

    // Ask user to input the expression
    cout << "Please type the parenthesis expression ";
    cout << "then press ENTER!" << endl;
    cin >> expr;

    // Check the validity
    bool bo = IsValid(expr);

    // Notify the user
    cout << endl;
    cout << "The " << expr << " expression is ";
    if(bo)
        cout << "valid";
    else
        cout << "invalid";
    cout << endl;

    return 0;
}
```

If we run the code and supply the following expression:

```
{ ( ) [ { } ] }
```

It will say that the expression is valid, as we can see in the following output:

```
Terminal
Please type the parenthesis expression then press ENTER!
{()[{}]}

The {()[{}]} expression is valid

Process returned 0 (0x0)   execution time : 26.543 s
Press ENTER to continue.
```

You can try other parentheses expressions to ensure that the code we have built works.

Building a Queue ADT

A **queue** data type is a list with some restrictions to the effect that the inserting operation (**enqueue**) can only be performed from one side (called the **back**) and the removing operation (**dequeue**) can only be performed from the other side (called the **front**). Similar to the `Stack` data type, we can develop the `Queue` data type by using the `LinkedList` data type. For the `Enqueue()` operation, we can adopt the `InsertTail()` operation in the `LinkedList` data type since we are going to insert an element from the back, which is similar to the `Tail` node in the `LinkedList` data type. Also, for the `Dequeue()` operation, we will use the implementation of the `RemoveHead()` operation in the `LinkedList` data type. The `Queue` data type is also known as the **First In First Out** (**FIFO**) data type since the element that is inserted from the back of `Queue` will travel to the front side before it can be removed. Let's take a look at the following diagram showing the queue:

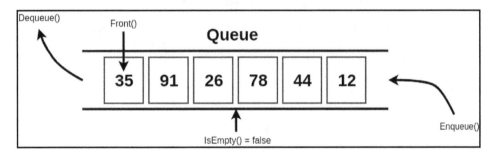

As we can see in the preceding diagram, there's a line of queueing numbers which has two sides opened. We insert a number from the right side (which is the backside in the **Queue**) and it then travels to the left side until it's at the frontside and is ready to dequeue. This `Queue` data type is similar to a queue in real life, for instance, a queue at a theatre, where we have to stand in a line from the back of the queue and wait until all of the people in front of us have been served.

The following is the declaration of the `Queue` data type. It's quite similar to the declaration of the `Stack` data type, so please take a look:

```
template <typename T>
class Queue
{
private:
    int m_count;
    Node<T> * m_front;
    Node<T> * m_back;

public:
```

```
Queue();
bool IsEmpty();
T Front();
void Enqueue(T val);
void Dequeue();
};
```

Similar to a `Stack` data type, the `Queue` data type also adopts the `LinkedList` data type. However, it has two private nodes—`m_front` and `m_back` instead of `Head` and `Tail` in the `LinkedList` data type. It also has a `Front()` operation to retrieve the front-most element's value, an `Enqueue()` operation to insert a new element in the back, and a `Dequeue()` operation to remove the front-most element.

Getting a value from Queue ADT

As we discussed earlier, we can only fetch the front value of the queue. For this purpose, we are going to implement the `Front()` operation to get the value of the front element. The implementation should be as follows:

```
template <typename T>
T Queue<T>::Front()
{
    // Just return the value
    // of m_front node
    return m_front->Value;
}
```

Since it just returns the value of the front element, the time complexity for this operation is *O(1)* for both best and worst case. Also, don't forget to invoke the `IsEmpty()` operation before invoking the `Front()` operation to ensure that the queue is not empty. The implementation of the `IsEmpty()` operation for the `Queue` data type is completely the same as the implementation of the `IsEmpty()` operation in the `Stack` data type.

Inserting an element into the Queue ADT

Inserting a new item in the Queue data type can only be performed from the back side, which means the newly inserted item will be pointed by the m_back pointer, and the Next pointer of the current element will point to this new element to create a new chaining node. However, it can be applied if there's at least one element before we insert the new element. If Queue is empty when we are going to insert a new element, we have to set the new element to be the front and the back element. Let's explore the following Enqueue() operation's implementation:

```
template <typename T>
void Queue<T>::Enqueue(T val)
{
    // Create a new Node
    Node<T> * node = new Node<T>(val);

    if(m_count == 0)
    {
        // If the queue is empty
        // the new node will be
        // m_front and m_back
        node->Next = NULL;
        m_front = node;
        m_back = m_front;
    }
    else
    {
        // If there's at least one element
        // in the queue, the current m_back element
        // won't be the Back element anymore
        // so the Next pointer of the current m_back
        // point to the new node
        m_back->Next = node;

        // The new Node now become the Back position
        m_back = node;
    }

    // One element is added
    m_count++;
}
```

As we can see in the preceding code snippet, there are two conditions when inserting a new element in the Queue data type. However, it doesn't depend on the number of elements inside the data type, so the time complexity for this operation is always *O(1)* for both best and worst case.

Removing an element from the Queue ADT

Removing an element can also be performed from the front side only, which is done by using the Dequeue() operation. This is similar to the RemoveHead() operation in the LinkedList data type—removing the current front node and then assigning the next element as the new front element. The implementation should be as follows:

```cpp
template <typename T>
void Queue<T>::Dequeue()
{
    // Do nothing if list is empty
    if(m_count == 0)
        return;

    // Save the current Front
    // to a new node
    Node<T> * node = m_front;

    // Point the Front pointer
    // to the element next to the current Front
    m_front = m_front->Next;

    // Now it's safe to remove
    // the first element
    delete node;

    // One element is removed
    m_count--;
}
```

Similar to the Enqueue() operation, the Dequeue() operation does not depend on the number of items inside the data type. The time complexity of this operation is *O(1)* for both best and worst case.

Consuming the Queue ADT

Now, let's create a new Queue instance that contains the different elements, as shown in the earlier diagram. The element will be inserted by using the Enqueue() operation. We can then display all queue elements by using the Front() and Dequeue() operations. The code should be as follows:

```cpp
// Project: Queue.cbp
// File : main.cpp
#include <iostream>
#include "Queue.h"

using namespace std;

int main()
{
    // NULL
    Queue<int> queueInt = Queue<int>();

    // Enqueue several numbers to the queue
    queueInt.Enqueue(35);
    queueInt.Enqueue(91);
    queueInt.Enqueue(26);
    queueInt.Enqueue(78);
    queueInt.Enqueue(44);
    queueInt.Enqueue(12);

    // list the element of queue
    while(!queueInt.IsEmpty())
    {
        // Get the front element
        cout << queueInt.Front() << " - ";

        // Remove the front element
        queueInt.Dequeue();
    }
    cout << "END" << endl;

    return 0;
}
```

In contrast to the `Stack` data type, the first element inserted into the queue will be the first element that will be removed if we invoke the `Dequeue()` operation. We should get the following output if we build and run the `Queue.cbp` project:

```
Terminal
35 - 91 - 26 - 78 - 44 - 12 - END

Process returned 0 (0x0)   execution time : 0.006 s
Press ENTER to continue.
```

Building a Deque ADT

A **dequeue**, which stands for **double-ended queue**, is a queue that can insert and remove items from two sides: the **front** and **back**. To build this data structure, we are going to adopt the `DoublyLinkedList` data type we already built in the previous chapter. Similar to the `Queue` data type, the `Dequeue` data type also has the `Front()` operation to fetch the front-most element's value. The `Enqueue()` operation in the `Queue` data type will become `EnqueueBack()` in the `Dequeue` data type, and the `Dequeue()` operation in the `Queue` data type will become `DequeueFront()` in the `Dequeue` data type. However, since we adopt the `DoublyLinkedList` data type instead of `LinkedList`, the implementation will be different. Besides those operations, we are also going to build the following operations:

- The `Back()` operation to fetch the back-most element's value.
- The `EnqueueFront()` operation to insert a new element into the front side. It will be similar to the implementation of the `InsertHead()` operation in the `DoublyLinkedList` data type.
- The `DequeueBack()` operation to remove an element from the back side. It will be similar to the implementation of the `RemoveTail()` operation in the `DoublyLinkedList` data type.

Let's take a look at the following diagram of the **Deque** data type:

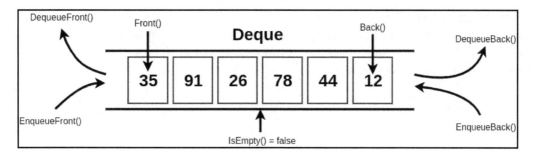

Based on the preceding requirement, the declaration of the `Deque` data structure should be as follows:

```
template <typename T>
class Deque
{
private:
    int m_count;
    DoublyNode<T> * m_front;
    DoublyNode<T> * m_back;

public:
    Deque();
    bool IsEmpty();
    T Front();
    T Back();
    void EnqueueFront(T val);
    void EnqueueBack(T val);
    void DequeueFront();
    void DequeueBack();
};
```

Notice that we now use the `DoublyNode` data type instead of the `Node` data type since we are going to use the implementation of the `DoublyLinkedList` data type for the `Deque` data type.

Fetching a value from a Deque

The implementation of the `Front()` and `IsEmpty()` operations for the `Deque` data type is the same as the implementation of the `Front()` and `IsEmpty()` operations for the `Queue` data type. For the `Back()` operation, it just returns the value of the `m_back` node. The implementation should be as follows:

```
template <typename T>
T Deque<T>::Back()
{
    // Just return the value
    // of m_back node
    return m_back->Value;
}
```

Since the implementation of this operation doesn't depend on the number of `Deque` elements, the complexity of this operation is *O(1)* for both best and worst case.

Enqueueing an element into the Deque ADT

There are two ways to enqueue a new element into the `Deque` data type—from the front side and from the back side. To enqueue a new element from the front side, we can use the `EnqueueFront()` operation, which will create a new `DoublyNode` node and then assigns the `Next` pointer of this new node to the current `m_front` node. Also, if the current `m_front` exists, the `Previous` pointer of the current `m_front` node points to the new node. Now, the `m_front` node will change to the new node. If it's the only node that resides in the `Deque` data type, the `m_back` node will also point to this new node. The implementation of the `EnqueueFront()` operation should be as follows:

```
template <typename T>
void Deque<T>::EnqueueFront(T val)
{
    // Create a new Node
    DoublyNode<T> * node = new DoublyNode<T>(val);

    // The current m_front will no longer become a m_front
    // so the Next pointer of the new Node will
    // point to the current m_front
    node->Next = m_front;

    // If the current m_front is exist,
    // the previous pointer of the current m_front
    // should point to the node
```

```
        if(m_front != NULL)
            m_front->Previous = node;

        // The new Node now become the m_front
        m_front = node;

        // If the deque is empty
        // The m_back is also the m_front
        if(m_count == 0)
            m_back = m_front;

        // One element is added
        m_count++;
    }
```

Similar to the `EnqueueFront()` operation, the `EnqueueBack()` operation will create a new `DoublyNode` node. The `Next` pointer of the current `m_back` node will point to this new node, and the `Previous` pointer of this new node will point to the current `m_back` node. Now, we have a new back-most element, so we assign the `m_back` node to the new node. For simplicity, if there's no element before we enqueue a new element, just ignore the preceding step and invoke the `EnqueueFront()` operation instead. The implementation of the `EnqueueBack()` operation should be as follows:

```
    template <typename T>
    void Deque<T>::EnqueueBack(T val)
    {
        // If the deque is empty,
        // just simply invoke EnqueueFront()
        if(m_count == 0)
        {
            EnqueueFront(val);
            return;
        }

        // Create a new Node
        DoublyNode<T> * node = new DoublyNode<T>(val);

        // The current m_back will no longer become a m_back
        // so the Next pointer of the current m_back will
        // point to the new node
        m_back->Next = node;

        // Also, the previous pointer of the new node
        // should point to the current m_back
        node->Previous = m_back;
```

```
    // The new Node now become the m_back
    m_back = node;

    // One element is added
    m_count++;
}
```

The two enqueueing operations we have built do not depend on the number of deque elements so their complexity is *O(1)* for both best and worst case.

Dequeuing an element from the Deque ADT

Similar to enqueueing a new element, dequeuing an element in the Deque data type can also be performed from both the front and back sides. When we are going to dequeue from the front side, which is done by using the DequeueFront() operation, we initially assign the new m_front to the Next pointer of the current m_front node. If the new, current m_front exists then it points its Previous pointer to NULL. Now, it's safe to delete the frontmost element. The implementation of the DequeueFront() operation should be as follows:

```
template <typename T>
void Deque<T>::DequeueFront()
{
    // Do nothing if deque is empty
    if(m_count == 0)
        return;

    // Save the current m_front
    // to a new node
    DoublyNode<T> * node = m_front;

    // Point the m_front Pointer
    // to the element next to the current m_front
    m_front = m_front->Next;

    // Now it's safe to remove
    // the first element
    delete node;

    // If there's still any element in the deque,
    // the previous pointer of the m_front
    // should point to NULL
    if(m_front != NULL)
        m_front->Previous = NULL;
```

```
        // One element is removed
        m_count--;
    }
```

If we are going to dequeue an element from the back side, which is done by using the DequeueBack() operation, we initially assign the new m_back node to the Previous pointer of the current m_back node. Then, we just point the Next pointer of the new, current m_back node to NULL so that it no longer points to the back-most element. Now, it's safe to delete the back-most element. The implementation of the DequeueBack() operation should be as follows:

```cpp
template <typename T>
void Deque<T>::DequeueBack()
{
    // Do nothing if deque is empty
    if(m_count == 0)
        return;

    // If deque element is only one
    // just simply call DequeueFront()
    if(m_count == 1)
    {
        DequeueFront();
        return;
    }

    // Save the current m_back
    // to a new node
    DoublyNode<T> * node = m_back;

    // Point the m_back Pointer
    // to the element before the current m_back
    m_back = m_back->Previous;

    // Set the new Next pointer of the new m_back
    // to NULL since we are going to delete
    // the last element
    m_back->Next = NULL;

    // Now it's safe to remove
    // the last element
    delete node;

    // One element is removed
    m_count--;
}
```

Both the `DequeueFront()` and `DequeueBack()` operations we have designed do not depend on the number of the deque element, so we can say that the complexity of these two operations is *O(1)* for both best and worst cases.

Consuming the Deque ADT

We are going to create a deque containing the elements shown in the preceding diagram. Since the `Deque` data type is similar to the `Queue` data type, we are going to use the `Back()` operation to peek at the element's value. The elements' value will be displayed from back to front. The code will be as follows:

```cpp
// Project: Deque.cbp
// File : main.cpp
#include <iostream>
#include "Deque.h"

using namespace std;

int main()
{
    // NULL
    Deque<int> deque = Deque<int>();

    // Enqueue several numbers to the deque
    // 26
    deque.EnqueueFront(26);
    // 26 - 78
    deque.EnqueueBack(78);
    // 26 - 78 - 44
    deque.EnqueueBack(44);
    // 91 - 26 - 78 - 44
    deque.EnqueueFront(91);
    // 35 - 91 - 26 - 78 - 44
    deque.EnqueueFront(35);
    // 35 - 91 - 26 - 78 - 44 - 12
    deque.EnqueueBack(12);

    // list the element of queue
    while(!deque.IsEmpty())
    {
        // Get the front element
        cout << deque.Back() << " - ";

        // Remove the front element
        deque.DequeueBack();
```

```
    }
    cout << "END" << endl;

    return 0;
}
```

And if we run the preceding code, we get the following output:

```
😕😑🗔  Terminal
12 - 44 - 78 - 26 - 91 - 35 - END

Process returned 0 (0x0)    execution time : 0.003 s
Press ENTER to continue.
```

Summary

In this chapter, we have successfully built others linear data types: the Stack, Queue, and Deque data types. We can use the Stack data type if we need storage that only has one side to insert and remove an element, we can use the Queue data type if we need storage which has to insert and remove the element from a different side, and if we need storage that can be accessed from two sides, both the front and back sides, we can use the Deque data type. Fortunately, the time complexity for all of the operations in these three data types is O(1), and doesn't depend on the number of the elements in the data type. In the next chapter, we are going to discuss various sorting algorithms to arrange the elements inside the data types we have discussed so far.

QA section

- Specify three basic operations in the Stack data type!
- What does LIFO refer to and with which data type (covered in this chapter) is it associated?
- Give an example of stack implementation in real life
- What is stack implementation in a programming language?
- What is deque also known as?
- What is the difference between queue and deque?
- Why is the complexity of the data types *O(1)*? Can you guess why the number of elements in the data type doesn't affect the complexity?

Further reading

For reference, you can refer to the following links:

- http://www.geeksforgeeks.org/stack-data-structure/
- http://www.geeksforgeeks.org/queue-data-structure/
- http://www.geeksforgeeks.org/deque-set-1-introduction-applications/
- https://visualgo.net/en/list?slide=4
- https://visualgo.net/en/list?slide=5
- https://visualgo.net/en/list?slide=7

4
Arranging Data Elements Using a Sorting Algorithm

In the previous chapter, we discussed several linear data structures, such as linked list, stack, queue, and dequeue. In this chapter, we are going to arrange data elements in a list using some sorting algorithm techniques. The following are the popular sorting algorithms that we are going to discuss in this chapter:

- Bubble sort
- Selection sort
- Insertion sort
- Merge sort
- Quick sort
- Counting sort
- Radix sort

Technical requirements

To follow along with this chapter, as well as the source code, you are going to require the following:

- A desktop PC or Notebook with Windows, Linux, or macOS
- GNU GCC v5.4.0 or above
- Code Block IDE v17.12 (for Windows and Linux OS) or Code Block IDE v13.12 (for macOS)
- You will find the code files on GitHub at `https://github.com/PacktPublishing/CPP-Data-Structures-and-Algorithms`

Bubble sort

Bubble sort is a simple sorting algorithm, but it has a slow process time. It will divide an input list into two parts—a sublist of items already sorted on the right side and a sublist of items remaining to be sorted in the rest of the list. If we are going to sort a list of elements in ascending order, the algorithm will move the greatest value to the right position followed by the second greatest value and so on, similar to air bubbles when they rise to the top. Suppose we have an array of unsorted elements and are going to sort them using the bubble sort algorithm. The following are the steps required to perform the sorting process:

1. Compare each pair of adjacent items, for instance `array[0]` with `array[1]`, `array[1]` with `array[2]`, and so on.
2. Swap that pair if the items are not in the correct order. Since we are going to sort in ascending order, the correct order will be `array[0] <= array[1]`, `array[1] <= array[2]`, and so on.
3. Repeat the first and second steps until the end of the array is reached.
4. By now, the largest item is in the last position. We can omit this item and repeat step **1** until step **3** until no swap item is found.

Let's create an unsorted array containing six elements—`{43, 21, 26, 38, 17, 30}`. By using the bubble sort algorithm, we are going to sort this array. We will pick the first pair of adjacent items, `43` and `21`. Since `43` is greater than `21`, we have to swap the position and now the array becomes `{21, 43, 26, 38, 17, 30}`. Again, we compare `43` to `26` and need to swap them, and since `43` is the greatest item in the array, each pair of adjacent items in comparison will swap the pair so that `43` will be the last position in the array. By now, the array will be `{21, 26, 38, 17, 30, 43}`.

The element `43` is now in the correct position, so we don't need to include it in the repeated step. In the remaining unsorted elements, we do the same process as we did in the preceding step. First, we compare `21` and `26`, so no swapping is necessary, and then compare `26` and `38`, where again no swapping is necessary. When we compare `38` and `17`, we need to swap these items so the array becomes `{21, 26, 17, 38, 30, 43}`. Again, we compare `38` and `30`, and they need to be swapped so that `38` is now in the correct position. The array will then be `{21, 26, 17, 30, 38, 43}`. This function will go on until there is nothing to be sorted.

Now, we can go further and develop C++ code for this sorting algorithm. We will have a function named `BubbleSort()` that passes an array and the length of the array as arguments. The array we pass to this function will be sorted, so we need the `swap()` function provided by C++ STL in the `std` namespace. In this function, we have the `unsortedElements` variable to hold the remaining unsorted elements. In the beginning, this variable is set with the length of the array. We then iterate all unsorted elements until there are no swapped items, which is marked by the `isSwapped` variable. As we discussed earlier, when we iterate all unsorted elements, we swap each pair of adjacent items if they are not in the correct position. The code should be as follows:

```cpp
// Project: Bubble_Sort.cbp
// File    : Bubble_Sort.cpp

#include <iostream>

using namespace std;

void BubbleSort(int arr[], int arrSize)
{
    // Flag for swapping element
    bool isSwapped;

    // The value will be decreased
    // every time one element has been sorted
    int unsortedElements = arrSize;
    do
    {
        // If there's at least two element are swapped
        // it will be true
        isSwapped = false;

        // Iterate through the array's element
        for(int i = 0; i < unsortedElements - 1; ++i)
        {
            if (arr[i] > arr[i+1])
            {
                swap(arr[i], arr[i+1]);
                isSwapped = true;
            }
        }

        // After iteration, the last element has been sorted
        // so it will be ignored in the next iteration
        --unsortedElements;
    }
    // Do comparison again if there's swapped element
```

```
        // otherwise, all array's elements have been sorted
        while(isSwapped);
    }

    int main()
    {
        cout << "Bubble Sort" << endl;

        // Initialize a new array
        int arr[] = {43, 21, 26, 38, 17, 30};
        int arrSize = sizeof(arr)/sizeof(*arr);

        // Display the initial array
        cout << "Initial array: ";
        for (int i=0; i < arrSize; ++i)
            cout << arr[i] << " ";
        cout << endl;

        // Sort the array with BubbleSort algorithm
        BubbleSort(arr, arrSize);

        // Display the sorted array
        cout << "Sorted array : ";
        for (int i=0; i < arrSize; ++i)
            cout << arr[i] << " ";
        cout << endl;

        return 0;
    }
```

As we can see in the preceding code, we used the isSwapped flag to indicate whether the do...while iteration is needed or not. It's useful to stop the iteration if we pass a sorted array to the BubbleSort() function, so it will only need to iterate through the input array elements once. So, the time complexity of this function is *O(N)* in the best case if we pass a sorted array on the function. And since there's a nested for iteration in the do...while iteration, the bubble sort time complexity for the worst case is *O(N2)*. If we build and run the preceding code, we should see the following output on the screen:

```
⊗ ⊜ ⊡   Terminal
Bubble Sort
Initial array: 43 21 26 38 17 30
Sorted array : 17 21 26 30 38 43

Process returned 0 (0x0)   execution time : 0.020 s
Press ENTER to continue.
```

Selection sort

Similar to bubble sort, **selection sort** also divides an input list into two parts—a sublist of items already sorted in the left side and a sublist of items remaining to be sorted in the rest of the list. If we are going to sort the input list in ascending order, the lowest items will be in the leftmost position in the input list. These are the steps to perform a selection sort on a given input list:

1. Find the first index of the unsorted sublist and mark it as `minIndex`. If it's the first sorting iteration, the index should be `0`.
2. Iterate through the elements of the unsorted sublist, starting at its first element (the first time, it should be index `1` through n - 1) and compare the current value element in the iteration with the first index of the unsorted sublist. If the value of the current index is lower than the value of the first index, set the current index to `minIndex`.
3. After finishing the unsorted elements iteration, swap each value of the first index of the unsorted `sublist` and the `minIndex`.
4. Repeat step **1** and step **3** until the unsorted sublist has only one item remaining.

Let's borrow the unsorted array we used in the preceding bubble sort algorithm, which has the items `{43, 21, 26, 38, 17, 30}`, and then perform the selection sort algorithm on it. In the first iteration, we will pick `array[0]` as the first index of the unsorted sublist. Then, we iterate through `array[1]` to `array[5]` and find that **17** is the lowest item in the array. We can now swap `array[0]` and `array[4]` as in the following diagram:

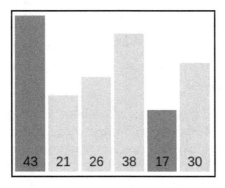

Now, `array[0]` stores the sorted item. We can pick `array[1]` as the first index of the unsorted sublist that holds **21**. Through the iteration of the unsorted sublist, it is found that **21** is the lowest item, so it's not swapped with anything. Please see the following diagram:

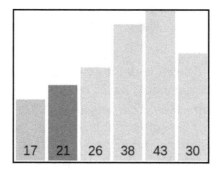

Now, we've got `array[2]` as the first index of the unsorted sublist; it holds **26**. Similar to the previous iteration, it won't be swapped with anything since it's the lowest item in the unsorted sublist, as we can see in the following diagram:

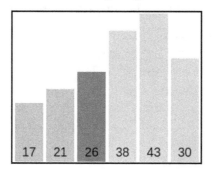

As of now, `array[0]`, `array[1]`, and `array[2]` have been sorted. The process will go on until there is nothing left to be sorted.

Since we have now understood the concept of selection sort, we can develop a code to make performing selection sorts a lot easier. Similar to the `BubbleSort()` function, the selection sort function will also pass an array that needs to be sorted and the length of the array. We then pick the first position of each unsorted sublist to be swapped with the lowest item in the current unsorted list. This will be repeated until the unsorted sublist remains at one item. The code should be as follows:

```
// Project: Selection_Sort.cbp
// File    : Selection_Sort.cpp
```

```cpp
#include <iostream>

using namespace std;

void SelectionSort(int arr[], int arrSize)
{
    // variable to store the index of the minimum value
    // in each iteration
    int minIndex;

    // Iterate until the N-1 elements
    for(int i = 0; i < arrSize - 1; ++i)
    {
        // Set the first unsorted element
        // as the minimum value
        minIndex = i;

        // Iterate through the unsorted elements only
        for(int j = i + 1; j < arrSize; ++j)
        {
            // set the new minimum value
            // if the saved minimum value is higher
            // than the current index value
            if (arr[j] < arr[minIndex])
                minIndex = j;
        }

        // Swap the the first unsorted element
        // with the minimum value
        swap(arr[i], arr[minIndex]);
    }
}

int main()
{
    cout << "Selection Sort" << endl;

    // Initialize a new array
    int arr[] = {43, 21, 56, 78, 97, 30};
    int arrSize = sizeof(arr)/sizeof(*arr);

    // Display the initial array
    cout << "Initial array: ";
    for (int i = 0; i < arrSize; ++i)
        cout << arr[i] << " ";
    cout << endl;

    // Sort the array with SelectionSort algorithm
```

```
        SelectionSort(arr, arrSize);

        // Display the sorted array
        cout << "Sorted array : ";
        for (int i = 0; i < arrSize; ++i)
            cout << arr[i] << " ";
        cout << endl;

        return 0;
    }
```

As we can see in the preceding code, there's a nested `for` loop in a `for` loop. The outer `for` loop is used to iterate the unsorted sublist while the inner `for` loop is used to find the lowest item. Contrary to bubble sort, selection sort cannot detect whether an input list is sorted at the beginning of the process, so the time complexity of this sorting algorithm is *O(N2)* for both the best and worst cases. If we build and run the preceding code, we are going to see the following output on the screen:

```
⊗ ⊖ ⊕  Terminal
Selection Sort
Initial array: 43 21 26 38 17 30
Sorted array : 17 21 26 30 38 43

Process returned 0 (0x0)   execution time : 0.002 s
Press ENTER to continue.
```

Insertion sort

Insertion sort is a sorting algorithm that is similar to arranging a hand of poker cards. This sorting algorithm will also divide the list into a sorted and unsorted sublist in the sorting process. For clarity, we pick an item as a reference, then go through the sorted sublist and find the correct position based on performing a comparison. This process is repeated until all the items are sorted, which means that we have to iterate through all of the array's elements.

Let's use our previous array {43, 21, 26, 38, 17, 30} and then perform an insertion sort algorithm on it. First, we set `array[0]` as the sorted sublist, so we pick `array[1]` as the reference. Now, we compare the reference item, which is **21**, with the sorted sublist. See the following diagram:

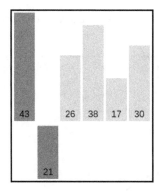

Since **21** is lower than **43**, **43** will be shifted to `array[1]` and since no more items are in the sorted sublist, **21** is put into `array[0]`. Now, `array[0]` and `array[1]` are in the sorted sublist, as we can see in the following diagram:

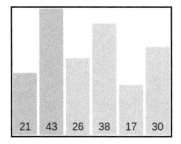

Now, we move to `array[2]`, which is **26**. We will set it as a reference item rather than iterating through the sorted sublist that contains **21** and **43**. We will have something similar to the following figure:

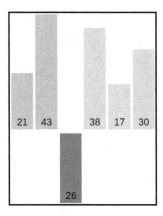

When **26** is compared with **43**, **43** will be shifted to the place where **26** is. And since **26** is greater than **21**, **26** now occupies `array[1]`. By now, the array will be as follows:

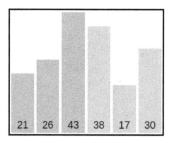

Again, we pick **38** as the reference and then iterate through to the sorted sublist, which is **21**, **26**, and **43**. Please see the following diagram:

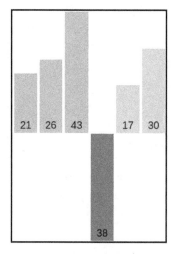

When the reference item is compared with **43**, **43** will be shifted to the place of the reference item since it's lower than **43**. Then, the reference item is compared with **26**. Since it's greater than **26**, **38** will be in-between **26** and **43** as we can see in the following diagram:

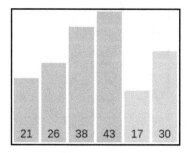

We do the same preceding iteration for the remaining items, **17** and **30**, until we've got a sorted array as follows:

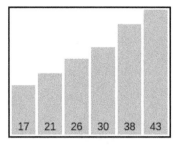

Now, let's design C++ code based on the preceding explanation. We need to iterate each element to be the reference item and based on this reference item, we can iterate the sorted sublist. The code should be as follows:

```cpp
// Project: Insertion_Sort.cbp
// File    : Insertion_Sort.cpp

#include <iostream>

using namespace std;

void InsertionSort(int arr[], int arrSize)
{
    // Iterate to all array's element
    for(int i = 0; i < arrSize; ++i)
    {
        // Set the current element
        // as reference value
        int refValue = arr[i];

        // variable to shift the element
        // to right position
        int j;

        // Iterate through the sorted element
        // to insert the reference value
        // in right position
        for(j = i - 1; j >= 0; --j)
        {
            // if the value of the current index
            // is greater than the reference value then
            // move the current value to right side
            // otherwise, put the reference value
            // in the current index
```

```cpp
                if(arr[j] > refValue)
                    arr[j+1] = arr[j];
                else
                    break;
            }

            // here's the line to put the reference value
            // in the current index (the right position)
            arr[j + 1] = refValue;
        }
    }

int main()
{
    cout << "Insertion Sort" << endl;

    // Initialize a new array
    int arr[] = {43, 21, 26, 38, 17, 30};
    int arrSize = sizeof(arr)/sizeof(*arr);

    // Display the initial array
    cout << "Initial array: ";
    for (int i=0; i < arrSize; ++i)
        cout << arr[i] << " ";
    cout << endl;

    // Sort the array with InsertionSort algorithm
    InsertionSort(arr, arrSize);

    // Display the sorted array
    cout << "Sorted array : ";
    for (int i=0; i < arrSize; ++i)
        cout << arr[i] << " ";
    cout << endl;

    return 0;
}
```

As we can see in the `InsertionSort()` function, similarly to the `SelectionSort()` function there's also a nested `for` loop in a `for` loop. The outer `for` loop is used to iterate the unsorted sublist while the inner `for` loop is used to find the correct position to insert the `refValue`. Indeed, this will make the time complexity of this sorting algorithm become *O(n2)* for the worst case scenario. Fortunately, in the inner `for` loop, we have an `if` comparison that will break the inner `for` loop if the reference value is greater than the biggest item in the sorted sublist. Imagine we pass a sorted list to the `InsertionSort()` function. This `if` comparison will ignore the inner `for` loop since it will only execute once, so for the best case scenario the time complexity of this sorting algorithm is *O(n)*. The output on the screen should be as follows when we build and run the preceding code:

```
Insertion Sort
Initial array: 43 21 26 38 17 30
Sorted array : 17 21 26 30 38 43

Process returned 0 (0x0)    execution time : 0.013 s
Press ENTER to continue.
```

Merge sort

Merge sort is an efficient sorting algorithm that divides the input array into two parts of a sublist. It sorts each sublist and then merges them. To sort each sublist, the algorithm divides the sublist in two again. If this sublist of the sublist can be divided into two halves, then it will be. The idea of the merge sort is that it will merge all the sorted sublists into the fully sorted list. Suppose we have an array containing these elements, {7, 1, 5, 9, 3, 6, 8, 2}, as shown in the following diagram:

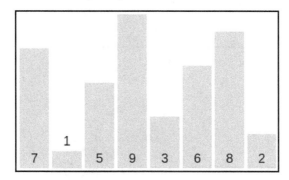

We can divide the array into two sublists, which are [**7, 1, 5, 9**] and [**3, 6, 8, 2**]. Then, the first sublist can be divided as well to become [**7, 1**] and [**5, 9**]. We can sort these sublists and they will be [**1, 7**] and [**5, 9**], and then we can merge this sublist so that it becomes [**1, 5, 7, 9**], as shown in the following diagram:

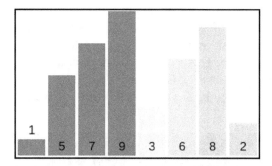

By now, we have one sorted sublist. We need to sort another sublist, [**3, 6, 8, 2**]. We can divide this sublist to become [**3, 6**] and [**8, 2**], and then sort them partially to become [**3, 6**] and [**2, 8**]. These sublists can be merged and become [**2, 3, 6, 8**], as we can see in the following diagram:

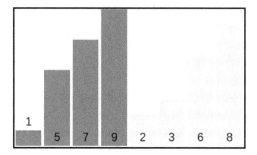

By now, we have two sorted sublists. Now, we can merge these two sublists to become [**1, 2, 3, 5, 6, 7, 8, 9**], as shown in the following diagram:

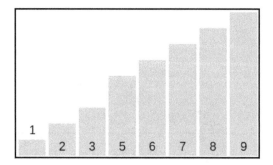

When designing a code for a merge sort, we need to have two functions to perform it. The first function is the Merge() function, which passes an array, a start index, a middle index, and an end index. This function is used when we have an array where each half part has been sorted, for instance, [**1, 5, 7, 9, 2, 3, 6, 8**] as we did in the preceding diagram. The function's implementation should be as follows:

```
void Merge(
    int arr[],
    int startIndex,
    int middleIndex,
    int endIndex)
{
    // Numbers of elements that will be sorted
    // from startIndex until endIndex
    int totalElements = endIndex - startIndex + 1;

    // Temporary array to store merged array
    int * tempArray = new int[totalElements];

    // Index of left subarray
    // arr[startIndex ... middleIndex]
    int leftIndex = startIndex;

    // Index of right subarray
    // arr[middleIndex + 1 ... endIndex]
    int rightIndex = middleIndex + 1;

    // Index of merged array
    int mergedIndex = 0;

    // Merge the two subarrays
    while (leftIndex <= middleIndex && rightIndex <= endIndex)
    {
        if(arr[leftIndex] <= arr[rightIndex])
        {
            // Store the left subarray's element
            // if it's lower than the right one
            tempArray[mergedIndex] = arr[leftIndex];

            // Go to next left subarray index
            ++leftIndex;
        }
        else
        {
            // Store the right subarray's element
            // if it's lower than the left one
            tempArray[mergedIndex] = arr[rightIndex];
```

```
            // Go to next right subarray index
            ++rightIndex;
        }

        // Go to next merged array index
        ++mergedIndex;
    }

    // If there're any remaining element in left subarray
    // that is not stored to merged array yet
    while (leftIndex <= middleIndex)
    {
        tempArray[mergedIndex] = arr[leftIndex];

        // Go to next left subarray index
        ++leftIndex;

        // Go to next merged array index
        ++mergedIndex;
    }

    // If there're any remaining element in right subarray
    // that is not stored to merged array yet
    while (rightIndex <= endIndex)
    {
        tempArray[mergedIndex] = arr[rightIndex];

        // Go to next right subarray index
        ++rightIndex;

        // Go to next merged array index
        ++mergedIndex;
    }

    // Now, the merged array has been sorted
    // Copy the elements to the original array
    for (int i = 0; i < totalElements; ++i)
    {
        arr[startIndex + i] = tempArray[i];
    }

    // Remove the temporary array tempArray
    delete[] tempArray;

    return;
}
```

As we can see in the preceding code, we need `tempArray` to store the sorted array as a result of the two sorted sublists being merged. It will rearrange the array by merging these two sublists. After this is completed, put all of the elements of the `tempArray` in the correct order. This will copy the temporary array into the original array.

If we have a really random array, we need another function, named `MergeSort()`, to separate the array into two sublists. The function's implementation should be as follows:

```
void MergeSort(
    int arr[],
    int startIndex,
    int endIndex)
{
    // Only perform sort process
    // if the end index is higher than start index
    if(startIndex < endIndex)
    {
        // Find middle index
        int middleIndex = (startIndex + endIndex) / 2;

        // Sort left subarray
        // arr[startIndex ... middleIndex]
        MergeSort(arr, startIndex, middleIndex);

        // Sort right subarray
        // arr[middleIndex + 1 ... endIndex]
        MergeSort(arr, middleIndex + 1, endIndex);

        // Merge the left and the right subarray
        Merge(arr, startIndex, middleIndex, endIndex);
    }

    return;
}
```

As we can see in the preceding code, the `MergeSort()` function will call itself incursively until the halved sublist cannot be divided any more. It then invokes the `Merge()` function we created previously to merge the two sorted sublists. To invoke the `MergeSort()` function, we can make the following `main()` function using the preceding array we used in the previous illustration:

```
int main()
{
    cout << "Merge Sort" << endl;

    // Initialize a new array
```

```cpp
    int arr[] = {7, 1, 5, 9, 3, 6, 8, 2};
    int arrSize = sizeof(arr)/sizeof(*arr);

    // Display the initial array
    cout << "Initial array: ";
    for (int i=0; i < arrSize; ++i)
        cout << arr[i] << " ";
    cout << endl;

    // Sort the array with MergeSort algorithm
    MergeSort(arr, 0, arrSize - 1);

    // Display the sorted array
    cout << "Sorted array : ";
    for (int i=0; i < arrSize; ++i)
        cout << arr[i] << " ";
    cout << endl;

    return 0;
}
```

As we can see in the `main()` function, we invoked the `MergeSort()` function and passed an input array and the range of the element we desired to sort, which is from index `0` to the last element. The output of the preceding code (that has been saved in the `Merge_Sort.cpp` file) should be as follows:

```
    Terminal
Merge Sort
Initial array: 7 1 5 9 3 6 8 2
Sorted array : 1 2 3 5 6 7 8 9

Process returned 0 (0x0)   execution time : 0.013 s
Press ENTER to continue.
```

Now, we need to find the time complexity of this sorting algorithm. As we discussed earlier, we have to divide the input array into two halved sublists, divide these sublists into another two halved sublists, and so on until only one element remains in the sublists. The sublist elements will be passed to the `Merge()` function, where the time complexity of the `Merge()` function is $O(N)$ since it only contains one level while in the loop. The analysis for the `MergeSort()` function that invokes the `Merge()` function will be as follows:

- Level 1: `Merge(N/2`^{0}`)`
- Level 2: `Merge(N/2`^{1}`)`
- Level 3: `Merge(N/2`^{2}`)`
- Level 4: `Merge(N/2`^{4}`)`
- Level n: `Merge(N/2`^{x}`)`

From the preceding analysis, we will have the level N when there's only one element in a sublist so that it cannot be divided any more. In this case, we will have the following formula:

$$\frac{N}{2^x} = 1 \Rightarrow N = 2^x \Rightarrow x = \log(N)$$

Based on the preceding formula, for level N, we will have the time complexity before we call the `Merge()` function, which is *log N*. Since the time complexity of the `Merge()` function itself is $O(N)$, the time complexity of the merge sort algorithm is $O(N \bullet log N)$ for both the best and worst case scenarios.

Quick sort

Quick sort is almost the same as the other sorting algorithms we have discussed so far as it divides the input array into two sublists, which are the left sublist and the right sublist. In quick sort, the process of dividing the array into two sublists is called **partitioning**. The partition process will pick an item to become a **pivot** and it will then use the pivot to divide the input into two sublists. If we are going to sort an array in ascending order, all items that are lower than the pivot will be moved to the left sublist, and the rest will be in the right sublist. After running the partition process, we will ensure that the pivot is in the correct position in the array. Although we can choose the item that will be the pivot, we will always choose the first item of the array as the pivot in this discussion.

Suppose we have an array {25, 21, 12, 40, 37, 43, 14, 28}. We are going to sort the array by using the quick sort algorithm. Please see the following diagram:

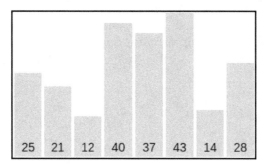

First, we choose the first item as the pivot, which is **25**. We then iterate through the remaining elements and compare each item with the pivot. When we compare **21** and **12**, they are lower than the pivot so they will be in the left sublist, and won't be moved. The elements **40**, **37**, and **43**, are also not moved. However, they will be in the right sublist. Then, we compare **14** with the pivot, and we can see that its value is lower. We need to move it to the left sublist. To do that, we swap it with the first element in the right sublist, which is **40**. The last is element **28**, but we don't need to move it since it's lower than the pivot. By now, the array should be as follows:

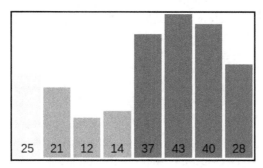

To complete the partition, we can swap the pivot with the last item in the left sublist, which is **14**. Although we have moved **14**, it will be in the left sublist. By now, the pivot is in the correct position and the array should be as follows:

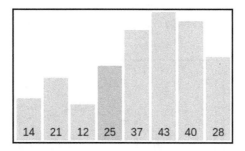

As shown in the preceding diagram, we have two unsorted sublists: [**14, 12, 21**] as the left sublist and [**37, 43, 40, 28**] as the right sublist. We will use the quick sort algorithm to sort these sublists. Starting from the left sublist, we pick **14** as the pivot. We then compare **21** with the pivot and mark it as the right sublist. When we find **12**, we swap it with **21** since it should be in the left sublist. The array should be as follows:

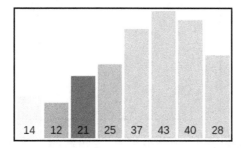

As shown in the preceding diagram, **14** is the pivot, **12** is in the left sublist, and **21** is in the right sublist. To complete the partition, we need to swap the pivot with the last item of the left sublist. Because it only contains one element, we just swap **14** with **12**, the only left sublist item remaining. By now, the array should be as follows:

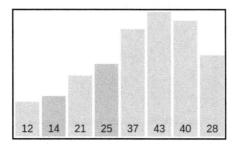

As we can see in the preceding diagram, **14** is in the right position. Fortunately, **12** and **21** are also in the right position, so we now have all of the left sublist sorted. Now, we move to the right sublist and pick **37** as the pivot. It compares with **43**, and so it should be in the right sublist. It then compares with **40**, which is also in the right sublist. When it is compared with **28**, we have to swap **28** with **43** since **28** is lower than the pivot. The array should look as follows:

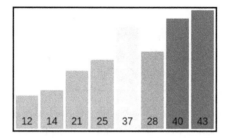

Now, we can swap the pivot with the last item in the left sublist and then the pivot will be in the right position afterwards. The array should be as follows:

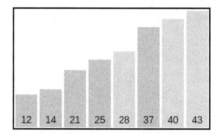

Fortunately, **28** is now in the right position as well, so we can move it to the right sublist. We pick **43** as the pivot and then compare it with **43** and mark **43** as being the right sublist. Since we don't have any elements in the left sublist, with the result that the pivot is in the correct position automatically, the last item, which is **43**, is automatically in the right position as well. The fully sorted array should be as follows:

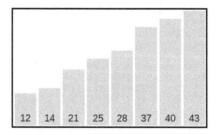

Now, let's create a C++ code to solve the quick sort algorithm. We need a `Partition()` function that will divide an input array into left and right sublists and put the pivot in the correct position. Then, we need a `QuickSort()` function to call the `Partition()` function to recursively invoke itself to sort the left and right sublists. The code should be as follows:

```cpp
// Project: Quick_Sort.cbp
// File   : Quick_Sort.cpp

#include <iostream>

using namespace std;

int Partition(
    int arr[],
    int startIndex,
    int endIndex)
{
    // Set the first item as pivot
    int pivot = arr[startIndex];

    // Left sublist and right sublist
    // are initially empty
    int middleIndex = startIndex;

    // Iterate through arr[1 ... n - 1]
    for (int i = startIndex + 1; i <= endIndex; ++i)
    {
        if (arr[i] < pivot)
        {
            // the current item is on the left sublist
            // prepare a seat by shifting middle index
            ++middleIndex;

            // the arr[middleIndex] is
            // the member of right sublist,
            // swap it to the current item which is
            // member of left list
            swap(arr[i], arr[middleIndex]);
        }
    }

    // By now, the arr[middleIndex] item is
    // member of left sublist.
    // We can swap it with the pivot
    // so the pivot will be in the correct position
    // which is between left sublist and right sublist
    swap(arr[startIndex], arr[middleIndex]);
```

```
        // return the index of pivot
        // to be used by next quick sort
        return middleIndex;
}

void QuickSort(
    int arr[],
    int startIndex,
    int endIndex)
{
    // Only perform sort process
    // if the end index is higher than start index
    if (startIndex < endIndex)
    {
        // Retrieve pivot position from Partition() function
        // This pivotIndex is the index of element that is already
        // in correct position
        int pivotIndex = Partition(arr, startIndex, endIndex);

        // Sort left sublist
        // arr[startIndex ... pivotIndex - 1]
        QuickSort(arr, startIndex, pivotIndex - 1);

        // Sort right sublist
        // arr[pivotIndex + 1 ... endIndex]
        QuickSort(arr, pivotIndex + 1, endIndex);
    }
}

int main()
{
    cout << "Quick Sort" << endl;

    // Initialize a new array
    int arr[] = {25, 21, 12, 40, 37, 43, 14, 28};
    int arrSize = sizeof(arr)/sizeof(*arr);

    // Display the initial array
    cout << "Initial array: ";
    for (int i=0; i < arrSize; ++i)
        cout << arr[i] << " ";
    cout << endl;

    // Sort the array with QuickSort algorithm
    QuickSort(arr, 0, arrSize - 1);

    // Display the sorted array
    cout << "Sorted array : ";
```

```
        for (int i=0; i < arrSize; ++i)
            cout << arr[i] << " ";
        cout << endl;

        return 0;
    }
```

If we build and run the preceding code, we should see the following output on the screen:

```
Terminal
Quick Sort
Initial array: 25 21 12 40 37 43 14 28
Sorted array : 12 14 21 25 28 37 40 43

Process returned 0 (0x0)    execution time : 0.008 s
Press ENTER to continue.
```

Since quick sort is similar to merge sort in dividing an input array into two sublists, the time complexity of quick sort is $O(N \cdot log\ N)$ for the best case scenario. In the worst case scenario, we may pick the lowest or the greatest element as a pivot so that we have to iterate through all elements. In this case, the time complexity will be $O(N^2)$.

Counting sort

Counting sort is a sorting algorithm that arranges items based on a key. Suppose we have an array containing unsorted items with a range between **0** to **9**; we can sort it by counting the number of items based on the range as the key. Let's say we have an array of these items—{9, 6, 5, 6, 1, 7, 2, 4, 3, 5, 7, 7, 9, 6}. In a simple explanation, we just need to count the frequency of the occurrence of each item. We then iterate through the range from **0** to **9** to output the items in a sorted order. Initially, we will have an array containing the following items:

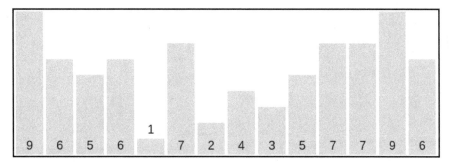

Now, we count the occurrence frequency of each item. Items **1**, **2**, **3**, **4** will occur only once, items **5** and **9** occur twice, items **6** and **7** occur three times, and item **8** never occurs. This can be seen in the following diagram:

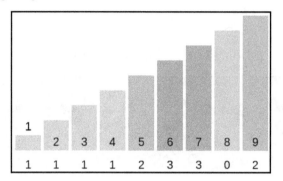

Based on this collection, we can reconstruct the array from the lowest item so that we end up with the following result:

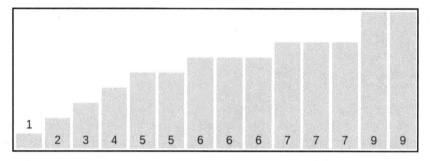

Creating C++ code for counting sort is quite simple; we just need to prepare the `counterArray[]` array with the item range as its length and then put the occurrence of the item in that array. We can reconstruct the array based on the `counterArray[]` array. The code should be as follows:

```cpp
// Project: Counting_Sort.cbp
// File    : Counting_Sort.cpp

#include <iostream>

using namespace std;

void CountingSort(int arr[], int arrSize)
{
    // Create key/counting array
    // with assumption that all element value
    // are from 0 to 9
```

```
    int counterSize = 10;
    int * counterArray = new int [counterSize];

    // Increase the respective counter by 1
    for(int i = 0; i < arrSize; ++i)
    {
        ++counterArray[arr[i]];
    }

    // Counter for iterating the arrCounter array
    int arrCounter = 0;

    for(int i = 0; i < counterSize; ++i)
    {
        while(counterArray[i] > 0)
        {
            // Restore element to list
            arr[arrCounter++] = i;

            // Decrease counter by 1
            --counterArray[i];
        }
    }
}

int main()
{
    cout << "Counting Sort" << endl;

    // Initialize a new array
    int arr[] = {9, 6, 5, 6, 1, 7, 2, 4, 3, 5, 7, 7, 9, 6};
    int arrSize = sizeof(arr)/sizeof(*arr);

    // Display the initial array
    cout << "Initial array: ";
    for (int i=0; i < arrSize; ++i)
        cout << arr[i] << " ";
    cout << endl;

    // Sort the array with BubbleSort algorithm
    CountingSort(arr, arrSize);

    // Display the sorted array
    cout << "Sorted array : ";
    for (int i=0; i < arrSize; ++i)
        cout << arr[i] << " ";
    cout << endl;
```

```
                return 0;
        }
```

As we can see in the preceding code, we have two `for` loop iterations. The first iteration is used to iterate through the array elements and put them into the respective key. The second one is used to reconstruct the initial array so that it will become a sorted list. Please note that, even though there is a `while` loop inside the second `for` loop, it doesn't make the time complexity of `CountingSort()` become $O(N^2)$. This is because the second `for` loop iterates through the counter (which is the key in counting sort) and only the `while` loop iterates through the array elements, so that, for both best and worst case scenarios, the time complexity of this counting sort is $O(N + k)$, where k is the number of keys. However, we can ignore the k variable if k is very small so that the time complexity will be $O(N)$. The output of the preceding code should be as follows:

```
🔴🟡🟢  Terminal
Counting Sort
Initial array: 9 6 5 6 1 7 2 4 3 5 7 7 9 6
Sorted array : 1 2 3 4 5 5 6 6 6 7 7 7 9 9

Process returned 0 (0x0)   execution time : 0.002 s
Press ENTER to continue.
```

Radix sort

Radix sort is a sorting algorithm that is used if the items we are going to sort are in a large range, for instance, from 0 to 9999. In this sorting algorithm, we sort from the least significant (rightmost) digit until the most significant digit (leftmost). We are going to involve the Queue data structure we learned in Chapter 3, *Constructing Stacks and Queues* since we will be putting the equal digit in the queue. This means we need ten queues to represent the digits from **0** to **9**. Suppose we have an array with the following elements—**{429, 3309, 65, 7439, 12, 9954, 30, 4567, 8, 882}** as we can see in the following diagram:

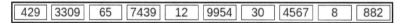

| 429 | 3309 | 65 | 7439 | 12 | 9954 | 30 | 4567 | 8 | 882 |

Then, we populate each item based on the least significant digit (the last digit) and store them in their respective queue bucket. The diagram for this is as follows:

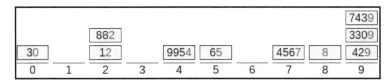

Since we put them in the queue, we can dequeue each bucket from **0** to **9**. In the preceding diagram, we enqueue the bucket from the top so we dequeue it from the bottom. The diagram should be as follows:

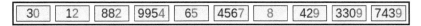

Now, we can repeat the process, but this time for the second least significant digit (the second digit from the left). If the item contains only one digit, the rest of the digits will be **0**. The collection should be as follows:

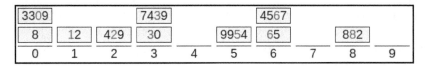

Again, we dequeue each bucket from **0** to **9** and should have the following array:

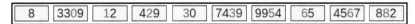

Move to the third digit from the left, and we can collect them into buckets as follows:

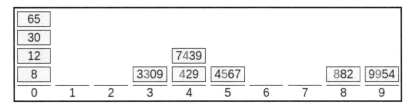

From the preceding diagram, we can rearrange the array by dequeuing each bucket from **0** to **9** as follows:

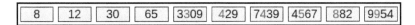

Now, the last digit's position has to be collected (this is the most significant digit). Then, we will have the following bucket diagram:

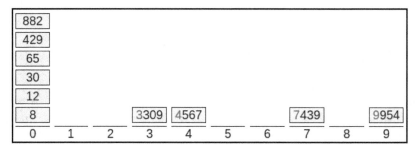

Finally, we can get a the fully sorted array by dequeuing all of the buckets from the lowest digit to the greatest digit, as shown in the following diagram:

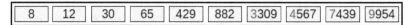

Now, let's design the code for this sorting algorithm in the C++ language. The first thing we need to know in performing this algorithm is the greatest item in the inputted array. This is because we need to iterate through the digit of the greatest item. Once we have found the greatest item, we can iterate through the number of digits in the item by diving it by an exponential, starting from 1, then 10, 100, and so on. To get the selected digit, we can divide the selected item by its current exponential and then find the modulus, 10, of the result. The code should be as follows:

```cpp
// Project: Radix_Sort.cbp
// File   : Radix_Sort.cpp

#include <iostream>
#include "Queue.h"

using namespace std;

void RadixSort(int arr[], int arrSize)
{
    // Create ten buckets for each digits
    // (0 - 9)
    Queue<int> * buckets = new Queue<int>[10];

    // Find the largest element
    int largestElement = arr[0];
    for(int i = 0; i < arrSize; ++i)
    {
        if(largestElement < arr[i])
```

```
            largestElement = arr[i];
    }

    // Iterate through every digit
    // using exponetial (10^exp) to find the digit
    for(int exp = 1; largestElement/exp > 0; exp *= 10)
    {
        // Iterate the array's elements
        for(int i = 0; i < arrSize; ++i)
        {
            // Move element into respective bucket
            buckets[(arr[i]/exp)%10].Enqueue(arr[i]);
        }

        // Reconstruct the array starting from
        // the smallest digit in the buckets
        // Reset the array counter before reconstructing
        int arrCounter = 0;
        for(int i = 0; i < 10; ++i)
        {
            // Get all elements from the buckets
            while(!buckets[i].IsEmpty())
            {
                // Get the front element
                // then restore element to array
                arr[arrCounter++] = buckets[i].Front();

                // Remove the front element
                buckets[i].Dequeue();
            }
        }
    }

    return;
}

int main()
{
    cout << "Radix Sort" << endl;

    // Initialize a new array
    int arr[] = {429, 3309, 65, 7439, 12, 9954, 30, 4567, 8, 882};
    int arrSize = sizeof(arr)/sizeof(*arr);

    // Display the initial array
    cout << "Initial array: ";
    for (int i=0; i < arrSize; ++i)
        cout << arr[i] << " ";
```

```
        cout << endl;

        // Sort the array with QuickSort algorithm
        RadixSort(arr, arrSize);

        // Display the sorted array
        cout << "Sorted array : ";
        for (int i=0; i < arrSize; ++i)
            cout << arr[i] << " ";
        cout << endl;

        return 0;
}
```

As we can see in the preceding code, we can skip the first `for` loop since it's only there to find out the greatest item. The second `for` loop is used to iterate to the number of digits, or we can notate it as `d`. Each iteration of `d` will iterate through all of the array elements to collect all of the items based on the key (`k`) as we did for counting sort. So, the time complexity of the code inside the second `for` loop will be the same as the time complexity of the counting sort. So, the time complexity of the `RadixSort()` function will be $O(d \cdot (N+k))$, and since we can ignore the `k` variable if it's very small, the time complexity of a radix sort will be $O(d \cdot N)$ for both the best and worst case scenarios. The output on the screen will be as follows if we build and run the preceding code:

```
Terminal
Radix Sort
Initial array: 429 3309 65 7439 12 9954 30 4567 8 882
Sorted array : 8 12 30 65 429 882 3309 4567 7439 9954

Process returned 0 (0x0)   execution time : 0.014 s
Press ENTER to continue.
```

Summary

By now, we have understood the sorting algorithms concept and have implemented all common sorting algorithms in C++. We have looked at the slowest sorting algorithms that give the time complexity as $O(N^2)$: bubble sort, selection sort, and insertion sort. However, if we are lucky, we can have a time complexity of $O(N)$ for both bubble sort and insertion sort since they can detect whether we pass a sorted list. However, for selection sort, we will still have a time complexity of $O(N^2)$ even after the input list is sorted.

Other sorting algorithms that are faster than the three preceding algorithms are merge sort and quick sort. Their time complexity is $O(N \log N)$ since they have to divide the input list into two sublists. The last, and the fastest, sorting algorithm, are counting sort and radix sort since their time complexity is $O(N)$.

In the next chapter, we are going to discuss a technique to search for an item in an array or a list by using a sorting algorithm.

QA section

- Can we sort the left sublist and right sublist from the partition method in quick sort using other sorting algorithms?
- Suppose we have an array which consists of {**4, 34, 29, 48, 53, 87, 12, 30, 44, 25, 93, 67, 43, 19, 74**}. What sorting algorithm will give you the fastest time performance?
- Why can merge sort and quick sort have $O(N \bullet \log N)$ for their time complexity?
- What sorting algorithm is similar to arranging a hand of poker cards?
- What is the best sorting algorithm if we are going to sort an array which consists of {**293, 21, 43, 1024, 8, 532, 70, 8283**}?

Further reading

For reference purposes, you can refer to the following links:

- https://www.geeksforgeeks.org/sorting-algorithms/
- https://visualgo.net/en/sorting

5
Finding out an Element Using Searching Algorithms

In the previous chapter, we discussed various techniques to arrange a list by sorting it. Now, in this chapter, we are going to discuss various techniques to search a specific value on a list and find the index where it's stored. Several searching algorithms we are going to discuss in this chapter need a sorted list, so we can apply one of the sorting algorithms we discussed in the previous chapter. By the end of this chapter, we will be able to understand and apply the following searching algorithms:

- Linear search
- Binary search
- Ternary search
- Interpolation search
- Jump search
- Exponential search
- Sublist search

Technical requirements

To follow along with this chapter, including the source code, we require the following:

- Desktop PC or Notebook with Windows, Linux, or macOS
- GNU GCC v5.4.0 or above
- Code Block IDE v17.12 (for Windows and Linux OS), or Code Block IDE v13.12 (for macOS)
- You will find the code files on GitHub at `https://github.com/PacktPublishing/CPP-Data-Structures-and-Algorithms`

Linear search

Linear search is a simple searching algorithm to find out an item in a list using a sequential method. It means that we start looking at the first item in the list, then move to the second item, the third item, the fourth item, and so on. In chapter 2, *Storing Data in Lists and Linked Lists* and chapter 3, *Constructing Stacks and Queues*, when we discussed data structure, we designed a searching algorithm for each data structure we had. Actually, the searching algorithm uses a linear searching algorithm.

Developing a linear search algorithm

To refresh our memory about linear algorithms, let's pick a random array that contains {43, 21, 26, 38, 17, 30, 25, 18}. We then have to find the index where 30 is stored. As we can see in the array, 30 is in index 5 (since the array is zero-based indexing); however, if we find an unexisting item, the algorithm should return −1. The following is the method of linear search named LinearSearch():

```
int LinearSearch(
    int arr[],
    int startIndex,
    int endIndex,
    int val)
{
    // Iterate through the start index
    // to the end index and
    // return the searched value's index
    for(int i = startIndex; i < endIndex; ++i)
    {
        if(arr[i] == val)
        {
            return i;
        }
    }

    // return -1 if no val is found
    return -1;
}
```

As we can see in the LinearSearch() implementation, we pass an array, startIndex, endIndex, and the value we are going to search for. The algorithm then iterates through the array from startIndex to endIndex. The algorithm will return the index if the value is found. If the value is not stored in the array, it will simply return −1.

Implementing the linear search algorithm

Now, let's create a `main()` function to invoke a `LinearSearch()` function, as follows:

```cpp
int main()
{
    cout << "Linear Search" << endl;

    // Initialize a new array
    int arr[] = {43, 21, 26, 38, 17, 30, 25, 18};
    int arrSize = sizeof(arr)/sizeof(*arr);

    // Define value to be searched
    int searchedValue = 30;

    // Find the searched value using Linear Search
    int i = LinearSearch(arr, 0, arrSize - 1, searchedValue);

    // Notify user the result
    // if the return is not -1,
    // the searched value is found
    if(i != -1)
    {
        cout << searchedValue << " is found in index ";
        cout << i << endl;
    }
    else
    {
        cout << "Could not find value " << searchedValue;
        cout << endl;
    }

    return 0;
}
```

In the preceding `main()` function, we try to find the position of value 30. The following output occurs if we build and run the preceding code that is written in the `Linear_Search.cpp` file:

```
Terminal
Linear Search
30 is found in index 5

Process returned 0 (0x0)    execution time : 0.053 s
Press ENTER to continue.
```

From the `LinearSearch()` function, we see that it has to iterate all array elements until it finds the searched value. In the best case scenario, the searched value will be at the first index, so the time complexity would be *O(1)*. However, the searched value might not be found in the array, and the algorithm has to iterate until the end of the array's element; that is the worst case scenario, with the *O(N)* time complexity.

Binary search

Binary search is a searching algorithm to find the position of the searched value in a list by dividing the list into left and right sublists. Prior to performing this searching algorithm, we have to sort the list using the sorting algorithms we discussed in the Chapter 4, *Arranging Data Elements Using a Sorting Algorithm*.

Developing binary search algorithm

Suppose we have a sorted array containing these 15 elements {3, 8, 11, 15, 16, 23, 28, 30, 32, 39, 42, 44, 47, 48, 50} and we need to find the position of 16. The first thing the binary search does is to find the middle element, then compares it with the searched value. Since we've got 15 elements on the list, the middle index is 7 (since the array is a zero-based index), and the value of the index is 30. Then, we compare 30 with our searched value, which is 16. Since the middle value is greater than the value we are looking for, the searched value must be to the left of the middle index. So, we can take the left subarray and have these elements: {3, 8, 11, 15, 16, 23, 28}. Again, we perform the binary search on this subarray and find the middle value is 15, which is lower than 16, so we take the right subarray and get these elements: {16, 23, 28}. We now have only three elements to be sorted, and, by performing the binary search on this subarray, we will find the position of the value 16. The C++ code for the binary search algorithm is as follows:

```cpp
int BinarySearch(
    int arr[],
    int startIndex,
    int endIndex,
    int val)
{
    // Only perform searching process
    // if the end index is higher than
    // or equals to start index
    if(startIndex <= endIndex)
    {
        // Find middle index
```

```
int middleIndex = startIndex + (endIndex - startIndex) / 2;

// If the middle index's value is the searched value
// then return the index
if(arr[middleIndex] == val)
{
    return middleIndex;
}
// If the middle index's value is greater than the searched
  value
// then perform another Binary Search to the left sub
  array
// arr[startIndex ... middleIndex - 1]
else if(arr[middleIndex] > val)
{
    return BinarySearch(arr, startIndex, middleIndex - 1,
      val);
}
// If the middle index's value is lower than the searched
  value
// then perform another Binary Search to the right sub
  array
// arr[middleIndex + 1 ... endIndex]
else
{
    return BinarySearch(arr, middleIndex + 1, endIndex,
      val);
}
}

// Just in case no any value found
return -1;
}
```

As we can see in the preceding `BinarySearch()` function, we call the function recursively for a sublist it has after performing the `BinarySearch()` function. The function will find the position of the searched value if it finds the middle value equals the searched value.

As we can see in `BinarySearch()` function implementation, we use recursion instead of iteration to repeat function invocation. The usage of recursion will make our function simpler and more natural; however, recursion will be an infinite loop if you miss a basis case.
If you are interested in learning more about recursion, you can refer to the book *Learning C++ Functional Programming, Chapter 4, Repeating Method Invocation Using Recursive Algorithms*, published by *Packt Publishing*.

Implementing binary search algorithm

The following is the `main()` function which invokes the `BinarySearch()` function:

```cpp
int main()
{
    cout << "Binary Search" << endl;

    // Initialize a new array
    int arr[] = {3, 8, 11, 15, 16, 23, 28, 30, 32, 39, 42, 44, 47,
     48, 50};
    int arrSize = sizeof(arr)/sizeof(*arr);

    // Define value to be searched
    int searchedValue = 16;

    // Find the searched value using Binary Search
    int i = BinarySearch(arr, 0, arrSize - 1, searchedValue);

    // Notify user the result
    // if the return is not -1,
    // the searched value is found
    if(i != -1)
    {
        cout << searchedValue << " is found in index ";
        cout << i << endl;
    }
    else
    {
        cout << "Could not find value " << searchedValue;
        cout << endl;
    }

    return 0;
}
```

As shown in the preceding code, we are going to find the position of value `16` in the array containing 15 elements. The following screenshot demonstrates the output that we should see on the console if we run the preceding code we can find in the `Binary_Search.cpp` file:

```
Binary Search
16 is found in index 4

Process returned 0 (0x0)   execution time : 0.007 s
Press ENTER to continue.
```

The time complexity of binary search algorithm is $O\ (log\ N)$ in the worst case, since we have to divide the array into two subarray, then again divide each subarray into two subarrays, until we find the searched value, or until the subarray cannot be divided anymore; however, this searching algorithm can give $O(1)$ time complexity in the best case scenario, if the searched value is stored in the middle position (for instance, if we search for 30 in the preceding array).

Ternary search

Ternary search is a searching algorithm that divides an input array into three subarrays—an array of the first third, an array of the last third, and an array between these two areas. It needs to pick two indexes, which are called `middleLeftIndex` and `middleRightIndex`. These two indexes are calculated based on the first index and the last index of the input array.

Developing ternary search algorithm

Suppose we have an array as we have in a binary search, {3, 8, 11, 15, 16, 23, 28, 30, 32, 39, 42, 44, 47, 48, 50}, and want to search for a value of 16. The array contains 15 elements, so we will have the fifth index as the middle-left index (`middleLeftIndex = 4`), and ninth index as the middle-right index (`middleRightIndex = 8`). By using these two indexes, we can find the searched value in each area using the ternary search algorithm itself (recursive invocation). The code of a ternary search algorithm in C++ is as follows:

```
int TernarySearch(
    int arr[],
    int startIndex,
    int endIndex,
    int val)
{
    // Only perform searching process
    // if the end index is higher than
    // or equals to start index
    if(startIndex <= endIndex)
    {
        // Find index of area of the first third
        int middleLeftIndex = startIndex + (endIndex - startIndex)
        / 3;

        // Find index of area of the last third
```

```
int middleRightIndex =
    middleLeftIndex + (endIndex - startIndex) / 3;

// If val is at middleLeftIndex
// then return middleLeftIndex
if(arr[middleLeftIndex] == val)
{
    return middleLeftIndex;
}
// If val is at middleRightIndex
// then return middleRightIndex
else if(arr[middleRightIndex] == val)
{
    return middleRightIndex;
}
// If val is at the are of the first third
// then perform another Ternary Search to this subarray
// arr[startIndex ... middleLeftIndex - 1]
else if(arr[middleLeftIndex] > val)
{
    return TernarySearch(
        arr,
        startIndex,
        middleLeftIndex - 1,
        val);
}
// If val is at the area of the last third
// then perform another Ternary Search to this subarray
// arr[middleRightIndex + 1 ... endIndex]
else if(arr[middleRightIndex] < val)
{
    return TernarySearch(
        arr,
        middleRightIndex + 1,
        endIndex,
        val);
}
// The val is at the area
// between middleLeftIndex and middleRightIndex
// arr[middleLeftIndex + 1 ... middleRightIndex - 1]
else
{
    return TernarySearch(
        arr,
        middleLeftIndex + 1,
        middleRightIndex - 1,
        val);
}
```

```
    }

    // Just in case no any value found
    return -1;
}
```

As we can see in the preceding `TernarySearch()` function implementation, after defining `middleLeftIndex` and `middleRightIndex`, we compare the elements at the two indexes with the searched value to guess where the searched value is stored.

Applying the ternary search algorithm

To invoke the `TernarySearch()` function, we can use the following `main()` function:

```cpp
int main()
{
    cout << "Ternary Search" << endl;

    // Initialize a new array
    int arr[] = {3, 8, 11, 15, 16, 23, 28, 30, 32, 39, 42, 44, 47,
        48, 50};
    int arrSize = sizeof(arr)/sizeof(*arr);

    // Define value to be searched
    int searchedValue = 16;

    // Find the searched value using Ternary Search
    int i = TernarySearch(arr, 0, arrSize - 1, searchedValue);

    // Notify user the result
    // if the return is not -1,
    // the searched value is found
    if(i != -1)
    {
        cout << searchedValue << " is found in index ";
        cout << i << endl;
    }
    else
    {
        cout << "Could not find value " << searchedValue;
        cout << endl;
    }

    return 0;
}
```

If we build and run the preceding code, we are going to see the following output on the console:

```
😕 😕 😕   Terminal
Ternary Search
16 is found in index 4

Process returned 0 (0x0)    execution time : 0.020 s
Press ENTER to continue.
```

Since the area of the ternary search is always one third, the time complexity of this search algorithm is *O(log3 N)* for the worst case. For the best case, the time complexity is *O(1)*.

Interpolation search

Interpolation search is an improvement of the binary search algorithm in picking the middle index. Instead of always picking the middle element to be checked to a searched value like in a binary search, the middle index is not always at the middle position in an interpolation search. The algorithm will calculate the middle index based on the searched value, and pick the nearest element from the searched value. Similar to the binary search, in the interpolation search we have to pass an array we want to search and define the lowest index and the highest index, then calculate the middle index using the following formula:

$$middleIndex = lowIndex + \left[(val - array[lowIndex]) \cdot \frac{(highIndex - lowIndex)}{array[highIndex] - array[lowIndex]}\right]$$

Developing interpolation search algorithm

Let's borrow the array we used in the binary search algorithm, which is {3, 8, 11, 15, 16, 23, 28, 30, 32, 39, 42, 44, 47, 48, 50}, and find value 16. As we discussed earlier, in binary search, we've got 30, 15, and 23 as the middle index when it runs recursively, before we find the position of 16 (which means it needs four invocation of `BinarySearch()` function). However, by using interpolation search, we just need two invocation of an interpolation search function. Let's prove it.

Imagine we use the `BinarySearch()` function, but just replace the `middleIndex` calculation with the formula in the preceding section. First, we pass the array and have `lowIndex` = 0, `highIndex` = 14, and `val` = 16 (since we are going to search value 16). Based on those values, we can calculate the middle index as follows:

$$middleIndex = 0 + \left[(16 - 3) \cdot \frac{(14 - 0)}{(50 - 3)} \right]$$

The result of the preceding calculation is 3.87, and as an integer value, it will be 3. The `array[3]` is 15 and it doesn't equal to 16, but is lower than it. So we can eliminate the `array[0]` until `array[3]`, and start the search from index 4. Now, we have `lowIndex` = 4, `highIndex` = 14, and `val` = 16. The middle index can be calculated as follows:

$$middleIndex = 4 + \left[(16 - 16) \cdot \frac{(14 - 4)}{(50 - 16)} \right]$$

The result of the preceding calculation is obvious, which is 4. We now have `middleIndex` = 4, and, since 16 is stored at index 4, we have successfully found the position of the searched value, and just need two invocations of the interpolation search function.

Because interpolation search is just an improvement of binary search, the implementation of interpolation search in C++ is similar to the binary search implementation, except the way we calculate the middle index. The implementation of `InterpolationSearch()` should be as follows:

```
int InterpolationSearch(
    int arr[],
    int lowIndex,
    int highIndex,
    int val)
{
    if(lowIndex <= highIndex)
    {
        // Find middle index
        int middleIndex =
            lowIndex + (
                (val - arr[lowIndex]) * (highIndex - lowIndex) /
                (arr[highIndex] - arr[lowIndex]));

        // If the middle index's value is the searched value
        // then return the index
        if(arr[middleIndex] == val)
        {
```

```
            return middleIndex;
    }
    // If the middle index's value is greater than the searched
     value
    // then perform another Interpolation Search to the left
     sub array
    // arr[lowIndex ... middleIndex - 1]
    else if(arr[middleIndex] > val)
    {
        return InterpolationSearch(arr, lowIndex, middleIndex -
         1, val);
    }
    // If the middle index's value is lower than the searched
     value
    // then perform another Interpolation Search to the right
     sub array
    // arr[middleIndex + 1 ... highIndex]
    else
    {
        return InterpolationSearch(arr, middleIndex + 1,
        highIndex, val);
    }
}

// Just in case no any value found
return -1;
}
```

Applying interpolation search algorithm

We can use the main() function similar to binary search to find the value 16, as shown in the following code:

```
int main()
{
    cout << "Interpolation Search" << endl;

    // Initialize a new array
    int arr[] = {3, 8, 11, 15, 16, 23, 28, 30, 32, 39, 42, 44, 47,
     48, 50};
    int arrSize = sizeof(arr)/sizeof(*arr);

    // Define value to be searched
    int searchedValue = 16;

    // Find the searched value using Interpolation Search
```

```
        int i = InterpolationSearch(arr, 0, arrSize - 1,
         searchedValue);

        // Notify user the result
        // if the return is not -1,
        // the searched value is found
        if(i != -1)
        {
            cout << searchedValue << " is found in index ";
            cout << i << endl;
        }
        else
        {
            cout << "Could not find value " << searchedValue;
            cout << endl;
        }

        return 0;
    }
```

This is the output that we should see if we build and run the preceding code, it will be similar to a binary search, as we can see in the following screenshot:

As we discussed earlier, the time complexity of binary search is *O(log N)*; however, the interpolation search is faster than the binary search, since the interpolation search improves the calculation of the middle index. The time complexity of the interpolation is *O(log (log N))* and still, for the best case, the time complexity of the algorithm is *O(1)*.

Jump search

Jump search is a searching algorithm to find the position of a searched value in a sorted list by dividing the array into several fixed-size blocks, jumping to the first index of the block, then comparing the value of the block's first index with the searched value. If the value of the block's first index is greater than the searched value, it jumps backward to the previous block, then starts a linear search of the block.

Developing jump search algorithm

Suppose we have an array containing {8, 15, 23, 28, 32, 39, 42, 44, 47, 48} elements, and we want to find the position of value 39. We will set the jump step by the square root elements number. Since the element number of the array is 10, the step will be $\sqrt{10}$ = 3. We will now compare the value of index 0, 3, 6, and 9. When the algorithm compares array[0] with 39, the value of array[0] is lower than the searched value. It then jumps to array[3] and compares its value with 39. Since the value is lower than the searched value, it jumps to array[6] and finds that 42 is greater than 39. It then jumps backward to array[6], and performs the linear search on array[6], array[7], and array[8] to find the value 39 and get the position of the value. The implementation of jump search in C++ code is as follows:

```
int JumpSearch(
    int arr[],
    int arrSize,
    int val)
{
    // It's impossible to search value
    // in array contains zero or less element
    if (arrSize <= 0)
    {
        return -1;
    }

    // Defining step used to jump the array
    int step = sqrt(arrSize);

    // Start comparing from index 0
    int blockIndex = 0;

    // Increase the blockIndex by the step
    // if blockIndex is lower than array size
    // and the value of element in blockIndex
    // is still lower than searched value
    while (blockIndex < arrSize && arr[blockIndex] < val)
    {
        blockIndex += step;
    }

    // After find the blockIndex,
    // perform Linear Search to the sub array
    // defined by the blockIndex
    // arr[blockIndex - step .... blockIndex or arrSize]
    return LinearSearch(
```

```
        arr,
        blockIndex - step,
        min(blockIndex, arrSize),
        val);
}
```

Applying jump search algorithm

If we want to find the position of 39 in the array, as we did earlier in this chapter, we can use the following `main()` function:

```
int main()
{
    cout << "Jump Search" << endl;

    // Initialize a new array
    int arr[] = {8, 15, 23, 28, 32, 39, 42, 44, 47, 48};
    int arrSize = sizeof(arr)/sizeof(*arr);

    // Define value to be searched
    int searchedValue = 39;

    // Find the searched value using Jump Search
    int i = JumpSearch(arr, arrSize, searchedValue);

    // Notify user the result
    // if the return is not -1,
    // the searched value is found
    if(i != -1)
    {
        cout << searchedValue << " is found in index ";
        cout << i << endl;
    }
    else
    {
        cout << "Could not find value " << searchedValue;
        cout << endl;
    }

    return 0;
}
```

If we build and run the preceding code, we are going to see the following output on the console:

```
Terminal
Jump Search
39 is found in index 5

Process returned 0 (0x0)    execution time : 0.004 s
Press ENTER to continue.
```

Since we decide the jump step with √N, where N is the array's elements number, we will have the time complexity of jump search as $O(\sqrt{N})$ for both best and worst cases.

Exponential search

Exponential search is similar to a jump search, since it also divides the input array into several subarrays; however, in exponential search, the step we jump is increased exponentially (2^n). In exponential search, we initially compare the second index (blockIndex = 1), then compare array[1] with the searched value. If the array[1] is still lower than the searched value, we increase the blockIndex exponentially to become 2, 4, 8, and so on, until the array[blockIndex] is higher than the searched value. Then we can perform the binary search to the subarray defined by the blockIndex.

Developing exponential search algorithm

Let's use the array we used in jump search, {8, 15, 23, 28, 32, 39, 42, 44, 47, 48}, to perform an exponential search, and we will also find value 39. First, we apply setblockIndex = 1, then compare array[1] with the searched value, 39. Since 15 is lower than 39, the algorithm sets blockIndex = 2. array[2] is still lower than 39, then moves to array[4]. And since its value is still lower than 39, it moves to array[8] and finds that it's now greater than 39. After that, the algorithm performs the binary search from array[4] to array[8] to find the searched value. The implementation of the exponent search in C++ will be as follows:

```
int ExponentialSearch(
    int arr[],
    int arrSize,
    int val)
{
    // It's impossible to search value
    // in array contains zero or less element
```

```
if (arrSize <= 0)
{
    return -1;
}

// Start comparing from index 1
int blockIndex = 1;

// Increase the blockIndex exponentially
// if blockIndex is lower than array size
// and the value of element in blockIndex
// is still lower than searched value
while (blockIndex < arrSize && arr[blockIndex] < val)
{
    blockIndex *= 2;
}

// After find the blockIndex,
// perfom Binary Search to the sub array
// defined by the blockIndex
// arr[blockIndex / 2 .... blockIndex or arrSize]
return BinarySearch(
    arr,
    blockIndex / 2,
    min(blockIndex, arrSize),
    val);
}
```

As we can see in the preceding code, we don't need to calculate the step as we did in the jump search, since the step is increased by exponential value.

Invoking the ExponentialSearch() function

To invoke the preceding ExponentialSearch() function, we can use the following main() function code:

```
int main()
{
    cout << "Exponential Search" << endl;

    // Initialize a new array
    int arr[] = {8, 15, 23, 28, 32, 39, 42, 44, 47, 48};
    int arrSize = sizeof(arr)/sizeof(*arr);

    // Define value to be searched
    int searchedValue = 39;
```

```
// Find the searched value using blockIndex Search
int i = ExponentialSearch(arr, arrSize, searchedValue);

// Notify user the result
// if the return is not -1,
// the searched value is found
if(i != -1)
{
    cout << searchedValue << " is found in index ";
    cout << i << endl;
}
else
{
    cout << "Could not find value " << searchedValue;
    cout << endl;
}

return 0;
}
```

If we build and run the preceding code, we are going to be displaying similar output to a jump search, as follows:

```
Terminal
Exponential Search
39 is found in index 5

Process returned 0 (0x0)   execution time : 0.003 s
Press ENTER to continue.
```

To find the performance of this searching algorithm, we have to calculate all processes in the algorithm, which are `while` loop and a binary search invocation. In the `while` loop process, the algorithm takes `O(log i)`, where i is the index of the searched value. The second process is the invocation of binary search. As we know, the time complexity of binary search is *O(log N)*; however, after the `while` loop process, the number of array elements are no longer `N`, but i. So, the second process' time complexity will be *O(log i)* as well. As a result, whole processes in exponential search will be:

```
O(log i) + O(log i) = 2 O(log i)
```

Since we can omit a constant value, the time complexity of this searching algorithm is `O(log i)`, where i is the index of the searched value.

Sublist search

Sublist search is used to detect a presence of one list in another list. Suppose we have a single-node list (let's say the first list), and we want to ensure that the list is present in another list (let's say the second list), then we can perform the sublist search to find it. For instance, the first list contains these elements: `23 -> 30 -> 41`, and the second list contains these elements: `10 -> 15 -> 23 -> 30 -> 41 -> 49`. At a glance, we see that the first list presents in the second list.

The sublist search algorithm works by comparing the first element of the first list with the first element of the second list. If the two values don't match, it goes to the next element of the second list. It does this until the two values match, then checks the succeeding elements of the first list with the succeeding elements of the second list. If all elements match, then it returns true, otherwise, it returns false.

Designing sublist search algorithm

Let's design the C++ program for this searching algorithm. First, we are going to develop a `SublistSearch()` function that will compare the first element of the first list with all elements of the second list. The code should be as follows:

```cpp
bool SublistSearch(
    Node * firstList,
    Node * secondList)
{
    // If both are NULL,
    // just return true
    if(firstList == NULL && secondList == NULL)
    {
        return true;
    }

    // If one is NULL but the other is not,
    // just return false
    if((firstList != NULL && secondList == NULL) ||
       (firstList == NULL && secondList != NULL))
    {
        return false;
    }

    // Compare the value, if not match,
    // check next element of second list
    if (firstList->Value == secondList->Value)
```

```
        {
            // If matched, check deeper
            if(CompareAllMatchedElements(
                firstList,
                secondList))
            {
                return true;
            }
        }

        // Check next element of the first list
        return SublistSearch(firstList, secondList->Next);
    }
```

As we can see in the preceding `SublistSearch()` function implementation, it calls itself when moving to the next element of the second list. And when it finds that `firstList->Value == secondList->Value`, it performs the `CompareAllMatchedElements()` function to ensure the remaining second list elements match all the second list's elements. The implementation of the `CompareAllMatchedElements()` function will be as follows:

```
bool CompareAllMatchedElements(
    Node * ptr1,
    Node * ptr2)
{
    // ptr2 cannot be NULL
    // since it will be compared
    // to ptr1
    if(ptr1 != NULL && ptr2 == NULL)
        return false;

    // It's the end of the first list element
    if(ptr1 == NULL)
        return true;

    // Compare value of each list
    if(ptr1->Value == ptr2->Value)
    {
        // Compare next element
        return CompareAllMatchedElements(
            ptr1->Next,
            ptr2->Next);
    }
    else
    {
        return false;
    }
```

```
                    }
```

In the preceding code, we also see the `CompareAllMatchedElements()` function invokes itself to prove that the next element of the two lists remains the same. This function will return `false` if it finds one element that doesn't match. Also, if it has iterated all elements of the first list, it will return `true`.

Performing sublist search algorithm

To perform the sublist search, we can invoke the `SublistSearch()` function and pass two lists. The following `main()` function will create two lists and invoke the `SublistSearch()` function:

```cpp
int main()
{
    cout << "Sublist Search" << endl;

    // Initialize first list
    // 23 -> 30 -> 41
    Node * node1_c = new Node();
    node1_c->Value = 41;
    Node * node1_b = new Node();
    node1_b->Value = 30;
    node1_b->Next = node1_c;
    Node * node1_a = new Node();
    node1_a->Value = 23;
    node1_a->Next = node1_b;

    // Print the first list
    cout << "First list : ";
    PrintNode(node1_a);

    // Initialize second list
    // 10 -> 15 -> 23 -> 30 -> 41 -> 49
    Node * node2_f = new Node();
    node2_f->Value = 49;
    Node * node2_e = new Node();
    node2_e->Value = 41;
    node2_e->Next = node2_f;
    Node * node2_d = new Node();
    node2_d->Value = 30;
    node2_d->Next = node2_e;
    Node * node2_c = new Node();
    node2_c->Value = 23;
    node2_c->Next = node2_d;
```

```
Node * node2_b = new Node();
node2_b->Value = 15;
node2_b->Next = node2_c;
Node * node2_a = new Node();
node2_a->Value = 10;
node2_a->Next = node2_b;

// Print the second list
cout << "Second list: ";
PrintNode(node2_a);

// Notify user the result
// if the return is true
// the searched value is found
cout << "Result: second list is ";
if(SublistSearch(node1_a, node2_a))
{
    cout << "found";
}
else
{
    cout << "not found";
}
cout << " in first list." << endl;

return 0;
}
```

And if we build and run the preceding code, we will see the following output on the screen:

```
Terminal
Sublist Search
First list : 23 -> 30 -> 41 -> NULL
Second list: 10 -> 15 -> 23 -> 30 -> 41 -> 49 -> NULL
Result: second list is found in first list.

Process returned 0 (0x0)   execution time : 0.175 s
Press ENTER to continue.
```

If we notate N as the number of first elements and M as the number of second elements, we will have the time complexity of the sublist search as $O(M \cdot N)$, since the algorithm will iterate through each element of both the first and second lists.

Summary

In this chapter, we discussed various searching algorithms, from the fastest searching algorithm to the slowest searching algorithm. To get a faster searching algorithm, we can use the interpolation search with $O(log\ (log\ N))$, since it can find the nearest middle index from a searched value. The others are binary search with $O(log\ N)$ and exponential search with $O(log\ i)$, where i is the index of searched value. The moderate searching algorithm is a jump search, which has $O(\sqrt{N})$ and the slowest algorithm is a linear algorithm with $O(N)$ complexity, since it has to check all list elements; however, contrary to other searching algorithms we discussed in this chapter, the linear algorithm can also be applied to an unsorted list.

In the next chapter, we are going to discuss several common algorithms that are frequently used in `string` data type to gain the best performance.

QA section

- What is the simplest search algorithm?
- How does linear search algorithm work?
- Which is fastest—binary search algorithm or ternary search algorithm?
- Why does interpolation search algorithm become an improvement of binary search algorithm?
- If we have to choose between binary search algorithm and exponential search algorithm, which should we pick to get the fastest execution time possibilities?
- What is a similarity between jump search algorithm and exponential search algorithm?
- If we need to detect a presence of one list in another list, which search algorithm should we use?

Further reading

For further reference, you can refer to the following links:

- https://www.geeksforgeeks.org/linear-search/
- https://www.geeksforgeeks.org/binary-search/
- https://www.geeksforgeeks.org/jump-search/
- https://www.geeksforgeeks.org/interpolation-search/
- https://www.geeksforgeeks.org/exponential-search/
- https://www.geeksforgeeks.org/binary-search-preferred-ternary-search/

6
Dealing with the String Data Type

In the previous chapters, we have discussed several simple data structures, such as lists, linked lists, strings, stacks, and queues. Now, starting from this chapter, we are going to discuss non-linear data types. This chapter will discuss the `string` data type, including how to construct, use, and solve several problems in the `string` data type. The following are topics that will be discussed in this chapter:

- Introducing the `string` data type in C++
- Finding out whether a string is an anagram or palindrome
- Creating a sequence of binary digits as binary string
- Generating a subsequence of a string
- Searching a pattern in a string

Technical requirement

To follow along with this chapter, including the source code, we require the following:

- Desktop PC or Notebook with Windows, Linux, or macOS
- GNU GCC v5.4.0 or above
- Code Block IDE v17.12 (for Windows and Linux OS), or Code Block IDE v13.12 (for macOS)
- You will find the code files on GitHub at `https://github.com/PacktPublishing/CPP-Data-Structures-and-Algorithms`

String in C++

String is a data type that stores a collection of characters. This collection can form a word or some information that can be understood by humans, it can also form a sentence from several words. In this section, we are going to discuss how to construct and use the `string` data type in C++.

Constructing a string using character array

In C++, a string can be composed by using an array of characters. When we compose a string using an array, we have to reserve a space to store a *NULL* character (**\0**) at the last array's element to indicate the end of the string. Suppose we want to create a `string` variable containing a name of a person called **James**; we need an array with at least six elements, since **James** is composed of five characters. Please take a look at the following diagram:

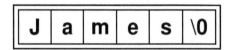

As we can see in the preceding diagram, we need an array with at least six elements to store a string containing five letters. There are several ways to create a string using character arrays. These are some of them:

```
char name[] = "James";
char name[] = {'J', 'a', 'm', 'e', 's', '\0'};
char name[6] = "James";
char name[6] = {'J', 'a', 'm', 'e', 's', '\0'}
```

From the preceding pieces of code, the first line and second line are used to construct arrays that set their length automatically based on initial elements. In the third and fourth lines, we specify the length of the array. However, we can choose any one of the four preceding lines of code to create a string variable named `name` and containing `James` as its value.

The problem comes when we need to modify the string by adding one character. For example, since the array cannot be extended, we have to create another array with our desired length, then copy the old array into the new one. To solve the problem, we can use `std::string` class provided by C++, which we will discuss in the next subchapter.

Using std::string for more flexibility features

There is a `std::string` data type in the **C++ Standard Template Library** (**STL**). We can use it to replace characters in an array, since it has more flexibility features. The biggest advantage to using this data type instead of a characters array is that the size of `std::string` can be extended dynamically in runtime. Other functionalities that it has are as follows:

- `getline()`: This function is used to get input from the user and then store it to a character stream in memory
- `push_back()`: This function is used to insert a character at the end of the string
- `pop_back()`: This function is used to remove the last character from the string
- `size()`: This function is used to retrieve the number of character in the string
- `begin()`: This function returns an iterator pointing to the first character of the string
- `end()`: This function returns an iterator pointing to the last character of the string
- `rbegin()`: This function returns a reverse iterator pointing to the last character of the string
- `rend()`: This function returns a reverse iterator pointing at the first character of the string

We will use some of the preceding functions in a discussion later on in this chapter.

Playing with words

A collection of characters is used to construct a word or a sentence. The position of each character in a word matters, since different character positions can cause the word to have different meanings. For example, when you rearrange the characters in *God*, you will get *Dog*.

There are two methods in strings to find another word from a word, or to ensure a word has exactly the same spelling both forward and backward. Let's play with them.

Rearranging a word to create an anagram

An **anagram** is a word that is produced by rearranging the letters of the word itself. Let's take a look at the word *ELBOW*. We can say that *BELOW* is anagram of *ELBOW*, since *BELOW* uses all the original letters of *ELBOW* exactly once. Not only from one word, an anagram can also be created from, and can create, two or more words: *SCHOOL MASTER* is an anagram of *THE CLASSROOM*, or *FOURTH OF JULY* is an anagram of *JOYFUL FOURTH*.

Checking whether two strings are an anagram or not is quite easy. We just need to sort the two and compare the sorted strings. They are an anagram if both sorted strings are exactly the same. Take a look at the following C++ code:

```cpp
bool IsAnagram(
    string str1,
    string str2)
{
    // Anagram is not case sensitive
    // so we convert all characters
    // to uppercase
    transform(
        str1.begin(),
        str1.end(),
        str1.begin(),
        ::toupper);
    transform(
        str2.begin(),
        str2.end(),
        str2.begin(),
        ::toupper);

    // Anagram does not care about space
    // so we remove all spaces if any
    str1.erase(
        remove(
            str1.begin(),
            str1.end(),
            ' '),
            str1.end());
    str2.erase(
        remove(
            str2.begin(),
            str2.end(),
            ' '),
            str2.end());
```

```
        // Then, we sort string1 and string2
        sort(str1.begin(), str1.end());
        sort(str2.begin(), str2.end());

        // If they both are anagram,
        // they will be exactly same after sorted
        return str1 == str2;
}
```

As we can see in the preceding IsAnagram() function, beside sorting the two strings, we transform the strings into uppercase, since anagram is not case sensitive. We also remove all spaces in the strings, since space doesn't matter in an anagram. After we have sorted the two strings, we can just compare them to determine if they are an anagram.

When invoking the IsAnagram() function, we need to pass two strings as the argument. In the following main() function, we ask the user to input the string using the getline() function before invoking the IsAnagram() function. The implementation of the main() function should be as follows:

```
int main()
{
    cout << "Anagram" << endl;

    // Input string1
    string string1;
    cout << "Input string 1 -> ";
    getline(cin, string1);

    // Input string2
    string string2;
    cout << "Input string 2 -> ";
    getline(cin, string2);

    // Check if they are anagram
    cout << "'" << string1 << "' and '";
    cout << string2 << "' are ";
    if(IsAnagram(string1, string2))
    {
        cout << "anagram";
    }
    else
    {
        cout << "NOT anagram";
    }
    cout << endl;
```

```
        return 0;
    }
```

The preceding code can be found in `Anagram.cpp`. If we build and run the file, we will get the following output on the screen:

```
Anagram
Input string 1 -> Fourth of July
Input string 2 -> Joyful Fourth
'Fourth of July' and 'Joyful Fourth' are anagram

Process returned 0 (0x0)   execution time : 32.331 s
Press ENTER to continue.
```

From the preceding code, we can see that the *spaces*, *uppercase letters*, and *lowercase letters* don't matter. We have a result that *Fourth of July* and *Joyful Fourth* are an anagram.

The time complexity of the `IsAnagram()` function will be *O(N log N)*, where *N* is the total characters on the one string, since we use `std::sort()` to sort the string. `std::sort()` is doing comparison similar to quick sort.

Detecting whether a word is a palindrome

A **palindrome** is a string, or sequence of characters, that has the exact same spelling both forward and backward. *NOON*, *MADAM*, *RADAR*, and *ROTATOR* are some examples of the palindrome. Similar to the anagram, we can also construct a palindrome from more than one word; for instance, *A NUT FOR A JAR OF TUNA*, or *NO LEMON NO MELON*.

To check if a string is palindrome, we have to compare each pair of characters, left character and right character, starting from the most left and the most right character, then moving to the middle. Please see the following diagram:

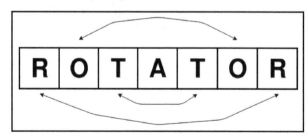

Using the word **ROTATOR**, as we can see in the preceding diagram, we need to check the character at index 0 with 6, 1 with 5, and 2 with 4. Since all comparisons are true, the string is a palindrome.

In C++, we can do it by iterating string elements. The iteration will break if it finds unmatched pair characters, or it has iterated through `N/2` elements. The code to check a palindrome is as follows:

```cpp
bool IsPalindrome(
    string str)
{
    // Palindrome is not case sensitive
    // so we convert all characters
    // to uppercase
    transform(
        str.begin(),
        str.end(),
        str.begin(),
        ::toupper);

    // Palindrome does not care about space
    // so we remove all spaces if any
    str.erase(
        remove(
            str.begin(),
            str.end(),
            ' '),
        str.end());

    // --- Palindrome detector ---
    // Starting from leftmost and rightmost elements
    // of the str
    int left = 0;
    int right = str.length() - 1;

    // Comparing the current leftmost
    // and rightmost elements
    // until all elements are checked or
    // until unmatched characters are found
    while(right > left)
    {
        if(str[left++] != str[right--])
        {
            return false;
        }
    }
```

```
        // If all characters which are compared
        // are same, it must be palindrome
        return true;
        // --- End of palindrome detector ---
    }
```

Similar to the `IsAnagram()` function, the preceding `IsPalindrome()` implementation also converts all characters to uppercase and removes spaces. After that, it runs a `while` loop procedure and compares each pair of characters. If it successfully iterates through all string elements, we can say that the string is a palindrome. Otherwise, it will return `FALSE`, and it means the string is not a palindrome.

To ease our understanding of the flow of the `IsPalindrome()` function, we will use the `while` loop iteration; however, the C++ STL has provided the `std::equal()` functionality to compare each pair of string elements. We can replace the preceding code, from `// --- Palindrome detector ---` until `// --- End of palindrome detector ---`, with the following single line of code:

```
return std::equal(str.begin(), str.begin() + str.size() /
2, str.rbegin());
```

To check whether a string is a palindrome or not, we need to invoke the `IsPalindrome()` function and pass a string to it. We can ask the user to input a string by using the `getline()` function, as we can see in the following `main()` function:

```
int main()
{
    cout << "Palindrome" << endl;

    // Input string
    string str;
    cout << "Input string -> ";
    getline(cin, str);

    // Check if it is palindrome
    cout << "'" << str << "' is ";
    if(IsPalindrome(str))
    {
        cout << "a palindrome";
    }
    else
    {
        cout << "NOT a palindrome";
```

```
        }
        cout << endl;

        return 0;
    }
```

We can find the following code in the `Palindrome.cpp` file. If we build and run the file, we will get the following output on the console:

```
Terminal
Palindrome
Input string -> A nut for a jar of tuna
'A nut for a jar of tuna' is a palindrome

Process returned 0 (0x0)    execution time : 13.151 s
Press ENTER to continue.
```

In the `IsPalindrome()` function, we have to iterate string elements *N/2* times, so the time complexity is *O(N/2)*. And since we can omit constant, we can say that the time complexity of the `IsPalindrome()` function is *O(N)*.

Constructing a string from binary digits

A **binary string** is a string that represents a number in binary format and only contains 0 and 1. Supposing we have a number 3, the binary string will be 11, or the binary string of 9 is 1001.

Binary string is usually used to hold non-traditional data, such as pictures. Suppose we have the following black and white image:

If black is represented by 0 and white is represented by 1, we can create the following binary string to represent the preceding image:

```
11111111111111111111111111111111111111
11111111111111111111111111111111111111
11111111111111111111111111111111111111
11111111111111000000000011111111111111
11111111111110000000000000111111111111
11111111111000000000000000011111111111
11111111110000000000000000001111111111
11111111100000000000000000000111111111
11111111100000000000000000000011111111
11111111000000000000000000000011111111
11111110000000000000000000000011111111
11111110000000000000000000000011111111
11111110000000000000000000000011111111
11111110000000000000000000000000111111
11111110000000000000000000000000111111
11111100000000000000000000000000111111
11111100000000000000000000000000111111
11111110000000000000000000000000111111
11111110000000000000000000000000111111
11111110000000000000000000000001111111
11111110000000000000000000000001111111
11111110000000000000000000000001111111
11111110000000000000000000000011111111
11111110000000000000000000000111111111
11111111000000000000000000000111111111
11111111100000000000000000000111111111
11111111110000000000000000001111111111
11111111111000000000000000011111111111
11111111111100000000000000111111111111
11111111111110000000000001111111111111
11111111111111100000000111111111111111
11111111111111111111111111111111111111
11111111111111111111111111111111111111
11111111111111111111111111111111111111
```

Converting decimal to binary string

As we have discussed in the previous section, the binary string of 9 is 1001. We can convert a decimal number into a binary digit by dividing the number by 2 until it cannot be divided any more, and collect the remainder of each division. Here's the steps to convert 9 into binary digit:

```
9 is divided by 2 is 4, remainder is 1
4 is divided by 2 is 2, remainder is 0
```

```
2 is divided by 2 is 1, remainder is 0
1 is divided by 2 is 0, remainder is 1
```

Look at the remainder of each division, and read it from the bottom to the top. So that's why we have `1001` as a binary digit of 9. Now, let's try another larger number, which is `500`. Here are the steps to convert `500` to binary digit:

```
500 is divided by 2 is 250, remainder is 0
250 is divided by 2 is 125, remainder is 0
125 is divided by 2 is 62,  remainder is 1
62  is divided by 2 is 31,  remainder is 0
31  is divided by 2 is 15,  remainder is 1
15  is divided by 2 is 7,   remainder is 1
7   is divided by 2 is 3,   remainder is 1
3   is divided by 2 is 1,   remainder is 1
1   is divided by 2 is 0,   remainder is 1
```

From our preceding calculation, we can see that the binary digit of `500` is `111110100`, since we have to read the remainder from bottom to top. Now, it's time to write a C++ code to convert a decimal number to a binary string. We will use the `do...while` iteration, and it will last if the division result is more than `0`. The code should be as follows:

```cpp
string DecimalToBinaryString(
    int decimalNumber)
{
    // Initial result
    string binaryString = "0";

    // Only perform this procedure
    // if decimalNumber is greater than 0
    if(decimalNumber > 0)
    {
        // Reset result
        binaryString = "";

        // Declare a variable for division process
        div_t dv{};

        // Initialize the division quot
        dv.quot = decimalNumber;

        // Perform these procedure
        // until the quot is 0
        do
        {
            dv = div(dv.quot, 2);
            binaryString = to_string(dv.rem) + binaryString;
```

```
                    }
                    while(dv.quot);
                }

                // return the binary string
                return binaryString;
            }
```

In the preceding `DecimalToBinaryString()` function, we have to ensure the number passed to the function is greater than 0. After that, we perform `std::div()` to divide the number with 0 and convert the remainder to the `string` data type using the `to_string()` function, then concatenate string result into a `binaryString` variable. It will last for as long as `dv.quot` is greater than 0.

To invoke the `DecimalToBinaryString()` function, we just need to pass a single decimal number that we can get from the user, as shown in the following `main()` function:

```cpp
int main()
{
    cout << "Decimal To Binary String" << endl;

    // Input a decimal number
    int decNum;
    cout << "Input a decimal number -> ";
    cin >> decNum;

    // Convert to binary string
    string binaryString = DecimalToBinaryString(decNum);

    // Show the result to user
    cout << "Binary string of " << decNum;
    cout << " is '" << binaryString;
    cout << "'" << endl;

    return 0;
}
```

The preceding code can be found in the `Decimal_To_BinaryString.cpp` file. If we build and run the file, the following output will be displayed on the console:

```
Terminal
Decimal To Binary String
Input a decimal number -> 500
Binary string of 500 is '111110100'

Process returned 0 (0x0)    execution time : 2.867 s
Press ENTER to continue.
```

Since it divides the decimal number by 2 and divides the result by 2, again and again, the time complexity of the `DecimalToBinaryString()` function is $O(N \log N)$, where N is the decimal number.

Converting binary string to decimal

In this section, we are going to write a code to convert binary string into a decimal number. To do this, we are going to use 2 to the power of n formula (2^n) to get the decimal value. We will multiply the last digit of the binary digit with 2^0, then multiply the next binary digit with 2^1, and so on.

Let's use our binary digit from the previous section, which is **111110100**, and convert it to a decimal number. Please see the following diagram to find out the answer:

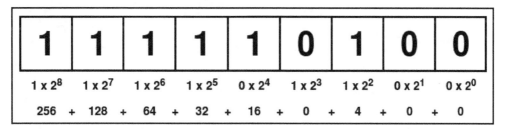

We will get the decimal number by adding all the results of 2^n multiplication. So, `256 + 128 + 64 + 32 + 16 + 0 + 4 + 0 + 0` equals `500`.

Now, let's write a C++ code to convert a binary string to a decimal number. We will iterate through all string characters, then multiply each character by 2^n. The code should be as follows:

```cpp
int BinaryStringToDecimal(
    string binaryString)
{
    // Initial result
    int decNumber = 0;

    // variable for current power base
    int n;

    // Declare reverse iterator
    string::reverse_iterator it;

    // Iterate all characters in binaryString
    // from the last character to the first character
    for (
        it = binaryString.rbegin(), n = 0;
        it != binaryString.rend();
        ++it, ++n)
    {
        // if character '1' is found
        // add decNumber with power of current base
        char c = *it;
        if(c == '1')
        {
            decNumber += pow(2, n);
        }
    }

    // return the decimal
    return decNumber;
}
```

As we can see in the preceding code, we call the reverse iteration to iterate the string elements backward. If we found character 1, we add decNumber with the current n value of 2^n. We just ignore if we found 0, since everything is multiplied by 0 is 0 and won't affect the result. After iteration is finished, we just need to return the value stored by the decNumber variable.

To invoke the preceding `BinaryStringToDecimal()` function, we can use the following `main()` method:

```cpp
int main()
{
    cout << "Binary String To Decimal" << endl;

    // Input binary string
    string binaryString;
    cout << "Input binary string -> ";
    getline(cin, binaryString);

    // Convert to decimal
    int decNumber = BinaryStringToDecimal(
        binaryString);

    // Show the result to user
    cout << "Decimal of '" << binaryString;
    cout << "' is " << decNumber << endl;

    return 0;
}
```

The preceding code can be found in the `BinaryString_To_Decimal.cpp` file. If we build and run the file, we will be shown the following output on the console:

```
⊗⊖⊡  Terminal
Binary String To Decimal
Input binary string -> 111110100
Decimal of '111110100' is 500

Process returned 0 (0x0)   execution time : 5.306 s
Press ENTER to continue.
```

It's quite easy to find out the time complexity of the `BinaryStringToDecimal()` function. Since we have to iterate through the string elements, its time complexity is *O(N)*, where *N* is the length of a binary string.

Subsequence string

Subsequence string is a string derived from another string by deleting some characters without changing the order of the remaining characters. Suppose we have a string: *donut*. The subsequences of this word would be—*d, o, do, n, dn, on, don, u, du, ou, dou, nu, dnu, onu, donu, t, dt, ot, dot, nt, dnt, ont, dont, ut, dut, out, dout, nut, dnut, onut,* and *donut*.

Generating subsequences from a string

To find out all subsequences of a string, we need to iterate through all characters of the string. We also create a bit counter variable to mark which element position should be considered to take as a subsequence, also known as a **power set**. The power set of S is the set of all subsets of S. Suppose we have three characters in a string, which are *xyz*. The power set of the string will be 2^n elements, which is as follows:

```
BIT -> SUBSET
===================
000 -> Empty subset
001 -> "x"
010 -> "y"
011 -> "xy"
100 -> "z"
101 -> "xz"
110 -> "yz"
111 -> "xyz"
```

By using the power set, we can create the code to generate subsequence of a string, as follows:

```
vector<string> GenerateSubsequences(
    string str)
{
    // Return value is stored
    // on vecString
    vector<string> vecString;

    // Retrieve str length
    int strLen = str.size();

    // bitCounter is used to check
    // character position
    int bitCounter = pow(2, strLen);

    // Check from 000..001 to 111..111
    // Empty subset is ignored
    for (int i = 1; i < bitCounter; ++i)
    {
        // Temporary variable
        // to store current subsequence
        string subsequence = "";

        // Construct the new subsequence string
        for (int j = 0; j < strLen; j++)
```

```
        {
            // Check if j-th bit in the bitCounter is set
            // If so, pick j-th character from str
            if (i & (1 << j))
            {
                subsequence += str[j];
            }
        }

        // Put it to vector
        vecString.push_back(subsequence);
    }

    // Return the vector
    return vecString;
}
```

As we can see in the preceding `GenerateSubsequences()` function, we generate subsequences by using a bit counter. We then construct a new subsequence based on bit, which is set in the bit counter variable. To invoke the `GenerateSubsequences()` function, we can use the following `main()` function:

```
int main()
{
    cout << "Subsequence Generator" << endl;

    // Input string
    string str;
    cout << "Input string -> ";
    getline(cin, str);

    // Generate subsequences
    vector<string> myvector = GenerateSubsequences(
        str);

    // Show the result to user
    cout << "All subsequences of '" << str;
    cout << "':" << endl;
    for (
        vector<string>::iterator it = myvector.begin();
        it != myvector.end();
        ++it)
    {
        cout << *it << " ";
    }
    cout << endl;
```

```
            return 0;
        }
```

The preceding code can be found in the `Subsequence_Generator.cpp` file. If we build and run the file, we will see the following output on the console:

```
Subsequence Generator
Input string -> donut
All subsequences of 'donut':
d o do n dn on don u du ou dou nu dnu onu donu t dt ot dot nt dnt ont dont ut du
t out dout nut dnut onut donut

Process returned 0 (0x0)   execution time : 2.131 s
Press ENTER to continue.
```

Since the `GenerateSubsequences()` function has iterated 2^n times (for bit counter), and inside this iteration it has had to iterate again through all string elements, the time complexity of this function is $O(N \cdot 2^N)$, where N is the length of the input string.

Checking whether a string is a subsequence of another string

We have successfully created code to generate subsequences of a string. Now we are going to create a C++ code to check if a string is a subsequence of another string. To do so, we will compare the character of two strings from the last character (the reason we compare from the last character of the string is the simplicity of checking the index against 0, rather than keeping track of the final index of both strings).

Suppose `str1` is a subsequence of a string of `str2`, x is the index of `str1`, and y is the index of `str2`. It means that we will compare `str1[x - 1]` with `str2[y -1]`. If matched, continue until all suspected subsequence string characters have been checked. If not, compare the last character of the suspected subsequence (`str1[x - 1]`) with the character before the last character of the string (`str2[y - 2]`). The code should be as follows:

```
bool IsSubSequence(
    string str1,
    string str2,
    int x,
    int y)
{
    // If all characters in str1
    // have been checked,
```

```
// it means that the str1 is subsequence
// of str2
if (x == 0)
{
    return true;
}

// There is some characters in str2
// that don't matched with str1
// so return false
if (y == 0)
{
    return false;
}

// If last characters of two strings are matching,
// continue to check another character
if (str1[x - 1] == str2[y - 1])
{
    return IsSubSequence(str1, str2, x - 1, y - 1);
}
// If not, check the second last of str2
else
{
    return IsSubSequence(str1, str2, x, y - 1);
}
}
```

As we can see in the preceding `IsSubSequence()` function implementation, if all characters of the suspected subsequence string have been iterated (x == 0), the process is done and the result is `true`; however, if all characters of the string have been iterated (y ==0), the result will be `false`. After that, we can recursively run the `IsSubSequence()` function. To invoke the function, we can use the following `main()` function implementation:

```
int main()
{
    cout << "Subsequence String" << endl;
    cout << "Check if 1st string is a ";
    cout << "subsequence of 2nd string" << endl;

    // Input first string
    string string1;
    cout << "Input 1st string -> ";
    getline(cin, string1);

    // Input second string
```

```
string string2;
cout << "Input 2nd string -> ";
getline(cin, string2);

// Check if str1 is subsequence of str2
cout << "'" << string1 << "' is ";
if(IsSubSequence(
    string1,
    string2,
    string1.size(),
    string2.size()))
{
    cout << "subsequence";
}
else
{
    cout << "NOT subsequence";
}
cout << " of '" << string2;
cout << "'" << endl;

return 0;
}
```

The preceding code can be found in the `Subsequence_String.cpp` file. If we build and run the file, we will get the following output on our console:

As we can see in the `IsSubSequence()` function implementation, the function is recursively invoked for all characters of the 2nd string, so that the time complexity of this function is $O(N)$, where N is the length of the 2nd string.

Pattern searching

Pattern searching is an algorithm to find out the location of a string in another string. This process is usually used in a word processor (such as Notepad or Sublime Text) to find a word position in a document. Let's look at the sentence—*the quick brown fox jumps over the lazy dog*. If we need to find out the position of the word *the*, we can use this algorithm and pass *the* as the pattern.

You might be confused with **Regular Expression** (**regex**) and pattern searching, the latter of which we are going to discuss in this section. With regex, we can check if a string satisfies a given pattern, while in this section we'll be discovering how to find a string (called a **pattern**) in another string. If you're interested in learning about RegEx in C++, you can go to http://www.cplusplus.com/reference/regex/.

To find the position of the pattern in a string, we have to iterate through the string's elements from the beginning until the last possible element. In our preceding example, we have a string containing 44 letters and want to search for a pattern of *the*, which contains three letters. For this, we just need to iterate the string 42 times, since it's impossible to find *the* in the 43rd and 44th character of the string.

In the string iteration, we start to iterate the pattern, then compare it with the characters of the string. If all characters of the pattern are matched with string characters, the pattern is found in the string. The following is the C++ code implementation:

```cpp
vector<int> SearchPattern(
    string targetString,
    string patternString)
{
    vector<int> vecIndex;

    // Retrieve string length
    int strLen = targetString.size();
    int patLen = patternString.size();

    // Only perform the following procedure
    // if pattern string is not longer than
    // target string
    if(patLen <= strLen)
    {
        // Iterate through target string elements
        // from the beginning until
        // the last possible element where
        // pattern is at the last position
```

```
        for(int i = 0; i <= strLen - patLen; ++i)
        {
            int j;

            // Start comparing pattern string
            for(j = 0; j < patLen; ++j)
            {
                // Quit from inner for-loop
                // if character is not matched
                if(targetString[i + j] !=
                    patternString[j])
                {
                    break;
                }
            }

            // If inner for-loop is done
            // it means that pattern is found
            // in the target string
            if(j == patLen)
            {
                // store the index in vector
                vecIndex.push_back(i);
            }
        }
    }

    // Return the vector
    return vecIndex;
}
```

As we can see in the preceding `SearchPattern()` function, we have to ensure that the pattern size is lower than or equal to the target string size (`patLen <= strLen`). Then, we iterate through the string elements from the beginning until the last possible element (`for(int i = 0; i <= strLen - patLen; ++i)`). Inside this iteration, we iterate through the pattern to find out if it matches the target string. To invoke the preceding `SearchPattern()` function, we can use the following `main()` function implementation:

```
int main()
{
    cout << "Pattern Searching" << endl;

    // Input target string
    string targetStr;
    cout << "Input target string -> ";
    getline(cin, targetStr);
```

```
        // Input pattern string
        string patternStr;
        cout << "Input pattern string -> ";
        getline(cin, patternStr);

        // Find the pattern
        vector<int> myvector = SearchPattern(
            targetStr,
            patternStr);

        // Show the result to user
        cout << "'" << patternStr << "' is ";
        if(myvector.size() > 0)
        {
            cout << "found at index ";
            for (
                vector<int>::iterator it = myvector.begin();
                it != myvector.end();
                ++it)
            {
                cout << *it << " ";
            }
        }
        else
        {
            cout << "NOT found";
        }
        cout << endl;

        return 0;
    }
```

The preceding code can be found in `Pattern_Searching.cpp`. If we build and run the file, we will have the following output on our console:

```
Terminal
Pattern Searching
Input target string -> the quick brown fox jumps over the lazy dog
Input pattern string -> the
'the' is found at index 0 31

Process returned 0 (0x0)   execution time : 4.915 s
Press ENTER to continue.
```

As we know, we have to iterate through all possible target string elements (`strLen` – `patLen`) and then iterate through pattern elements; the time complexity of the `SearchPattern()` function is $O(N \cdot (M - N))$, where N is the length of pattern string and M is the length of the target string.

Summary

In this chapter, we have discussed how to construct a string in C++ using `std::string`. We then used it to solve several problems in the `string` data type. We can rearrange a string to create another string, which is called an **anagram**. We also can detect if a string is a **palindrome** if it has the exact same spelling both forward and backward. We have discussed binary string, and can now convert a decimal number to binary string and vice versa.

Another string problem we have solved is checking whether a string is a subsequence of another string. Also, we have successfully generated all possible subsequences from a string. Finally, we have learned how a word processor (such as Notepad or Sublime Text) can find a word in a document using pattern searching.

In the next chapter, we are going to discuss another non-linear data structure, which is a tree structure, and the algorithm implementation of this data structure.

QA section

- What is the use of the `NULL` character in characters array?
- What is the difference between a `begin()` and an `rbegin()` iterator in `std::string`?
- How do you implement `rbegin()` and `rend()` in `std::string`?
- What is the difference between an anagram and a palindrome?
- What is the use of a binary string?
- What is a subsequence of string?
- What is the use of a bit counter variable when generating subsequences from a string?
- How many times is outer iteration performed in the pattern searching algorithm?

Further reading

For further reference, please visit the following links:

- https://en.wikipedia.org/wiki/String_(computer_science)
- https://www.geeksforgeeks.org/stdstring-class-in-c/
- https://en.wikipedia.org/wiki/Sort_(C%2B%2B)
- http://en.cppreference.com/w/cpp/algorithm/equal
- https://www.dcode.fr/binary-image
- http://en.cppreference.com/w/cpp/numeric/math/div
- https://en.wikipedia.org/wiki/Subsequence
- https://www.geeksforgeeks.org/power-set/
- https://en.wikipedia.org/wiki/Power_set
- https://www.geeksforgeeks.org/given-two-strings-find-first-string-subsequence-second/
- https://www.geeksforgeeks.org/subarraysubstring-vs-subsequence-and-programs-to-generate-them/
- https://www.geeksforgeeks.org/searching-for-patterns-set-1-naive-pattern-searching/
- https://www.dcode.fr/binary-image

7
Building a Hierarchical Tree Structure

In the previous chapter, we discussed using a string as a non-linear data structure and tried to construct, use, and solve several problems in the `string` data type. In this chapter, we are going to discuss another non-linear data structure, which is a tree that stores data in a hierarchical form.

In this chapter, we are going to discuss the following topics:

- Introducing the tree data structure
- Understanding the binary search tree
- Balancing the binary search tree
- Implementing the priority queue using a binary heap

Technical requirements

To follow along with this chapter, including the source code, you will require the following:

- A desktop PC or Notebook with Windows, Linux, or macOS
- GNU GCC v5.4.0 or above
- Code Block IDE v17.12 (for Windows and Linux OS) or Code Block IDE v13.12 (for macOS)
- You will find the code files on GitHub at `https://github.com/PacktPublishing/CPP-Data-Structures-and-Algorithms`

Building a binary tree ADT

A **binary tree** is a hierarchical data structure whose behavior is similar to a tree, as it contains root and leaves (a node that has no child). The *root* of a binary tree is the topmost node. Each node can have at most two children, which are referred to as the *left child* and the *right child*. A node that has at least one child becomes a *parent* of its child. A node that has no child is a *leaf*. Please take a look at the following binary tree:

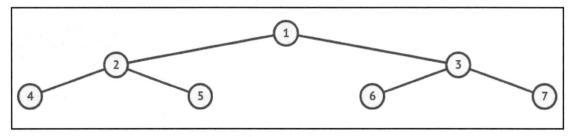

From the preceding binary tree diagram, we can conclude the following:

- The root of the tree is the node of element **1** since it's the topmost node
- The children of element **1** are element **2** and element **3**
- The parent of elements **2** and **3** is **1**
- There are four leaves in the tree, and they are element **4**, element **5**, element **6**, and element **7** since they have no child

This hierarchical data structure is usually used to store information that forms a hierarchy, such as a file system of a computer.

To implement the binary in code, we need a data structure so that it can store the element's key as well as pointers for left and right children. To do so, we can create the following `TreeNode` class in C++:

```cpp
class TreeNode
{
public:
    int Key;
    TreeNode * Left;
    TreeNode * Right;
};
```

The preceding `TreeNode` data structure will store each node of the tree containing the element key, along with the left and right pointers. We are also going to create a helper function to create a new node, as follows:

```
TreeNode * NewTreeNode(
    int key)
{
    // Create a new node
    TreeNode * node = new TreeNode;

    // Assign a key
    node->Key = key;

    // Initialize Left and Right pointer
    node->Left = NULL;
    node->Right = NULL;

    return node;
}
```

The preceding `NewTreeNode()` function will ease us into inserting a new `TreeNode` into an existing tree. Now, let's create a binary tree, as shown in the preceding diagram by using C++ code. Here are the steps:

1. Initialize the `root` node containing element 1 as follows:

```
// Creating root element
TreeNode * root = NewTreeNode(1);
```

2. After initializing the `root` node, we can add two children to the `root` node—element 2 and element 3, as follows:

```
/*
    Add children to root element
       1
      / \
     2   3
*/
root->Left = NewTreeNode(2);
root->Right = NewTreeNode(3);
```

3. Next, we have to add two children for element 2, which are element 4 and element 5, as follows:

```
/*
    Add children to element 2
         1
        /  \
       2    3
      / \
     4   5
*/
root->Left->Left = NewTreeNode(4);
root->Left->Right = NewTreeNode(5);
```

4. Finally, we are going to add two children for element 3, which are element 6 and element 7, as follows:

```
/*
    Add children to element 3
         1
        /  \
       2    3
      / \  / \
     4   5 6   7
*/
root->Right->Left = NewTreeNode(6);
root->Right->Right = NewTreeNode(7);
```

Building a binary search tree ADT

A **binary search tree** (**BST**) is a sorted binary tree, where we can easily search for any key using the binary search algorithm. To sort the BST, it has to have the following properties:

- The node's left subtree contains only a key that's smaller than the node's key
- The node's right subtree contains only a key that's greater than the node's key
- You cannot duplicate the node's key value

By having the preceding properties, we can easily search for a key value as well as find the maximum or minimum key value. Suppose we have the following BST:

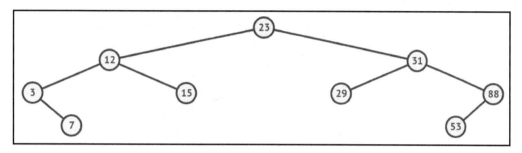

As we can see in the preceding tree diagram, it has been sorted since all of the keys in the root's left subtree are smaller than the root's key, and all of the keys in the root's right subtree are greater than the root's key. The preceding BST is a balanced BST since it has a balanced left and right subtree. We also can define the preceding BST as a balanced BST since both the left and right subtrees have an equal *height* (we are going to discuss this further in the upcoming section).

However, since we have to put the greater new key in the right subtree and the smaller new key in the left subtree, we might find an unbalanced BST, called a **skewed left** or a **skewed right BST**. Please see the following diagram:

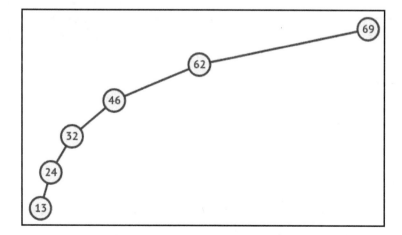

The preceding image is a sample of a *skewed left BST*, since there's no right subtree. Also, we can find a BST that has no left subtree, which is called a *skewed right BST*, as shown in the following diagram:

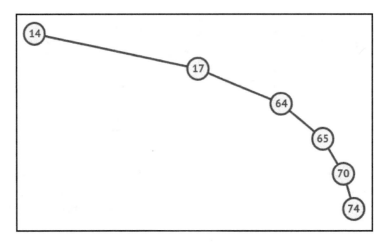

As we can see in the two skewed BST diagrams, the height of the BST becomes taller since the height equals to $N - 1$ (where N is the total keys in the BST), which is five. Comparing this with the balanced BST, the root's height is only three.

To create a BST in C++, we need to modify our `TreeNode` class in the preceding binary tree discussion, *Building a binary tree ADT*. We need to add the `Parent` properties so that we can track the parent of each node. It will make things easier for us when we traverse the tree. The class should be as follows:

```
class BSTNode
{
public:
    int Key;
    BSTNode * Left;
    BSTNode * Right;
    BSTNode * Parent;
};
```

There are several basic operations which BST usually has, and they are as follows:

- `Insert()` is used to add a new node to the current BST. If it's the first time we have added a node, the node we inserted will be a `root` node.
- `PrintTreeInOrder()` is used to print all of the keys in the BST, sorted from the smallest key to the greatest key.

- `Search()` is used to find a given key in the BST. If the key exists it returns `TRUE`, otherwise it returns `FALSE`.
- `FindMin()` and `FindMax()` are used to find the minimum key and the maximum key that exist in the BST.
- `Successor()` and `Predecessor()` are used to find the successor and predecessor of a given key. We are going to discuss these later in the upcoming section.
- `Remove()` is used to remove a given key from BST.

Now, let's discuss these BST operations further.

Inserting a new key into a BST

Inserting a key into the BST is actually adding a new node based on the behavior of the BST. Each time we want to insert a key, we have to compare it with the `root` node (if there's no root beforehand, the inserted key becomes a root) and check whether it's smaller or greater than the root's key. If the given key is greater than the currently selected node's key, then go to the right subtree. Otherwise, go to the left subtree if the given key is smaller than the currently selected node's key. Keep checking this until there's a node with no child so that we can add a new node there. The following is the implementation of the `Insert()` operation in C++:

```cpp
BSTNode * BST::Insert(BSTNode * node, int key)
{
    // If BST doesn't exist
    // create a new node as root
    // or it's reached when
    // there's no any child node
    // so we can insert a new node here
    if(node == NULL)
    {
        node = new BSTNode;
        node->Key = key;
        node->Left = NULL;
        node->Right = NULL;
        node->Parent = NULL;
    }
    // If the given key is greater than
    // node's key then go to right subtree
    else if(node->Key < key)
    {
        node->Right = Insert(node->Right, key);
```

```
        node->Right->Parent = node;
    }
    // If the given key is smaller than
    // node's key then go to left subtree
    else
    {
        node->Left = Insert(node->Left, key);
        node->Left->Parent = node;
    }

    return node;
}
```

As we can see in the preceding code, we need to pass the selected node and a new key to the function. However, we will always pass the root node as the selected node when performing the Insert() operation, so we can invoke the preceding code with the following Insert() function:

```
void BST::Insert(int key)
{
    // Invoking Insert() function
    // and passing root node and given key
    root = Insert(root, key);
}
```

Based on the implementation of the Insert() operation, we can see that the time complexity to insert a new key into the BST is *O(h)*, where *h* is the height of the BST. However, if we insert a new key into a non-existing BST, the time complexity will be *O(1)*, which is the best case scenario. And, if we insert a new key into a skewed tree, the time complexity will be *O(N)*, where *N* is the total number of keys in the BST, which is the worst case scenario.

Traversing a BST in order

We have successfully created a new BST and can insert a new key into it. Now, we need to implement the PrintTreeInOrder() operation, which will traverse the BST in order from the smallest key to the greatest key. To achieve this, we will go to the leftmost node and then to the rightmost node. The code should be as follows:

```
void BST::PrintTreeInOrder(BSTNode * node)
{
    // Stop printing if no node found
    if(node == NULL)
        return;
```

```
        // Get the smallest key first
        // which is in the left subtree
        PrintTreeInOrder(node->Left);

        // Print the key
        std::cout << node->Key << " ";

        // Continue to the greatest key
        // which is in the right subtree
        PrintTreeInOrder(node->Right);
    }
```

Since we will always traverse from the root node, we can invoke the preceding code as follows:

```
    void BST::PrintTreeInOrder()
    {
        // Traverse the BST
        // from root node
        // then print all keys
        PrintTreeInOrder(root);
        std::cout << std::endl;
    }
```

The time complexity of the PrintTreeInOrder() function will be $O(N)$, where N is the total number of keys for both the best and the worst cases since it will always traverse to all keys.

Finding out whether a key exists in a BST

Suppose we have a BST and need to find out if a key exists in the BST. It's quite easy to check whether a given key exists in a BST, since we just need to compare the given key with the current node. If the key is smaller than the current node's key, we go to the left subtree, otherwise we go to the right subtree. We will do this until we find the key or when there are no more nodes to find. The implementation of the Search() operation should be as follows:

```
    BSTNode * BST::Search(BSTNode * node, int key)
    {
        // The given key is
        // not found in BST
        if (node == NULL)
            return NULL;
        // The given key is found
        else if(node->Key == key)
```

```
            return node;
    // The given is greater than
    // current node's key
    else if(node->Key < key)
        return Search(node->Right, key);
    // The given is smaller than
    // current node's key
    else
        return Search(node->Left, key);
}
```

Since we will always search for a key from the `root` node, we can create another `Search()` function as follows:

```
bool BST::Search(int key)
{
    // Invoking Search() operation
    // and passing root node
    BSTNode * result = Search(root, key);

    // If key is found, returns TRUE
    // otherwise returns FALSE
    return result == NULL ?
        false :
        true;
}
```

The time complexity to find out a key in the BST is $O(h)$, where h is the height of the BST. If we find a key which lies in the root node, the time complexity will be $O(1)$, which is the best case. If we search for a key in a skewed tree, the time complexity will be $O(N)$, where N is the total number of keys in the BST, which is the worst case.

Retrieving the minimum and maximum key values

Finding out the minimum and maximum key values in a BST is also quite simple. To get a minimum key value, we just need to go to the leftmost node and get the key value. On the contrary, we just need to go to the rightmost node and we will find the maximum key value. The following is the implementation of the `FindMin()` operation to retrieve the minimum key value, and the `FindMax()` operation to retrieve the maximum key value:

```
int BST::FindMin(BSTNode * node)
{
    if(node == NULL)
        return -1;
    else if(node->Left == NULL)
```

```
            return node->Key;
        else
            return FindMin(node->Left);
    }

    int BST::FindMax(BSTNode * node)
    {
        if(node == NULL)
            return -1;
        else if(node->Right == NULL)
            return node->Key;
        else
            return FindMax(node->Right);
    }
```

 We return -1 if we cannot find the minimum or maximum value in the tree, since we assume that the tree can only have a positive integer. If we intend to store the negative integer as well, we need to modify the function's implementation, for instance, by returning NULL if no minimum or maximum values are found.

As usual, we will always find the minimum and maximum key values from the root node, so we can invoke the preceding operations as follows:

```
    int BST::FindMin()
    {
        return FindMin(root);
    }

    int BST::FindMax()
    {
        return FindMax(root);
    }
```

Similar to the Search() operation, the time complexity of the FindMin() and FindMax() operations is *O(h)*, where *h* is the height of the BST. However, if we find the maximum key value in a skewed left BST, the time complexity will be *O(1)*, which is the best case, since it doesn't have any right subtree. This also happens if we find the minimum key value in a skewed right BST. The worst case will appear if we try to find the minimum key value in a skewed left BST or try to find the maximum key value in a skewed right BST, since the time complexity will be *O(N)*.

Finding out the successor of a key in a BST

Other properties that we can find from a BST are the **successor** and the **predecessor**. We are going to create two functions named `Successor()` and `Predecessor()` in C++. But before we create the code, let's discuss how to find out the successor and the predecessor of a key of a BST. In this section, we are going to learn about the successor first, and then we will discuss the predecessor in the upcoming section.

There are three rules to find out the successor of a key of a BST. Suppose we have a key, `k`, that we have searched for using the previous `Search()` function. We will also use our preceding BST to find out the successor of a specific key. The successor of `k` can be found as follows:

1. If `k` has a right subtree, the successor of `k` will be the minimum integer in the right subtree of `k`. From our preceding BST, if `k = 31`, `Successor(31)` will give us `53` since it's the minimum integer in the right subtree of `31`. Please take a look at the following diagram:

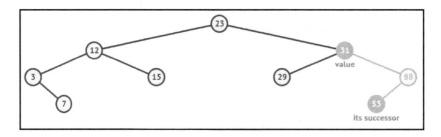

2. If `k` does not have a right subtree, we have to traverse the ancestors of `k` until we find the first node, `n`, which is greater than node `k`. After we find node `n`, we will see that node `k` is the maximum element in the left subtree of `n`. From our preceding BST, if `k = 15`, `Successor(15)` will give us `23` since it's the first greater ancestor compared with `15`, which is `23`. Please take a look at the following diagram:

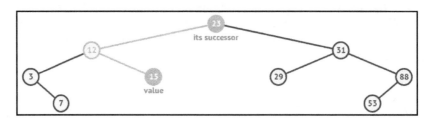

3. If k is the maximum integer in the BST, there's no successor of k. From the preceding BST, if we run Successor(88), we will get −1, which means no successor has been found, since 88 is the maximum key of the BST.

Based on our preceding discussion about how to find out the successor of a given key in a BST, we can create a Successor() function in C++ with the following implementation:

```cpp
int BST::Successor(BSTNode * node)
{
    // The successor is the minimum key value
    // of right subtree
    if (node->Right != NULL)
    {
        return FindMin(node->Right);
    }
    // If no any right subtree
    else
    {
        BSTNode * parentNode = node->Parent;
        BSTNode * currentNode = node;

        // If currentNode is not root and
        // currentNode is its right children
        // continue moving up
        while ((parentNode != NULL) &&
            (currentNode == parentNode->Right))
        {
            currentNode = parentNode;
            parentNode = currentNode->Parent;
        }

        // If parentNode is not NULL
        // then the key of parentNode is
        // the successor of node
        return parentNode == NULL ?
            -1 :
            parentNode->Key;
    }
}
```

However, since we have to find a given key's node first, we have to run `Search()` prior to invoking the preceding `Successor()` function. The complete code for searching for the successor of a given key in a BST is as follows:

```
int BST::Successor(int key)
{
    // Search the key's node first
    BSTNode * keyNode = Search(root, key);

    // Return the key.
    // If the key is not found or
    // successor is not found,
    // return -1
    return keyNode == NULL ?
        -1 :
        Successor(keyNode);
}
```

From our preceding `Successor()` operation, we can say that the average time complexity of running the operation is *O(h)*, where *h* is the height of the BST. However, if we try to find out the successor of a maximum key in a skewed right BST, the time complexity of the operation is *O(N)*, which is the worst case scenario.

Finding out the predecessor of a key in a BST

1. If k has a left subtree, the predecessor of k will be the maximum integer in the left subtree of k. From our preceding BST, if k = 12, Predecessor(12) will be 7 since it's the maximum integer in the left subtree of 12. Please take a look at the following diagram:

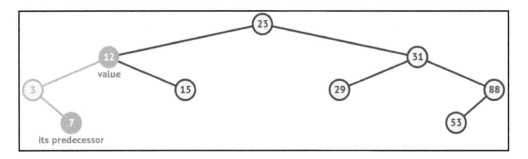

2. If k does not have a left subtree, we have to traverse the ancestors of k until we find the first node, n, which is lower than node k. After we find node n, we will see that node n is the minimum element of the traversed elements. From our preceding BST, if k = 29, Predecessor(29) will give us 23 since it's the first lower ancestor compared with 29, which is 23. Please take a look at the following diagram:

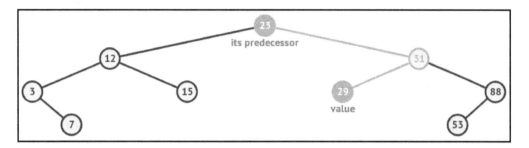

3. If k is the minimum integer in the BST, there's no predecessor of k. From the preceding BST, if we run Predecessor(3), we will get -1, which means no predecessor is found since 3 is the minimum key of the BST.

Now, we can implement the Predecessor() operation in C++ as follows:

```cpp
int BST::Predecessor(BSTNode * node)
{
    // The predecessor is the maximum key value
    // of left subtree
    if (node->Left != NULL)
    {
        return FindMax(node->Left);
    }
    // If no any left subtree
    else
    {
        BSTNode * parentNode = node->Parent;
        BSTNode * currentNode = node;

        // If currentNode is not root and
        // currentNode is its left children
        // continue moving up
        while ((parentNode != NULL) &&
               (currentNode == parentNode->Left))
        {
            currentNode = parentNode;
            parentNode = currentNode->Parent;
```

```
        }

        // If parentNode is not NULL
        // then the key of parentNode is
        // the predecessor of node
        return parentNode == NULL ?
            -1 :
            parentNode->Key;
    }
}
```

And, similar to the `Successor()` operation, we have to search for the node of a given key prior to invoking the preceding `Predecessor()` function. The complete code for searching for the predecessor of a given key in a BST is as follows:

```
int BST::Predecessor(int key)
{
    // Search the key's node first
    BSTNode * keyNode = Search(root, key);

    // Return the key.
    // If the key is not found or
    // predecessor is not found,
    // return -1
    return keyNode == NULL ?
        -1 :
        Predecessor(keyNode);
}
```

Similar to our preceding `Successor()` operation, the time complexity of running the `Predecessor()` operation is *O(h)*, where *h* is the height of the BST. However, if we try to find out the predecessor of a minimum key in a skewed left BST, the time complexity of the operation is *O(N)*, which is the worst case scenario.

Removing a node based on a given key

The last operation in the BST that we are going to discuss is removing a node based on a given key. We will create a `Remove()` operation in C++. There are three possible cases for removing a node from a BST, and they are as follows:

1. Removing a leaf (a node that doesn't have any child). In this case, we just need to remove the node. From our preceding BST, we can remove keys 7, 15, 29, and 53 since they are leaves with no nodes.

2. Removing a node that has only one child (either a left or right child). In this case, we have to connect the child to the parent of the node. After that, we can remove the target node safely. As an example, if we want to remove node 3, we have to point the `Parent` pointer of node 7 to node 12 and make the left node of 12 points to 7. Then, we can safely remove node 3.

3. Removing a node that has two children (left and right children). In this case, we have to find out the successor (or predecessor) of the node's key. After that, we can replace the target node with the successor (or predecessor) node. Suppose we want to remove node 31, and that we want 53 as its successor. Then, we can remove node 31 and replace it with node 53. Now, node 53 will have two children, node 29 in the left and node 88 in the right.

Also, similar to the `Search()` operation, if the target node doesn't exist, we just need to return `NULL`. The implementation of the `Remove()` operation in C++ is as follows:

```cpp
BSTNode * BST::Remove(
    BSTNode * node,
    int key)
{
    // The given node is
    // not found in BST
    if (node == NULL)
        return NULL;

    // Target node is found
    if (node->Key == key)
    {
        // If the node is a leaf node
        // The node can be safely removed
        if (node->Left == NULL && node->Right == NULL)
            node = NULL;
        // The node have only one child at right
        else if (node->Left == NULL && node->Right != NULL)
        {
            // The only child will be connected to
            // the parent's of node directly
            node->Right->Parent = node->Parent;

            // Bypass node
            node = node->Right;
        }
        // The node have only one child at left
        else if (node->Left != NULL && node->Right == NULL)
        {
            // The only child will be connected to
```

```
                        // the parent's of node directly
                        node->Left->Parent = node->Parent;

                        // Bypass node
                        node = node->Left;
                }
                // The node have two children (left and right)
                else
                {
                        // Find successor or predecessor to avoid quarrel
                        int successorKey = Successor(key);

                        // Replace node's key with successor's key
                        node->Key = successorKey;

                        // Delete the old successor's key
                        node->Right = Remove(node->Right, successorKey);
                }
        }
        // Target node's key is smaller than
        // the given key then search to right
        else if (node->Key < key)
            node->Right = Remove(node->Right, key);
        // Target node's key is greater than
        // the given key then search to left
        else
            node->Left = Remove(node->Left, key);

        // Return the updated BST
        return node;
}
```

Since we will always remove a node starting from the `root` node, we can simplify the preceding `Remove()` operation by creating the following one:

```
void BST::Remove(int key)
{
        root = Remove(root, key);
}
```

As shown in the preceding `Remove()` code, the time complexity of the operation is *O(1)* for both case **1** (the node that has no child) and case **2** (the node that has only one child). For case **3** (the node that has two children), the time complexity will be *O(h)*, where *h* is the height of the BST, since we have to find the successor or predecessor of the node's key.

Implementing the BST ADT

By now, we have a new ADT called BST class with the following declaration:

```
class BST
{
private:
    BSTNode * root;

protected:
    BSTNode * Insert(BSTNode * node, int key);
    void PrintTreeInOrder(BSTNode * node);
    BSTNode * Search(BSTNode * node, int key);
    int FindMin(BSTNode * node);
    int FindMax(BSTNode * node);
    int Successor(BSTNode * node);
    int Predecessor(BSTNode * node);
    BSTNode * Remove(BSTNode * node, int v);

public:
    BST();

    void Insert(int key);
    void PrintTreeInOrder();
    bool Search(int key);
    int FindMin();
    int FindMax();
    int Successor(int key);
    int Predecessor(int key);
    void Remove(int v);
};
```

To instantiate a BST class, we can write the following code:

```
// Instantiate BST instance
BST * tree = new BST;
```

By running the preceding code, we now have an instance of the BST class which is stored in the tree variable. For now, we can add several elements to the tree variable. We will create a tree containing exactly the same elements of our preceding BST. The following code snippet is used to insert several elements using the Insert() operation:

```
// Define key value to be inserted to BST
int keys[] = {23, 12, 31, 3, 15, 7, 29, 88, 53};

// Inserting keys
for(const int& key : keys)
    tree->Insert(key);
```

We can validate the elements by traversing the tree in order using the PrintTreeInOrder() operation, as follows:

```
// Traversing tree in order
// then print all keys
cout << "Tree keys: ";
tree->PrintTreeInOrder();
```

The preceding code snippet will print all of the keys in the tree in order, from the minimum key until the maximum key.

Now, we are going to invoke the Search() operation. We are going to try and find keys 31 and 18. As we already know, key 31 exists, but key 18 doesn't. Here is the code to invoke the operation:

```
// Search key 31
// it should be found
cout << "Search key 31: ";
bool b = tree->Search(31);
if(b)
    cout << "found";
else
    cout << "NOT found";
cout << endl;

// Search key 18
// it should NOT be found
cout << "Search key 18: ";
b = tree->Search(18);
if(b)
    cout << "found";
else
    cout << "NOT found";
cout << endl;
```

We can also find the minimum and maximum keys in the tree using the `FindMin()` and `FindMax()` operations, as follows:

```
// Retrieving minimum and maximum key
cout << "Min. Key : " << tree->FindMin();
cout << endl;
cout << "Max. Key : " << tree->FindMax();
cout << endl;
```

Again, to find the successor of a key we can use the `Successor()` operation, and to find the predecessor of a key we can use the `Predecessor()` operation. We will find the successor and predecessor of the keys we discussed in the previous section, that is, *Finding out the successor of a key in a BST* and *Finding out the predecessor of a key in a BST* section . The code will be as follows:

```
// Finding successor
// Successor(31) should be 53
// Successor(15) should be 23
// Successor(88) should be -1 or NULL
cout << "Successor(31) = ";
cout << tree->Successor(31) << endl;
cout << "Successor(15) = ";
cout << tree->Successor(15) << endl;
cout << "Successor(88) = ";
cout << tree->Successor(88) << endl;

// Finding predecessor
// Predecessor(12) should be 7
// Predecessor(29) should be 23
// Predecessor(3) should be -1 or NULL
cout << "Predecessor(12) = ";
cout << tree->Predecessor(12) << endl;
cout << "Predecessor(29) = ";
cout << tree->Predecessor(29) << endl;
cout << "Predecessor(3) = ";
cout << tree->Predecessor(3) << endl;
```

The last operation is `Remove()`. We will try to remove keys 15 and 53. Then, we will call the `PrintTreeInOrder()` operation again to prove that the selected keys have been removed. The code snippet will be as follows:

```
// Removing a key
cout << "Removing key 15" << endl;
tree->Remove(15);
cout << "Removing key 53" << endl;
tree->Remove(53);
```

```
// Printing all keys again
// Key 15 and 53 should be disappeared
cout << "Tree keys: ";
tree->PrintTreeInOrder();
```

The full code can be found in the `Binary_Search_Tree.cpp` file of
the `Binary_Search_Tree.cbp` project. If we build and run the project, we will get the
following output on the console:

```
Binary Search Tree
Tree keys: 3 7 12 15 23 29 31 53 88
Search key 31: found
Search key 18: NOT found
Min. Key : 3
Max. Key : 88
Successor(31) = 53
Successor(15) = 23
Successor(88) = -1
Predecessor(12) = 7
Predecessor(29) = 23
Predecessor(3) = -1
Removing key 15
Removing key 53
Tree keys: 3 7 12 23 29 31 88

Process returned 0 (0x0)    execution time : 0.021 s
Press ENTER to continue.
```

As we can see in the console's output, we've got all of the expected outputs for each
operation.

Building a balanced BST (AVL) ADT

As we discussed earlier in the *Building a binary search tree ADT* section, it's possible to have a
skewed tree (either left or right) and cause the time complexity of several operations to
become slow for *O(h)*, where *h* is the height of the tree. In this section, we are going to
discuss a balanced binary search tree to ensure that we won't get a skewed tree. There are
several implementations needed to create a balanced BST. However, we will only focus on
the *AVL* tree, which was invented by *Adelson-Velskii* and *Landis* in 1962, and is named after
the inventors.

To make a balanced BST, we have to know the height of each node in the tree. So, we need to modify the `BSTNode` class by adding a new property named `Height`, as follows:

```
class BSTNode
{
public:
    int Key;
    BSTNode * Left;
    BSTNode * Right;
    BSTNode * Parent;
    int Height;
};
```

This new property is used to track the height of each node. We will also create a new method to fetch the height of a node, which is named `GetHeight()`, with the following implementation:

```
int AVL::GetHeight(BSTNode * node)
{
    // Return the Height of the node
    // Return -1 if the node is NULL
    return node == NULL ?
        -1 :
        node->Height;
}
```

Let's see our preceding BST from the previous section. If it is a balanced BST, when we invoke `GetHeight(7)` it will return 0 since there's no edge in node 7.
Also, `GetHeight(15)` = `GetHeight(29)` = `GetHeight(53)` = 0. On the other hand, to get the tree's height, we just need to fetch the root's height, so in our preceding BST, we can invoke `GetHeight(23)`.

An AVL tree is basically a BST, but it has a balanced height. All operations in the AVL tree will be the same as they are in the BST, except for the `Insert()` and `Remove()` operations. To find the height of each node, we need to find the maximum height between the left subtree and the right subtree then add 1 to the result. The following code is used to fetch the height of a node:

```
std::max(GetHeight(T->Left), GetHeight(T->Right)) + 1;
```

We will add the preceding code to our new AVL `Insert()` and `Remove()` operations, which we will discuss in the upcoming sections.

Rotating nodes

The balanced BST can be achieved if the difference of the node's left height and the node's right height is no more than 1. Please see the following mathematical notation:

$$|GetHeight(node{-}{>}Left) - GetHeight(node{-}{>}Right)| \leq 1$$

Based on the preceding notation, we can initialize the `balance` variable with the following code:

```
int balance =
    GetHeight(node->Left) - GetHeight(node->Right);
```

If `balance == 2` then the tree is left heavy and we need to rotate the left subtree. In contrast, if `balance == -2` then the tree is right heavy and we need to rotate the right subtree. Please see the following diagram:

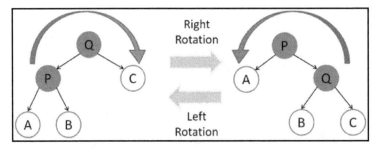

In the preceding diagram, we will get the right tree if we rotate the left tree to the right, and will get the left tree if we rotate the right tree to the left. Based on this explanation, we can create the `RotateLeft()` and `RotateRight()` operations as follows:

```
BSTNode * AVL::RotateLeft(BSTNode * node)
{
    // The node must have a right child

    // Create a new node as a result
    // that will be a balanced node
    BSTNode * balancedNode = node->Right;

    // the balanced node will replace
    // the current node
    balancedNode->Parent = node->Parent;

    // the current node will be child
    // of the balanced node
    node->Parent = balancedNode;
```

```cpp
    // The right child of current node
    // will be balanced node's left child
    node->Right = balancedNode->Left;

    // If balanced node has left child
    // point the parent to the current node
    if (balancedNode->Left != NULL)
        balancedNode->Left->Parent = node;

    // The left child of balanced node
    // will be the current node
    balancedNode->Left = node;

    // Refresh the node's height
    node->Height = std::max(
        GetHeight(node->Left),
        GetHeight(node->Right)) + 1;

    // Refresh the balanced node's height
    balancedNode->Height = std::max(
        GetHeight(balancedNode->Left),
        GetHeight(balancedNode->Right)) + 1;

    // return balancedNode
    return balancedNode;
}

BSTNode * AVL::RotateRight(BSTNode * node)
{
    // The node must have a left child

    // Create a new node as a result
    // that will be a balanced node
    BSTNode * balancedNode = node->Left;

    // the balanced node will replace
    // the current node
    balancedNode->Parent = node->Parent;

    // the current node will be child
    // of the balanced node
    node->Parent = balancedNode;

    // The left child of current node
    // will be balanced node's right child
    node->Left = balancedNode->Right;

    // If balanced node has right child
```

```
    // point the parent to the current node
    if (balancedNode->Right != NULL)
        balancedNode->Right->Parent = node;

    // The right child of balanced node
    // will be the current node
    balancedNode->Right = node;

    // Refresh the node's height
    node->Height = std::max(
        GetHeight(node->Left),
        GetHeight(node->Right)) + 1;

    // Refresh the balanced node's height
    balancedNode->Height = std::max(
        GetHeight(balancedNode->Left),
        GetHeight(balancedNode->Right)) + 1;

    // return balancedNode
    return balancedNode;
}
```

We will use the preceding `RotateLeft()` and `RotateRight()` operations in the upcoming `Insert()` and `Remove()` operations section.

Inserting a new key

Inserting a new key into an AVL tree is similar to inserting a new key in a BST. The difference is that we need to check the balance of the inserted node and the parent nodes. As we discussed earlier, we have the formula to make a balanced tree by balancing the left and right nodes. After that, we can decide if we have to rotate it left or right. The implementation of the `Insert()` operation in an AVL tree is as follows:

```
BSTNode * AVL::Insert(BSTNode * node, int key)
{
    // If AVL tree doesn't exist
    // create a new node as root
    // or it's reached when
    // there's no any child node
    // so we can insert a new node here
    if (node == NULL)
    {
        node = new BSTNode;
        node->Key = key;
        node->Left = NULL;
```

```
        node->Right = NULL;
        node->Parent = NULL;
        node->Height = 0;
    }
    // If the given key is greater than
    // node's key then go to right subtree
    else if(node->Key < key)
    {
        node->Right = Insert(node->Right, key);
        node->Right->Parent = node;
    }
    // If the given key is smaller than
    // node's key then go to left subtree
    else
    {
        node->Left = Insert(node->Left, key);
        node->Left->Parent = node;
    }

    // Get the balance
    int balance =
        GetHeight(node->Left) - GetHeight(node->Right);

    // If left heavy
    if (balance == 2)
    {
        // Get left subtree's height
        int balance2 =
            GetHeight(node->Left->Left) -
            GetHeight(node->Left->Right);

        if (balance2 == 1)
        {
            node = RotateRight(node);
        }
        else
        {
            node->Left = RotateLeft(node->Left);
            node = RotateRight(node);
        }
    }
    // If right heavy
    else if (balance == -2)
    {
        // Get right subtree's height
        int balance2 =
            GetHeight(node->Right->Left) -
            GetHeight(node->Right->Right);
```

```
            if (balance2 == -1)
                node = RotateLeft(node);
            else
            { // 1
                node->Right = RotateRight(node->Right);
                node = RotateLeft(node);
            }
        }

        // Refresh node's height
        node->Height = std::max(
            GetHeight(node->Left),
            GetHeight(node->Right)) + 1;

        // Return the updated AVL tree
        return node;
    }
```

Since the implementation of the `Insert()` operation of the AVL tree is similar to the `Insert()` operation of the BST, we can say that the time complexity of this operation is the same, which is *O(h)*. However, since we can ensure that the height is always balanced in an AVL tree, the height will always be *log N*. So, the time complexity of the `Insert()` operation of an AVL tree is *O(log N)*, where *N* is the total number of elements of the tree.

Removing a given key

Removing a key in an AVL tree is also the same as removing a key in a BST. We also need to check the balance after removing the key. Here is the implementation of the `Remove()` operation in the AVL class, which has been updated with balance checking:

```
BSTNode * AVL::Remove(BSTNode * node, int key)
{
    // The given node is
    // not found in AVL tree
    if (node == NULL)
        return NULL;

    // Target node is found
    if (node->Key == key)
    {
        // If the node is a leaf node
        // The node can be safely removed
        if (node->Left == NULL && node->Right == NULL)
            node = NULL;
        // The node have only one child at right
```

```
    else if (node->Left == NULL && node->Right != NULL)
    {
        // The only child will be connected to
        // the parent's of node directly
        node->Right->Parent = node->Parent;

        // Bypass node
        node = node->Right;
    }
    // The node have only one child at left
    else if (node->Left != NULL && node->Right == NULL)
    {
        // The only child will be connected to
        // the parent's of node directly
        node->Left->Parent = node->Parent;

        // Bypass node
        node = node->Left;
    }
    // The node have two children (left and right)
    else
    {
        // Find successor or predecessor to avoid quarrel
        int successorKey = Successor(key);

        // Replace node's key with successor's key
        node->Key = successorKey;

        // Delete the old successor's key
        node->Right = Remove(node->Right, successorKey);
    }
}
// Target node's key is smaller than
// the given key then search to right
else if (node->Key < key)
    node->Right = Remove(node->Right, key);
// Target node's key is greater than
// the given key then search to left
else
    node->Left = Remove(node->Left, key);

// Only perform rotation if node is not NULL
if (node != NULL)
{
    // Get the balance
    int balance =
        GetHeight(node->Left) - GetHeight(node->Right);
```

```cpp
        // If left heavy
        if (balance == 2)
        {
            // Get left subtree's height
            int balance2 =
                GetHeight(node->Left->Left) -
                GetHeight(node->Left->Right);

            if (balance2 == 1)
            {
                node = RotateRight(node);
            }
            else
            {
                node->Left = RotateLeft(node->Left);
                node = RotateRight(node);
            }
        }
        // If right heavy
        else if (balance == -2)
        {
            // Get right subtree's height
            int balance2 =
                GetHeight(node->Right->Left) -
                GetHeight(node->Right->Right);

            if (balance2 == -1)
                node = RotateLeft(node);
            else
            { // 1
                node->Right = RotateRight(node->Right);
                node = RotateLeft(node);
            }
        }

        // Refresh node's height
        node->Height = std::max(
            GetHeight(node->Left),
            GetHeight(node->Right)) + 1;

    }

    // Return the updated AVL tree
    return node;
}
```

Similar to the `Insert()` operation in the AVL tree, the time complexity of the `Remove()` operation in the AVL tree will be *O(log N)*, where *N* is the total number of elements of the tree since we can ensure that the tree is balanced.

Implementing AVL ADT

By now, we will have the AVL class declaration, as follows:

```
class AVL : public BST
{
private:
    BSTNode * root;

    int GetHeight(BSTNode * node);
    BSTNode * RotateLeft(BSTNode * node);
    BSTNode * RotateRight(BSTNode * node);
    BSTNode * Insert(BSTNode * node, int key);
    BSTNode * Remove(BSTNode * node, int key);

public:
    AVL();

    void Insert(int v);
    void Remove(int v);
};
```

As we can see in the preceding declaration code, we derive the AVL class from the BST class, which we discussed earlier. So, we just need to define the `Insert()` and `Remove()` operations. Also, since we have to maintain the tree's balance, we need to use the `RotateLeft()` and `RotateRight()` operations.

We are now going to balance our preceding skewed left BST tree example which contains the following keys: 69, 62, 46, 32, 24, and 13. To create an AVL tree, first we have to instantiate an AVL class instance as follows:

```
// Instantiate BST instance
AVL * avlTree = new AVL;
```

Next, we insert the first key, which is 69, as follows:

```
// Insert first key
avlTree->Insert(69);
```

Then, we insert key 62. The tree will look as follows:

```
/*
    Add key 62
        69
       /
     62
*/
avlTree->Insert(62);
```

Next, we will insert key 46. When the key is inserted, the tree becomes unbalance since 46 will be a child of 62. To keep it balanced, we will rotate it right the tree. The code will be as follows:

```
/*
    Add key 46
    it will rotate right since
    the balance = 2
        62
       /  \
     46    69
*/
avlTree->Insert(46);
```

Next, we insert 32 into the tree. After inserting the key, the tree is still balanced since the difference between the left subtree's height and right subtree's height is 1 (remember this notation—|GetHeight(node->Left) - GetHeight(node->Right)| ≤ 1). The code should be as follows:

```
/*
    Add key 32
        62
       /  \
     46    69
    /
  32
*/
avlTree->Insert(32);
```

The next key is 24. When we insert the key, the tree becomes unbalanced again. So, 32 will be the parent of 24 and 46. The parent of 32 will be 62. Please see the following code:

```
/*
    Add key 24
    it will rotate right since
    the balance = 2
            62
           /  \
        32      69
       /  \
     24    46
*/
avlTree->Insert(24);
```

The last key is 13. When we insert the key, the tree becomes unbalanced. Key 32 will become the root. Key 46 will be the left child of key 62. Key 62 will be the right child of the root node, which is 32. The code will be as follows:

```
/*
    Add key 13
    it will rotate right since
    the balance = 2
            32
           /  \
        24      62
       /       /  \
     13      46    69
*/
avlTree->Insert(13);
```

Building a binary heap ADT

A **binary heap** is a completely binary tree that is usually used to implement a priority queue. Please look at the following binary tree which is representing the priority queue:

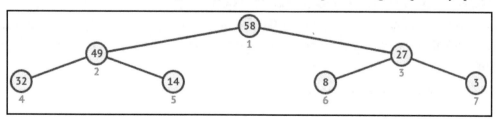

As we can see, each node has its own key and there's also a number below each node to indicate the priority of the element (in this example, the maximum element has higher priority). The priority queue is usually represented in an array, so we can have the following array as a representation of the preceding priority queue tree:

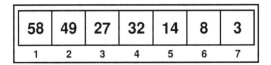

To create a binary heap in C++, we will have the `heapSize` variable, which will be increased when an element is inserted and will be decreased when an element is removed. There are four basic operations in a priority queue, and they are as follows:

- `IsEmpty()` is used to check whether the queue is empty
- `Insert()`, similar to the `Enqueue()` operation in a Queue data structure, is used to insert a new element into the queue
- `GetMax()`, similar to the `Peek()` operation in a Queue data structure, is used to fetch the element with the greatest order
- `ExtractMax()`, similar to the `Dequeue()` operation in a Queue data structure, is used to fetch the element with the greatest order before removing it from the queue

Now, let's discuss these operations further in the upcoming sections.

 We are going use a `vector` container in the C++ implementation of the Binary Heap ADT. However, since the binary heap we've developed starts from index 1 while the vector container starts from index 0, we won't use index 0 in the vector container, instead filling index 0 with -1 to indicate that it's not used.

Checking if the heap is empty

The `heapSize` variable can be used to indicate whether or not the heap is empty. We just need to check if `heapSize = 0` to determine that the heap is empty. The following is an implementation of the `IsEmpty()` operation:

```
bool BinaryHeap::IsEmpty()
{
    // Heap is empty if only
    // heapSize = 0
```

```
        return heapSize == 0;
    }
```

The preceding sample code will run on *O(1)* since it's just simply getting the `heapSize` value.

Inserting a new element into the heap

A new element will be inserted in the last vector. However, we need to shift the element up to ensure that it will be in the right place based on the value of the element. To do so, we need to create the `ShiftUp()` operation, which will swap two adjacent elements so that the vector will be in order. The implementation of the `ShiftUp()` operation will be as follows:

```cpp
void BinaryHeap::ShiftUp(int index)
{
    // Do nothing in root
    if (index == 1)
        return;

    if (vect[index] > vect[p(index)])
    {
        // Swap Upwards
        std::swap(vect[index], vect[p(index)]);

        // Recurse until root
        ShiftUp(p(index));
    }
}
```

After we have the `ShiftUp()` operation, we can create the `Insert()` operation as follows:

```cpp
void BinaryHeap::Insert(int key)
{
    // Add a new element in vector
    if (heapSize + 1 >= (int)vect.size())
        vect.push_back(0);

    // Store the key in the vector last position
    vect[++heapSize] = key;

    // Shift upwards
    ShiftUp(heapSize);
}
```

As we can see in the preceding `Insert()` operation, it invokes the `ShiftUp()` operation as well. Since the `ShiftUp()` operation has a time complexity of *O(log N)*, the `Insert()` operation will also be the same.

Fetching the element's maximum value

Fetching the element's maximum value is quite simple since it is stored in the root, or, in other words, it's in index `1`. To do so, we just need to return `vect[1]`:

```
int BinaryHeap::GetMax()
{
    // Return root's key
    return vect[1];
}
```

Since it's a simple implementation, the time complexity for the `GetMax()` operation is `O(1)`.

Removing the maximum element

To remove the maximum element from the priority queue, we will need to use the `ExtractMax()` operation. After we remove the element in root, we will place the minimum value in root to replace the maximum element which was just removed. Then, we need to shift the minimum value down to the leaf of the tree. To do so, we need to also create the `ShiftDown()` operation, as follows:

```
void BinaryHeap::ShiftDown(int i)
{
    // For non-existing index
    // just do nothing
    if(i > heapSize)
        return;

    // Initialize swapId
    int swapId = i;

    // Compare with left child, if exists
    if (l(i) <= heapSize && vect[i] < vect[l(i)])
        swapId = l(i);

    // Compare with right child, if exists
    if (r(i) <= heapSize && vect[swapId] < vect[r(i)])
        swapId = r(i);
```

```
        // Swap with the larger of the two children
        if (swapId != i)
        {
            // Swap downwards with the larger
            // of the two children
            std::swap(vect[i], vect[swapId]);

            // Recurse until the index
            ShiftDown(swapId);
        }
    }
```

As we discussed earlier, we will swap the last element of root and then shift down root. Here is the implementation of the ExtractMax() operation:

```
int BinaryHeap::ExtractMax()
{
    // Maximum value is in root
    int maxVal = vect[1];

    // Swap with the last existing leaf
    std::swap(vect[1], vect[heapSize--]);

    // Fix heap property downwards
    ShiftDown(1);

    // Return the maximum value
    return maxVal;
}
```

As we can see in the ShiftDown() operation, the time complexity of the implementation is *O(log N)*. Since the ExtractMax() operation invokes the ShiftDown() operation, the time complexity will be the same.

Implementing a binary heap as a priority queue

By now, we should have a BinaryHeap class implementation as follows:

```
class BinaryHeap
{
private:
    std::vector<int> vect;
    int heapSize;

    // three helper navigation function
```

```
    int p(int i) { return i>>1; } // i/2
    int l(int i) { return i<<1; } // i*2
    int r(int i) { return (i<<1)+1; } // i*2+1

    void ShiftUp(int index);
    void ShiftDown(int i);

public:
    BinaryHeap();

    bool IsEmpty();
    void Insert(int key);
    int ExtractMax();
    int GetMax();
};
```

We are going to create a priority queue using this `BinaryHeap` data structure. The following is the code snippet for the `BinaryHeap` data structure:

```
// Instantiate priority queue
BinaryHeap * priorityQueue = new BinaryHeap();
```

Before we insert a new element, we can check whether the queue is empty by using the following code snippet:

```
// Check if the queue is empty
// it should be TRUE
cout << "Is queue empty? ";
bool b = priorityQueue->IsEmpty();
if(b)
    cout << "TRUE";
else
    cout << "FALSE";
cout << endl;
```

To insert a new element, we can use the following code snippet:

```
// Insert a new element
priorityQueue->Insert(14);
cout << "Insert 14 to queue" << endl;
```

Again, we can check if the queue is empty by using the `IsEmpty()` operation, as we discussed earlier, and now it should say `FALSE`.

Then, we insert three new elements as follows:

```
// Insert others elements
priorityQueue->Insert(53);
priorityQueue->Insert(8);
priorityQueue->Insert(32);
```

Until now, the maximum value in the queue is 53. To ensure this, we can call the `GetMax()` operation, as follows:

```
// Peek the maximum element
// It should be 53
cout << "GetMax() = ";
cout << priorityQueue->GetMax();
cout << endl;
```

Also, we can extract the maximum value using the `ExtractMax()` operation, as follows:

```
// Extract maximum element
cout << "ExtractMax() = ";
cout << priorityQueue->ExtractMax();
cout << endl;
```

Now, if we invoke the `GetMax()` operation again, it should return 32. The full code can be found in the `Binary_Heap.cpp` file in the `Binary_Heap.cbp` project. If we build and run the project, we will get the following output on the console:

```
Terminal
Priority Queue
Is queue empty? TRUE
Insert 14 to queue
Is queue empty? FALSE
Insert 53, 8 and 32 to queue
GetMax() = 53
ExtractMax() = 53
GetMax() = 32

Process returned 0 (0x0)    execution time : 0.003 s
Press ENTER to continue.
```

Summary

In this chapter, we discussed the hierarchical data structure and stored information in the form of a tree. We started our discussion by creating a tree from several `TreeNodes`, and then built a binary search tree where we can search for a given key easily. Sometimes, we can have a skewed tree in a binary search tree, and so we build an AVL tree, which can balance all of the elements itself, so that now we can have a balanced binary tree. Another tree data structure implementation is the binary heap, which we used to build a priority queue, where we can access an element based on its priority.

In the next chapter, we are going to discuss how to construct and implement the hash structure in algorithm design.

QA section

- What is the difference between the `TreeNode` class in a binary tree and the `TreeNode` class in a binary search tree?
- What are the advantages of the binary search tree over the binary tree?
- How can the AVL tree have a balanced tree?

Further reading

For futher references, please visit these links:

- https://visualgo.net/en/bst
- https://www.geeksforgeeks.org/binary-tree-data-structure/
- https://en.wikipedia.org/wiki/Binary_search_tree
- http://en.cppreference.com/w/cpp/language/range-for
- https://en.wikipedia.org/wiki/Binary_heap
- https://visualgo.net/en/heap
- https://www.geeksforgeeks.org/binary-heap/

Associating a Value to a Key in a Hash Table

In the previous chapter, we discussed the hierarchical tree data type, which is a non-linear data type, that stores data in a tree-like structure. In this chapter, we are going to discuss another non-linear data type, the hash table, which stores data based on a key. The following topics are discussed in this chapter:

- Understanding hash tables
- Preventing a collision in a hash table
- Using a separate chaining technique to handle a collision
- Using an open addressing technique to handle a collision

Technical requirement

To follow along with this chapter, including the source code, we require the following:

- Desktop PC or Notebook with Windows, Linux, or macOS
- GNU GCC v5.4.0 or above
- Code::Blocks IDE v17.12 (for Windows and Linux OS), or Code::Blocks IDE v13.12 (for macOS)
- You will find the code files on GitHub at `https://github.com/PacktPublishing/CPP-Data-Structures-and-Algorithms`

Getting acquainted with hash tables

Suppose we want to store a collection of numbers, for instance, a phone number, and let's say we have approximately 1,000,000 numbers. In previous chapters, we also discussed several data structures, and here we can consider using one of them. We can use an array or a list, but we have to provide a million slots of data in the array. If we need to add some phone numbers again, we have to resize the array. Also, the operation of searching will be costly, since we have to use a linear search algorithm with time complexity *O(N)*, where the time consumption will increase if we add data to the list. Indeed, we can use a binary search algorithm with *O(log N)* time complexity if we manage to sort the elements of the list containing the bunch of phone numbers; however, the insert operation will be costly, since we have to maintain the sorted list.

Another data structure we can choose is the balanced binary search tree. It can give us a moderate time complexity, since it will be *O(log N)* to insert, search, and remove the operation; however, it still depends on the total number of elements in the tree.

Big data in small cells

To solve this problem, we are going to construct a **hash table** data type. This data type will have a **hash function** to convert a given big phone number into a small integer value. By using a hash table, we don't need to provide a million memory allocations; instead, we can determine a table size for the hash table. Afterward, we will map the integer value to the index of the hash table.

A phone number usually contains at least six to seven digits; however, for the sake of simplicity, we will use three-digit phone numbers in the example in this section. Here is a list of phone numbers we will use in several examples in upcoming sections:

No.	Phone Number	Name
1	434	Dylan
2	391	Dominic
3	806	Adam
4	117	Lindsey
5	548	Cameron
6	669	Terry
7	722	Brynn
8	276	Jody
9	953	Frankie
10	895	Vanessa

As we can see in the preceding list, we have **10** phone numbers, and each number is owned by a person as stated in the **Name** column. We are going to store data in **Phone Number** and **Name** column as a data pair in a hash table in the upcoming discussion.

Storing data in a hash table

In the preceding section, we have ten phone number to be inserted to a hash table. We will try to store them in a hash table which has seven slot. As we have discussed in preceding section, we need a hash function to get a hash key from the phone number so it can be stored to the hash table. The hash key can be found by find out the remainder if we divide the phone number by the total slot of the hash table, which is seven. Please see the following table which contain the mapping of hash key (slot number) with the data.

Hash Key	Data
0	[434, Dylan]
1	[806, Adam] - [722, Brynn] - [953, Frankie]
2	[548, Cameron]
3	[276, Jody]
4	[669, Terry]
5	[117, Lindsey]
6	[391, Dominic] - [895, Vanessa]

As we can see in the preceding table, there are several data that have same hash key, for instance, key **1** has three data and key **6** has two data. However, since each slot in the hash table can only contain one data, this cannot happen since it's called *collision* in hash table. To solve this problem, we are going to discuss how to prevent the collision in next section.

Collision handling

As we have discussed previously, there will be a possibility that one key is used by two values or more, since we map a big key to a small key. This situation is called a **collision**, where there is another key that will be mapped to an occupied slot. To solve this problem, we need a collision handling technique. And here are the ways to handle collisions:

- **Separate chaining** is a technique to point each cell in a hash table to a chaining node, or a linked list. The same hash key for a different value will be stored in the chaining node.
- **Open addressing** is a technique to store all elements in the hash table itself. If a collision is about to happen, the technique will find another slot by performing some calculation to ensure a collision will not happen.

Now, let's implement all collision handling techniques in a hash table by developing several ADTs in C++.

Implementing a separate chaining technique

Separate chaining is a collision handling technique that will make each cell in the hash table point to a chaining node containing values with the same hash key. We are going to create an ADT named `HashTable` to handle the preceding phone number list. Since the phone number contains only numbers, it will be stored in the `int` data type, and the owner of the phone number name will be stored in the `string` data type. However, if the phone number we have are saved as `123-456-789` format, we need to remove the dash (-) character first.

The `HashTable` will be four basic operations and they are:

- `Insert()` is used to insert a new `pair<int, string>` to the hash table. It passes an `int` as a key and a `string` as a value. It then finds a hash key for the inputted key. If the inputted key is found in the hash table, it will update the value of the key. If no key is found, it will append a new node to the linked list containing the inputted key and inputted value.
- `Search()` is used to find the value of the inputted key. It will return the value if the inputted key is found. If not, it will return an empty string.

- `Remove()` is used to delete an existing inputted key. If the inputted key is not found, it will do nothing.
- `IsEmpty()` is used to tell the user if the hash table has at least one element or not. If there is no element, it will return TRUE; otherwise, it returns FALSE.

Since we will have four operations, we are going to have the following class declaration:

```
#define TABLE_SIZE 7

class HashTable
{
    private:
        std::list<std::pair<int, std::string>>
            tableList[TABLE_SIZE];

        int HashFunction(int key);

    public:
        HashTable();

        void Insert(int key, std::string value);
        std::string Search(int key);
        void Remove(int key);
        bool IsEmpty();
};
```

As we can see in the preceding declaration, we have a `HashFunction()` declaration to generate a hash key for each inputted key. And since we need a chaining node, we declare a `tableList` in `std::list` data type containing `pair<int, string>` data.

Generating a hash key

As we have discussed earlier, a hash key is obtained by finding out the remainder when we divide the phone number with the total slot of table (table size). To generate the hash key, we will implement the `HashFunction()` function as follows:

```
int HashTable::HashFunction(int key)
{
    return key % TABLE_SIZE;
}
```

Since we have 10 data items, we define TABLE_SIZE as 7. By using this function, we can get a hash key for an inputted key in the operations of the HashTable. Since the implementation of the HashFunction() function is quite simple, the time complexity of this function will be *O(1)* for all cases.

Developing an Insert() operation

To insert a new pair of int and string to the hash table, we need to find out a hash key for the inputted key. Then, we traverse to chaining node in the cell pointed by the hash key to find if the the given new pair data exists. For instance, if the hash key is 5, we just need to go to cell 5 then traverse to the list in that cell to find out the inputted key. If the inputted key is found, we update the value of that key. If the key is not found, we add the pair of data to the back of the list. The implementation of Insert() operations should be as follows:

```cpp
void HashTable::Insert(int key, string value)
{
    bool isKeyFound = false;

    // Get hash key from hash function
    int hashKey = HashFunction(key);

    // Iterate through chaining node (linked list)
    // in selected cell
    for (auto &keyValue : tableList[hashKey])
    {
        // if the key is found
        // update the data
        if (keyValue.first == key)
        {
            isKeyFound = true;
            keyValue.second = value;
        }
    }

    // If key is not found,
    // append at the back
    if (!isKeyFound)
        tableList[hashKey].emplace_back(key, value);
}
```

As we can see in the preceding code implementation, because `emplace_back()` is similar to the `InsertTail()` operation in the `DoublyLinkedList` ADT, we have an $O(1)$ time complexity for the best case if there's no hash key stored before in the hash table; however, on average and in the worst cases, we will have an $O(N)$ time complexity if we have to traverse to the end of the list.

Developing a Search() operation

In a `Search()` operation, we will get the value of an inputted key. To do so, first we need to find out the hash key of the inputted key. Similar to the `Insert()` operation, we traverse to the chaining node in the cell pointed by the hash key to find if the key. If the key is found, we just need to return the value of the key. If not, the empty string will be returned instead. The implementation of the `Search()` operation should be as follows:

```
string HashTable::Search(int key)
{
    // Get hash key from hash function
    int hashKey = HashFunction(key);

    // Iterate through chaining node (linked list)
    // in selected cell
    for (auto &keyValue : tableList[hashKey])
    {
        // if the key is found
        // return the value of name
        if (keyValue.first == key)
        {
            return keyValue.second;
        }
    }

    // If this statement is reached
    // it means that the key is not found
    // so just return empty string
    return "";
}
```

Similar to the `Insert()` operation, the best case time complexity will be $O(1)$ if we found the inputted key in the first element of the list; however, we will get $O(N)$ for both the average and the worst cases, since we may have to traverse to the end of the list.

Developing a Remove() operation

In a `Remove()` operation, we erase a found key node from the chaining node in the cell pointed by hash key. Similar to the `Insert()` and `Search()` operation, we have to traverse to the linked list until we find the inputted key. If the inputted key is found, we just need to delete the node. If the inputted key doesn't exist, we simply do nothing. The implementation of the `Remove()` operation will be as follows:

```cpp
void HashTable::Remove(int key)
{
    // Get hash key from hash function
    int hashKey = HashFunction(key);

    // Get the cell
    auto &cell = tableList[hashKey];

    // Tranverse the chaining node (linked list)
    for (auto it = cell.begin(); it != cell.end(); ++it)
    {
        // if the key is found
        // then delete the list's element
        if (it->first == key)
        {
            cell.erase(it);
            break;
        }
    }

    // Note: if key is not found just do nothing
}
```

Again, we will have *O(1)* for the time complexity of the function for the best case if we found the key in the first element of the linked list. We will also have an *O(N)* time complexity for the average and the worst case if we have to traverse to all elements in the linked list.

Developing an IsEmpty() operation

Sometimes, we need to check whether a hash table is empty or not. To do so, we can check if each cell in the hash table has a list that contains at least one element. The implementation of the `IsEmpty()` operation should be as follows:

```
bool HashTable::IsEmpty()
{
    // Initialize total element
    int totalElement = 0;

    // Count all elements in table hash
    for (int i = 0; i < TABLE_SIZE; ++i)
    {
        totalElement += (int)tableList[i].size();

        // If the total element is not zero
        // the hash table must not be empty
        if totalElement > 0
            return false;
    }

    // If this statement is reached
    // it means that total element is zero
    return true;
}
```

As we can see in the preceding function implementation, we have to iterate the hash table and find out if the cell is empty or not. By using the preceding implementation, we can get an $O(1)$ time complexity in the best case if the first cell is not empty; however, on average and in the worst cases, the time complexity will be $O(TABLE\_SIZE)$.

Applying a HashTable ADT using a separate chaining technique in the code

Before we apply the HashTable ADT using the separate chaining technique to the code, let's see how a separate chaining technique works to handle collisions. First, we have phone number 434, owned by Dylan. The phone number will generate 0 for the hash key, so the data will be stored in cell 0. Next is phone number 391, owned by Dominic, which will be stored in cell 6. Phone number 806, owned by Adam in cell 1; phone number 117, owned by Lindsey in cell 5; phone number 548, owned by Cameron in cell 2; and phone number 669, owned by Terry in cell 4.

By now, everything has been running well, since no collision has occurred; however, if we store the 7th data to the hash table, which is phone number 722 owned by Brynn, it will have 2 as the hash key, but the hash key 2 has been occupied by phone number 548. In this situation, we will still store the data in cell 2, and link to the previous node in the same cell. After storing all data in the hash table, we will have the following diagram:

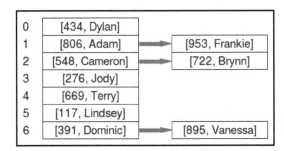

Now, it's time to apply our HashTable ADT to the phone number list we had at the beginning of this chapter. First, we have to instance a HashTable class in the code as follows:

```
HashTable * hashTable = new HashTable();
```

To prove that `HashTable` is initialized with an empty element, we can invoke the
`IsEmpty()` operation as follows:

```
// Check if hash table is empty
bool b = hashTable->IsEmpty();
if(b)
    cout << "Hash table is empty";
else
    cout << "Hash table is not empty";
cout << endl;
```

Then we can insert new data by using the `Insert()` operation, then checking if the hash
table is empty using the following code snippet:

```
// Adding a data then
// check if hash table is empty
cout << "Adding a data" << endl;
hashTable->Insert(434, "Dylan");
b = hashTable->IsEmpty();
if(b)
    cout << "Hash table is empty";
else
    cout << "Hash table is not empty";
cout << endl;
```

Afterward, we can insert all remaining data to the hash table as follows:

```
// Adding others data
hashTable->Insert(391, "Dominic");
hashTable->Insert(806, "Adam");
hashTable->Insert(117, "Lindsey");
hashTable->Insert(548, "Cameron");
hashTable->Insert(669, "Terry");
hashTable->Insert(722, "Brynn");
hashTable->Insert(276, "Jody");
hashTable->Insert(953, "Frankie");
hashTable->Insert(895, "Vanessa");
```

By now, we have all data stored in the hash table. We can search if a key is present in the hash table. Suppose we are going to search key 669, we can do the following:

```
// Search key 669
// it should be found
int key = 669;
cout << "Search value for key ";
cout << key << endl;
string name = hashTable->Search(key);
if(name != "")
{
    cout << "Value for key " << key;
    cout << " is " << name;
}
else
{
    cout << "Value for key " << key;
    cout << " is not found";
}
cout << endl;
```

Now, let's remove the 669 key. The key should be not found if we search it again. The code snippet is as follows:

```
// Remove key 669
// then search the key
// it should not be found
cout << "Remove node of key ";
cout << key << endl;
hashTable->Remove(key);name = hashTable->Search(key);
if(name != "")
{
    cout << "Value for key " << key;
    cout << " is " << name;
}
else
{
    cout << "Value for key " << key;
    cout << " is not found";
}
cout << endl;
```

As of now, we have tried all operations in the `HashTable` ADT. The following is the output we will have onscreen if we build and run the `Hash_Table_SC.cbp` project from the repository:

```
⊗ ⊖ ⊡   Terminal
Hash Table - Separate Chaining
Hash table is empty
Adding a data
Hash table is not empty
Search value for key 669
Value for key 669 is Terry
Remove node of key 669
Value for key 669 is not found

Process returned 0 (0x0)    execution time : 0.004 s
Press ENTER to continue.
```

Implementing the open addressing technique

As we discussed earlier at beginning of this chapter, an open addressing technique stores all elements in the hash table itself. A collision will not happen, since there is a calculation that will be performed if a collision is about to happen. Based on this calculation, we can have three types of open addressing technique—**Linear probing**, **quadratic probing**, and **double hashing**. The difference between the three is the formula for finding the next free space if the hash key of the given element has been occupied:

- In **linear probing**, if the hash key has been occupied by another element, we use the following formula to find the next free space— `(HashFunction(key) + n) % TABLE_SIZE`, then increase n from 0 until a free slot is found. Here is the explanation—If `HashFunction(key) % TABLE_SIZE` is occupied, then try `(HashFunction(key) + 1) % TABLE_SIZE`. If the slot is still occupied, try `(HashFunction(key) + 2) % TABLE_SIZE`. Repeat it by increasing n until a free slot is found.

- In **quadratic probing**, if the hash key has been occupied by another element, we use the following formula to find the next free space— (HashFunction(key) + n^2) % TABLE_SIZE, then increase n from 0 until a free slot is found. By using the formula, we increase the hash key quadratically. Here is the explanation—If HashFunction(key) % TABLE_SIZE is occupied, then try (HashFunction(key) + 1^2) % TABLE_SIZE. If the slot is still occupied, try (HashFunction(key) + 2^2) % TABLE_SIZE. Repeat it by increasing n until a free slot is found.

- In **double hashing**, if the hash key has been occupied by another element, we use the following formula to find the next free space— (HashFunction(key) + n*HashFunction(key)) % TABLE_SIZE, then increase n from 0 until a free slot is found. By using the formula, we increase the hash key quadratically. Here is the explanation—If (HashFunction(key) + 1*HashFunction(key)) % TABLE_SIZE is occupied, then try (HashFunction(key) + 2*HashFunction(key)) % TABLE_SIZE. If the slot is still occupied, try (HashFunction(key) + 3*HashFunction(key)) % TABLE_SIZE. Repeat it by increasing n until a free slot is found.

> Since the three types of open addressing technique are similar yet different in the formula for finding the next free slot, we will only discuss linear probing in this book.

There are also four basic operations in linear probing techniques, similar to separate the chaining technique. They are the Insert(), Search(), Remove(), and IsEmpty() operations. These four operations have totally the same functionality as operations in the separate chaining technique; however, we will add a new operation, PrintHashTable(), to prove that an inserted element is stored in the correct place. Based on the preceding requirement, we will have HashTable class declaration as follows:

```
#define TABLE_SIZE 7

class HashTable
{
    private:
        int currentSize;
        HashElement * *arr;
        HashElement * deletedElement;

        int HashFunction(int key);

    public:
```

```
        HashTable();

        void Insert(int key, std::string value);
        std::string Search(int key);
        void Remove(int key);
        bool IsEmpty();
        void PrintHashTable();
};
```

As we can see in the preceding code, we have put all the elements in an `arr` variable, and marked a slot that has been deleted as `deletedElement`. We will track the number of elements in the hash table using the `currentSize` variable. Also, we need a new data type named `HashElement` to be stored in the hash table. The implementation of the `HashElement` class is as follows:

```
class HashElement
{
    public:
        int Key;
        std::string Value;

        HashElement(int key, std::string value)
        {
            this->Key = key;
            this->Value = value;
        }
};
```

Since we need to reset `currentSize` and initialize the `arr` and `deletedElement` variables, we will have a `HashTable` constructor implementation as follows:

```
HashTable::HashTable()
{
    // Initialize current size as 0
    currentSize = 0;

    // Initialize table
    arr = new HashElement * [TABLE_SIZE];
    for(int i = 0 ; i < TABLE_SIZE ; ++i)
        arr[i] = NULL;

    // Specify deleted node content
    deletedElement = new HashElement(-1, "");
}
```

Now, let's develop all operations we need in this `HashTable` ADT in the upcoming section.

 We have a `HashFunction()` function in the linear probing technique; however, it is exactly the same as the `HashFunction()` function in the separate chaining technique. Therefore, we are not going to discuss it anymore in this section.

Developing the Insert() operation

To insert a new element in a hash table, first we obtain a hash key from the key's element using `HashFunction()`. After we have the hash key, we check if the slot is available. If it's not available, we check another free slot using the linear formula we discussed at the beginning of this section. Since the open addressing technique stored all elements in the hash table itself at the beginning of the `Insert()` function implementation, we need to check if all slots have been occupied. If there is no free slot, the function will do nothing. Each time there's a new element to be added, we increase the `currentSize` variable to track the total elements in the hash table. The implementation of the function will be as follows:

```cpp
void HashTable::Insert(int key, string value)
{
    // It's impossible to store a new element
    // if hash table doesn't have free space
    if (currentSize >= TABLE_SIZE)
        return;

    // Create a temporary element
    // to be inserted to hash table
    HashElement * temp =
        new HashElement(key, value);

    // Get hash key from hash function
    int hashIndex = HashFunction(key);

    // Find next free space
    // using linear probing
    while(arr[hashIndex] != NULL &&
        arr[hashIndex]->Key != key &&
        arr[hashIndex]->Key != -1)
    {
        ++hashIndex;
        hashIndex %= TABLE_SIZE;
    }
```

```
// If there's new element to be inserted
// then increase the current size
if(arr[hashIndex] == NULL ||
   arr[hashIndex]->Key == -1)
{
    ++currentSize;
    arr[hashIndex] = temp;
}
}
}
```

Please see the two bold statements in the preceding code snippet as follows:

```
++hashIndex;
hashIndex %= TABLE_SIZE;
```

That is the formula for calculating the next free slot in the linear probing technique. If we want to use quadratic probing or double hashing, we just need to replace the two bold statements with a correct calculation. In average and worst cases, the Insert() function will give *O(TABLE_SIZE)* for the time complexity. For the best case, it can give an *O(1)* time complexity.

Developing a Search() operation

Similar to the preceding Insert() operation, to search for a value of a key, we need to obtain the hash key of that given key using HashFunction(). Then, we check the cell which the index is the hash key. If the key in that cell matches with the given key, we just need to return the value of the key. If not, we have to find another possible slot using the linear probing calculation until the given key is found. If the given key is still not found, just return an empty string to notify the user that the given key doesn't exist in the hash table. The implementation of the Search() function is as follows:

```
string HashTable::Search(int key)
{
    // Get hash key from hash function
    int hashIndex = HashFunction(key);

    // Find the element with given key
    while(arr[hashIndex] != NULL) && arr[hashIndex]->Key !=
     deletedElement->Key)
    {
        // If element is found
        // then return its value
        if(arr[hashIndex]->Key == key)
            return arr[hashIndex]->Value;
```

```
        // Keep looking for the key
        // using linear probing
        ++hashIndex;
        hashIndex %= TABLE_SIZE;
    }

    //If not found return null
    return "";
}
```

As we can see in the preceding code, there are bold statements to indicate that it's a linear probing technique. We can change these statements with the quadratic probing or double hashing calculations if we want to replace with one of those techniques. The time complexity we will get from this operation is *O(TABLE_SIZE)* for the average and worst cases. In the best case, we can get an *O(1)* time complexity.

Developing the Remove() operation

To remove an element by using a given key, first we have to search the position of the element stored by using a hash key. If the given key is found, then delete the element. If not, find another possible slot using a linear probing calculation, then delete the element if it's found. Each time there's a new element to be removed, we decrease the currentSize variable to track the total elements in the hash table. The implementation of the Remove() operation will be as follows:

```
void HashTable::Remove(int key)
{
    // Get hash key from hash function
    int hashIndex = HashFunction(key);

    // Find the element with given key
    while(arr[hashIndex] != NULL &&
        arr[hashIndex]->Key != deletedElement->Key)
    {
        // If element is found
        // then mark the cell as deletedElement
        if(arr[hashIndex]->Key == key)
        {
            arr[hashIndex] = deletedElement;

            // Reduce size
            --currentSize;

            // No need to search anymore
```

```
            return;
        }

        // Keep looking for the key
        // using linear probing
        ++hashIndex;
        hashIndex %= TABLE_SIZE;
    }

    // Note: if key is not found just do nothing
}
```

Again, we have bold statements in the preceding code. They are the formula to find another possible slot in the linear probing technique. Consider changing those statements if you need to use quadratic probing or double hashing techniques. The time complexity we will get from the Remove() operation is *O(TABLE_SIZE)* in both average and worst cases. In the best case, we will get *O(1)* time complexity.

Developing an IsEmpty() operation

Since we have a currentSize variable that stores the total number of elements in the hash table, to see if the hash table is empty, we just need to check if the currentSize variable equals to 0. The implementation of the IsEmpty() operation will be as follows:

```
bool HashTable::IsEmpty()
{
    return currentSize == 0;
}
```

Differ with IsEmpty() operation in our previous separate chaining technique, it's guaranteed to have *O(1)* time complexity for all cases with a IsEmpty() operation in the linear probing technique, since we have tracked the size of the hash table each time we've performed Insert() and Remove() operation.

Developing a PrintHashTable() operation

By iterating the hash table, we can collect the pairs of key and value, then print them to the screen. We will use this `PrintHashTable()` operation to see if the new element we insert is stored in the right place. The implementation of the operation will be as follows:

```
void HashTable::PrintHashTable()
{
    // Iterate through array
    for(int i = 0 ; i < currentSize; ++i)
    {
        // Just print the element
        // if it exist
        if(arr[i] != NULL && arr[i]->Key != -1)
        {
            cout << "Cell: " << i;
            cout << " Key: " << arr[i]->Key;
            cout << " Value: " << arr[i]->Value;
            cout << std::endl;
        }
    }
}
```

Since the operation will iterate through the hash table until the size of the table, the time complexity of this operation is *O(TABLE_SIZE)* in all cases.

Applying an HashTable ADT using a linear probing technique in the code

Before we apply the `HashTable` ADT we built using the linear probing technique previously, we will first see how the linear probing technique handles a collision by applying it to the phone number list we had at the beginning of this chapter. We will also define `TABLE_SIZE` as 7, which is the same as our previous separate chaining techniques, as a comparison to separate the chaining technique.

First, we have phone number 434 owned by `Dylan`, which will be stored in cell 0. The next is phone number 391 owned by `Dominic`, which will be stored in cell 6. Phone number 806 owned by `Adam` in cell 1, phone number 117 owned by `Lindsey` in cell 5, phone number 548 owned by `Cameron` in cell 2, and phone number 669 owned by `Terry` in cell 4.

By now, all elements are stored in an appropriate hash key; however, if we insert the 7th data into the hash table, a collision will occur, since phone number 722 owned by `Brynn` has 2 as the hash key, and it's exactly the same as phone number 548 owned by `Cameron`. To prevent the collision, we use linear probing, which increases the hash key of collision element, then performs modulo to it. In this case, we will get 3 as a new hash key ((2 + 1) % 7). Since cell 3 is still free, we can store phone number 722 owned by `Brynn` in that cell.

Next, for 8th until 10th data, they won't be stored in the hash table even if we perform the `Insert()` operation, since there is no free space anymore in the hash table. The illustration will be as follows:

0	[434, Dylan]
1	[806, Adam]
2	[548, Cameron]
3	[722, Brynn]
4	[669, Terry]
5	[117, Lindsey]
6	[391, Dominic]

Now, let's apply the `HashTable` ADT we built using the linear probing technique in the code to the phone number list we had at the beginning of this chapter. The usage of `HashTable` using the linear probing technique is quite similar to the one we built using the separate chaining technique. We will try all operations as shown in the following `main()` function:

```cpp
int main()
{
    cout << "Hash Table - Open Addressing - Linear Probe";
    cout << endl;

    HashTable * hashTable = new HashTable();

    // Check if hash table is empty
    bool b = hashTable->IsEmpty();
    if(b)
        cout << "Hash table is empty";
    else
        cout << "Hash table is not empty";
    cout << endl;

    // Adding a data then
```

```
// check if hash table is empty
cout << "Adding a data" << endl;
hashTable->Insert(434, "Dylan");
b = hashTable->IsEmpty();
if(b)
    cout << "Hash table is empty";
else
    cout << "Hash table is not empty";
cout << endl;

// Adding others data
hashTable->Insert(391, "Dominic");
hashTable->Insert(806, "Adam");
hashTable->Insert(117, "Lindsey");
hashTable->Insert(548, "Cameron");
hashTable->Insert(669, "Terry");
hashTable->Insert(722, "Brynn");
hashTable->Insert(276, "Jody");
hashTable->Insert(953, "Frankie");
hashTable->Insert(895, "Vanessa");

// Print the table
hashTable->PrintHashTable();

// Search key 669
// it should be found
int key = 669;
cout << "Search value for key ";
cout << key << endl;
string name = hashTable->Search(key);
if(name != "")
{
    cout << "Value for key " << key;
    cout << " is " << name;
}
else
{
    cout << "Value for key " << key;
    cout << " is not found";
}
cout << endl;

// Remove key 669
// then search the key
// it should not be found
cout << "Remove node of key ";
cout << key << endl;
hashTable->Remove(key);
```

```
        name = hashTable->Search(key);
        if(name != "")
        {
            cout << "Value for key " << key;
            cout << " is " << name;
        }
        else
        {
            cout << "Value for key " << key;
            cout << " is not found";
        }
        cout << endl;

        return 0;
    }
```

And if we build and run the preceding code in the `Hash_Table_OP_LP.cbp` project, we will see the following output in the console:

From the preceding output, we can see that the order of all elements in the hash table is exactly the same with our previous diagram. We can say that we have successfully performed a linear probing technique.

Since an open addressing technique just stores all elements in the hash table itself, we have to define the TABLE_SIZE equal to or greater than the total of inserted elements, unless there will be some elements that cannot be stored in the hash table. We can use separate chaining technique to store all element in hash table.

There are several other hash table data types that have better performance, such as perfect hashing, cuckoo hashing, and hopscotch hashing. If you are interested in learning about these hashing methods, you can check links in the *Further reading* section.

Summary

In this chapter, we have discussed another non-linear data type called a **hash table**. Although a collision can happen to the hash table data type, we have learned how to handle it by using a separate chaining technique or open addressing technique. Regarding the open addressing technique, it has three different kinds of handling—**linear probing**, **quadratic probing**, and **double hashing**; however, they are relatively similar in terms of the implementation, except for the way in which we find the next free slot if the hash key we need to insert has been occupied.

In the next chapter, we are going to discuss common algorithm paradigms to design algorithms specifically for a certain purpose.

QA section

- What is collision in a hash table?
- Specify techniques to handle collision in a hash table!
- Specify four basic operations in a hash table?
- How does we obtain hash key for each data?
- Why do we need hash table data type although we have already had others data type such as array, list, and linked list?

Further reading

For further references, please visit these following links:

- https://www.geeksforgeeks.org/hashing-data-structure/
- https://www.geeksforgeeks.org/implementing-hash-table-open-addressing-linear-probing-cpp/
- https://visualgo.net/en/hashtable
- http://qa.geeksforgeeks.org/4988/qa.geeksforgeeks.org/4988/what-is-perfect-hashing
- https://www.geeksforgeeks.org/cuckoo-hashing/
- https://github.com/Tessil/hopscotch-map

Implementation of Algorithms in Real Life

9

So far, we have learned how to construct data structures and implement sorting and searching algorithms. In this final chapter, we are going to discuss the implementation of algorithms in real life. Here are the algorithms we are going to discuss:

- Greedy algorithms
- Divide and conquer algorithms
- Dynamic programming
- Brute-force algorithms
- Randomized algorithms
- Backtracking algorithms

Technical requirements

To follow along with this chapter, as well as the source code you require the following:

- Desktop PC or Notebook with Windows, Linux, or macOS
- GNU GCC v5.4.0 or above
- Code::Blocks IDE v17.12 (for Windows and Linux OS) or Code::Blocks IDE v13.12 (for macOS)
- You will find the code files on GitHub at `https://github.com/PacktPublishing/CPP-Data-Structures-and-Algorithms`

Greedy algorithms

Greedy algorithms work in levels. At each level, a decision is made that appears to be good, without regard for future consequences. Generally, this means that some local optimum is chosen. The strategy **take what you can get now** is the basis for these types of algorithm. When these algorithms terminate, we hope that the local optimum is equal to the global optimum. If this is the case, then the algorithm is correct; otherwise, the algorithm has produced a sub-optimal solution. If the absolute best answer is not required, then simple greedy algorithms are sometimes used to generate approximate answers, rather than using the more complicated algorithms generally required to generate an exact answer.

Local optimum is an optimization problem technique to find an optimal solution (either maximal or minimal) within several candidate solutions. This is in contrast to a global optimum, which is the optimal solution among all possible solutions, not just those in several candidate solutions.

Solving the coin-changing problem

Suppose you are working at a cash counter at a theme park. There, you are provided all different types of coins available in infinite quantities. You have to find the minimum number of coins for making change. That's an illustration of a coin-changing problem.

Let's consider the U.S. currency, to provide change, we repeatedly dispense the largest denomination. Thus, to give out $17.61 in change, we give out a $10 bill, a $5 bill, two $1 bills, two quarters, one dime, and one penny. By doing this, we are guaranteed to minimize the number of bills and coins.

Let's analyze how coin changing works. To get the value for minimum coin change (let's call it `changingNominal`), we have to find the largest denomination that is smaller than or equal to `changingNominal`. After we find the denomination, we subtract `changingNominal` with the denomination. Repeat this process until `changingNominal` is 0. The following is the solution of the coin-changing problem in C++ programming:

```cpp
void MinimalChangeCoin(double changingNominal)
{
    // All denominations of U.S. Currency
    double denom[] =
        {0.01, 0.05, 0.10, 0.25, 1, 2, 5, 10, 20, 50, 100};
    int totalDenom = sizeof(denom) / sizeof(denom[0]);

    // Initialize result as a vector
```

```
vector<double> result;

// Traverse through all denomination
for (int i = totalDenom - 1; i >= 0; --i)
{
    // Find denominations
    while (changingNominal >= denom[i])
    {
        changingNominal -= denom[i];
        result.push_back(denom[i]);
    }

    // If there's no any denomination
    // that can be given just exit the loop
    if (changingNominal < denom[0])
        break;
}

// Print result
for (int i = 0; i < result.size(); ++i)
    cout << result[i] << " ";
cout << endl;
}
```

As we can see in the preceding `MinimalChangeCoin()` function, the function will find the minimum coin change for the given `changingNominal`. For the best time performance, we check whether there's still any denomination remaining in each denomination list iteration. If `changingNominal` is smaller than the smallest available denomination, we don't need to continue the iteration. By doing this, we can have $O(1)$ time complexity for the best case. However, we will have $O(N^2)$ time complexity for both the average and the worst cases where `N` is the number of the denomination. To apply the preceding `MinimalChangeCoin()` function, we can use the following `main()` function:

```
int main()
{
    cout << "Coin Change Problem" << endl;

    // Initialize the change nominal
    float change = 17.61;

    // Getting the minimal
    cout << "Minimal number of change for ";
    cout << change << " is " << endl;
    MinimalChangeCoin(change);

    return 0;
```

```
    }
```

If we build and run the preceding code we will see the following output on the screen:

```
◉ ◉ ◉   Terminal
Coin Change Problem
Minimal number of change for 17.61 is
10 5 2 0.25 0.25 0.1 0.01

Process returned 0 (0x0)    execution time : 0.003 s
Press ENTER to continue.
```

This algorithm does not work in all monetary systems, but fortunately, we can prove that it does work in the U.S. monetary system.

Applying the Huffman coding algorithm

One of the applications of the greedy algorithms is **Huffman coding**. Huffman coding is used in compression algorithm because it's a lossless data compression. It will convert input character into code. The most frequent character will have the smallest code and the least frequent character will be the largest code. The variable length codes assigned to input characters are prefix codes.

There are mainly two major parts in Huffman coding; building a **Huffman tree** from input characters and traversing the Huffman tree and assigning codes to characters.

To build a Huffman tree, we need a node type that can hold a character and a frequency of the character. We are going to use a priority queue as a minimum heap, we name the node type MinHeapNode, with implementation as follows:

```cpp
class MinHeapNode
{
    public:
        // Input character
        char Data;

        // Frequency of the character
        unsigned Frequency;

        // Left and right child
        MinHeapNode * LeftChild, * RightChild;

        // Constructor
        MinHeapNode(char data, unsigned freq)
```

```
        {
            // Initialize left and right child
            LeftChild = NULL;
            RightChild = NULL;

            this->Data = data;
            this->Frequency = freq;
        }
    };
```

Then, we build the priority queue to construct the Huffman tree.

 As we had discussed in `Chapter 7`, *Building a Hierarchical Tree Structure*, we can use priority queue as representing of tree.

We will build a function named `HuffmanCodes()` that will construct a Huffman tree by using the given data with the following implementation:

```
    void HuffmanCodes(char data[], int freq[], int dataSize)
    {
        MinHeapNode * left, * right, * top;

        // Create a min heap & inserts all characters of data[]
        priority_queue<MinHeapNode*, vector<MinHeapNode*>, compare>
         minHeap;

        for (int i = 0; i < dataSize; ++i)
            minHeap.push(new MinHeapNode(data[i], freq[i]));

        // Iterate while size of heap doesn't become 1
        while (minHeap.size() != 1)
        {
            // Extract the two minimum
            // freq items from min heap
            left = minHeap.top();
            minHeap.pop();

            right = minHeap.top();
            minHeap.pop();

            // Create a new internal node with
            // frequency equal to the sum of the
            // two nodes frequencies. Make the
            // two extracted node as left and right children
            // of this new node. Add this node
```

```
        // to the min heap '$' is a special value
        // for internal nodes, not used
        top = new MinHeapNode(
            '$', left->Frequency + right->Frequency);

        top->LeftChild = left;
        top->RightChild = right;

        minHeap.push(top);
    }

    // Print Huffman codes using
    // the Huffman tree built above
    PrintCodes(minHeap.top(), "");
}
```

Huffman encoding can be computed by first creating a tree of nodes using the following steps:

1. Creating a leaf node for each symbol and addding it to the priority queue.

2. If there is more than one node in the queue, remove the node of highest priority (lowest probability) twice to get two nodes. Please see the following compare function implementation we used in the preceding `priority_queue` instance:

```
class compare
{
    public:
        bool operator()(
            MinHeapNode * left,
            MinHeapNode * right)
        {
            return(
                left->Frequency > right->Frequency);
        }
};
```

3. Create a new internal node with these two nodes as children and with the probability equal to the sum of the two nodes' probabilities.

4. Add the new node to the queue as follows:

```
top = new MinHeapNode(
    '$', left->Frequency + right->Frequency);
```

5. The remaining node is the `root` node; the tree is complete.

As we can see at the end of the `HuffmanCodes()` function implementation, we have the `PrintCodes()` function traverse the tree then display the data to user. The implementation of the function is as follows:

```
void PrintCodes(MinHeapNode * root, string str)
{
    if (!root)
        return;

    if (root->Data != '$')
    {
        cout << root->Data << ": ";
        cout << str << endl;
    }

    PrintCodes(root->LeftChild, str + "0");
    PrintCodes(root->RightChild, str + "1");
}
```

There are two details that must be considered with Huffman coding. First, the encoding information must be transmitted at the start of the compressed file, since otherwise it would be impossible to decode. There are several ways of doing this.

For small files, the cost of transmitting this table would override any possible savings in compression, and the result will probably be file expansion. Of course, this can be detected and the original left intact. For large files, the size of the table is not significant. The second problem is that, as described, this is a two-pass algorithm. The first pass collects the frequency data, and the second pass does the encoding. This is obviously not a desirable property for a program dealing with large files.

To understand Huffman encoding, let's take an example. Suppose we have a file that contains only the characters a, e, i, s, t, plus blank spaces and newlines. Suppose further that the file has **10 A's**, **15 E's**, **12 I's**, **3 S's**, **4 T's**, **13** blanks, and **1** newline. The following table shows that Huffman Coding uses fewer bits:

Character	Code	Frequency
A	111	10
E	10	15
I	00	12
S	11011	3
T	1100	4
space	01	13
newline	11010	1

Throughout this section, we will assume that the number of characters is C. Huffman's algorithm can be described as we maintain a forest of trees. The weight of a tree is equal to the sum of the frequencies of its leaves. C−1 times, select the two trees, T1 and T2, of smallest weight, breaking ties arbitrarily, and form a new tree with subtrees T1 and T2. At the beginning of the algorithm, there are C single-node trees—one for each character.

At the end of the algorithm, there is one tree, and this is an optimal Huffman coding tree. A worked example will make the operation of the algorithm clear. In the following tree, the weight of each sub-tree is shown in small type at the root. The two trees of lowest weight are merged together, creating multiple trees. We will name the new root T1, so that future merges can be stated unambiguously. We have made the left child arbitrarily; any tie-breaking procedure can be used. The total weight of the new tree is just the sum of the weights of the old trees, and can thus be easily computed:

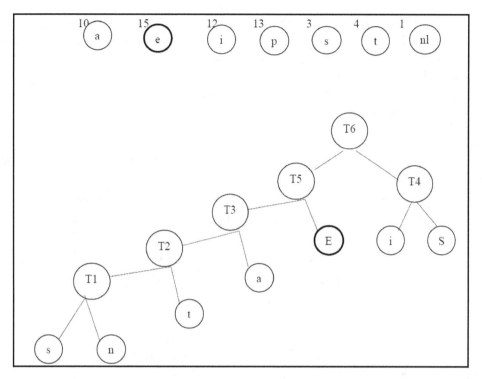

It is also a simple matter to create the new tree, since we merely need to get a new node, set the left and right pointers, and record the weight.

A simple implementation of the priority queue, using a list, would give an $O(C2)$ algorithm. The choice of priority queue implementation depends on how large c is. In the typical case of an ASCII character set, c is small enough that the quadratic running time is acceptable. In such an application, virtually all the running time will be spent on the disk I/O required to read the input file and write out the compressed version.

Divide and conquer algorithms

Another technique to design algorithms is **divide** and **conquer**.

The term *divide* shows that smaller problems are solved recursively—except, of course, base cases. The term *conquer* shows that the solution to the original problem is then formed from the solutions to the subproblems. You can think of a third part of this algorithm as *combine*. This combines the solutions to the subproblems into the solution for the original problem.

Traditionally, routines in which the text contains at least two recursive calls are called **divide and conquer algorithms**, while routines whose text contains only one recursive call and finally combines the solutions to the subproblems to solve the original problem. Because divide and conquer solves subproblems recursively, each subproblem must be smaller than the original problem, and there must be a base case for subproblems. We generally insist that the subproblems be disjointed; that is, be without overlapping.

We can easily remember the steps of a divide and conquer algorithm as *divide, conquer,* and *combine*. Here is how to view the steps of the algorithm, assuming that each divided step creates two subproblems:

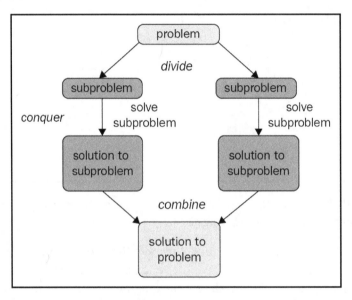

Some divide and conquer algorithms create more than two sub-problems. Because *divide* and *conquer* creates at least two subproblems, a divide and conquer algorithm makes multiple recursive calls. If we expand out two more recursive steps, result looks like this:

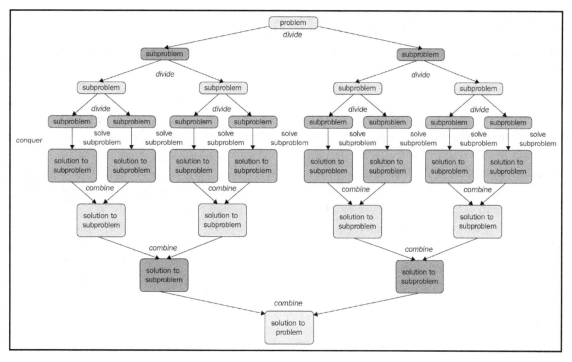

The following are some of the standard algorithms discussed in previous chapters that are Divide and Conquer algorithms:

- Binary Search is a searching algorithm. In each step, the algorithm compares the input element x with the value of the middle element in array. If the values match, return the index of middle. Otherwise, if x is less than the middle element, then the algorithm recurs for left side of the middle element; else, it recurs for right side of middle element.
- Quicksort is a sorting algorithm. The algorithm picks a pivot element, rearranges the array elements in such a way that all elements smaller than the pivot element move to left side of pivot, and all greater elements move to right side. Finally, the algorithm recursively sorts the subarrays on the left and right of the pivot element.
- Merge sort is also a sorting algorithm. The algorithm divides the array in two halves, recursively sorts them and finally merges the two sorted halves.

Here are some more examples of divide and conquer algorithm implementation solving selection problems and solving matrix multiplication.

Solving selection problems

The selection problem requires us to find the ith smallest element in a collection of S of n elements. Of particular interest is finding the median. This occurs when i = [n/2].

Although this algorithm runs in linear average time, it has a worst case of $O(N^2)$. Selection can easily be solved in *O(N logN)* worst-case time by sorting the elements, but for a long time it was unknown whether or not selection could be accomplished in *O(N)* worst-case time. The basic algorithm is a simple recursive strategy. Assuming that n is larger than the cutoff point where elements are simply sorted, an element v, known as the *pivot*, is chosen. The remaining elements are divided into two sets, S1 and S2. S1 contains elements that are confirmed to be no larger than v, and S2 contains elements that are no smaller than v. Finally, if i ≤ |S1|, then the ith smallest element in S can be found by recursively computing the kth smallest element in S1. If i = |S1|+1, then the pivot is the kth smallest element. Otherwise, the ith smallest element in S is the $(i - |S1| - 1)^{th}$ smallest element in S2. The main difference between this algorithm and quicksort is that there is only one subproblem to solve instead of two.

To get a good worst case, however, the key idea is to use one more level of indirection. Instead of finding the median from a sample of random elements, we will find the median from several subsets.

The basic pivot selection algorithm is as follows:

1. Arrange the N elements into N/5 groups of five elements, ignoring the (at most four) extra elements.
2. Find the median of each group. This gives a list M of N/5 medians.
3. Find the median of M. Return this as the pivot, v, then use as divider to get S1 and S2 sets as we discussed earlier.

We will use the term median of median of five partitioning to describe the quick select algorithm, which uses the pivot selection rule given. We will now show that median of five partitioning guarantees that each recursive subproblem is roughly 70% as large as the original.

Solving matrix multiplication calculations

A fundamental numerical problem is the multiplication of two matrices. The following is a simple $O(N^3)$ algorithm to compute C = AB, where A, B, and C are N×N matrices:

```
[A₁,₁ A₂,₂ ; A₂,₁ A₂,₂]  [B₁,₁ B₂,₂ ; B₂,₁ B₂,₂]  =  [C₁,₁ C₂,₂ ; C₂,₁ C₂,₂]
```

The algorithm follows on directly from the definition of matrix multiplication. To compute Ci, j, we compute the dot product of the ith row in A with the jth column in B. As usual, arrays begin at index 0. The C++ solution of the preceding problem is:

```cpp
void multiply(int A[][N], int B[][N], int C[][N])
{
    for (int i = 0; i < N; i++)
    {
        for (int j = 0; j < N; j++)
        {
            C[i][j] = 0;
            for (int k = 0; k < N; k++)
            {
                C[i][j] += A[i][k]*B[k][j];
            }
        }
    }
}
```

For a long time, it was assumed that $O(N^3)$ was required for matrix multiplication. But Strassen's algorithm improved this complexity. The basic idea of *Strassen*'s algorithm is to divide each matrix into quadrants. Then, it is easy to show that:

```
C₁,₁ = A₁,₁ B₁,₁ + A₁,₂ B₁,₂
C₁,₂ = A₁,₂ B₁,₂ + A₁,₂ B₂,₂
C₂,₁ = A₂,₁ B₁,₁ + A₂,₂ B₂,₁
C₂,₂ = A₂,₁ B₁,₂ + A₂,₂ B₂,₂
```

In the preceding formulas, we do eight multiplications for matrices of size N/2 x N/2 and 4 additions. The matrix additions take $O(N^2)$ time. If the matrix multiplications are done recursively, then the running time will be as follow:

```
T(N)  =  8T(N/2)  +  O(N²)
```

As usual, there are details to consider, such as the case when N is not a power of 2, but these are basically minor troubles. The *Strassen's* algorithm is worse than a simple $O(N^3)$ algorithm until N is fairly large. It does not generalize for the case where the matrices are sparse; that is, when they contain many zero entries. When run with floating point entries, it is less stable numerically than the classic algorithm.

Dynamic programming

By now, we have seen that a problem can be mathematically expressed recursively can also be expressed as a recursive algorithm, in many cases yielding a significant performance improvement over a more naive exhaustive search. Any recursive mathematical formula could be directly translated to a recursive algorithm, but the reality is that often the compiler will not do justice to the recursive algorithm, and an inefficient program will result. When we suspect that this is likely to be the case, we must provide a little more help to the compiler, by rewriting the recursive algorithm as a nonrecursive algorithm that systematically records the answers to the subproblems. One technique that makes use of this approach is known as dynamic programming.

Fibonacci numbers

We saw that the natural recursive program to compute the Fibonacci numbers is very inefficient. Here is the code to compute Fibonacci numbers in inefficient way:

```
long long fib(int n)
{
    if (n <= 1)
        return 1;
    else
        return fib(n - 1) + fib(n - 2);
}
```

It has a running time, T(N), that satisfies T(N) ≥ T (N−1) + T (N−2). Since T(N) satisfies the same recurrence relation as the Fibonacci numbers and has the same initial conditions, T(N) in fact grows at the same rate as the Fibonacci numbers and is thus exponential. On the other hand, since to compute F_N (Fibonacci number of N) all that is needed is F_N-1 and F_N-2, we only need to record the two most recently computed Fibonacci numbers. Please see the following fib2() function implementation:

```
long long fib2(int n)
{
    if(n <= 1)
        return 1;

    long long last = 1;
    long long nextToLast = 1;
    long long answer = 1;

    for(int i = 2; i <=n; ++i)
    {
        answer = last + nextToLast;
        nextToLast = last;
        last = answer;
    }

    return answer;
}
```

The reason that the recursive algorithm is so slow is because of the algorithm used to simulate recursion. To compute F_N, there is one call to F_N-1 and F_N-2. However, since F_N-1 recursively makes a call to F_N-2 and F_N-3, there are actually two separate calls to compute F_N-2. If one draws out the entire algorithm, then we can see that F_N-3 is computed three times, F_N-4 is computed five times, F_N-5 is computed eight times, and so on.

Dynamic programming and the coin-change problem

Given a value N, if we want to make changes for N cents, and we have an infinite supply of each of S = { S1, S2, .. , Sm} valued coins, how many ways can we make the change? The order of coins does not matter.

For example, for N = 4 and S = {1,2,3}, there are four solutions: {1,1,1,1}, {1,1,2}, {2,2}, and {1,3}. So, the output should be 4. For N = 10 and S = {2, 5, 3, 6}, there are five solutions: {2,2,2,2,2}, {2,2,3,3}, {2,2,6}, {2,3,5}, and {5,5}. So, the output should be 5.

To count the total number of solutions, we can divide all set solutions into two sets:

- Solutions that do not contain mth coin (or S_m)
- Solutions that contain at least one S_m

Let count (S[], m, n) be the function to count the number of solutions. S[] is the array of coins we have, m is the length of the array, and n is value we have as change. Then, it can be written as the sum of count (S[], m-1, n) and count (S[], m, n-Sm). Therefore, the problem has the optimal substructure property as the problem can be solved using solutions to subproblems. The implementation of the count () function will be as follows:

```
int count(int S[], int m, int n)
{
    int x, y;

    // Base case (n = 0)
    int table[n + 1][m];

    // Fill the enteries for 0 value case
    // (n = 0)
    for (int i = 0; i < m; ++i)
        table[0][i] = 1;

    // Fill rest of the table entries in bottom
    // up manner
    for (int i = 1; i < n + 1; ++i)
    {
        for (int j = 0; j < m; ++j)
        {
            //solutions count including S[j]
            x = (i - S[j] >= 0) ?
                table[i - S[j]][j] :
                0;

            //solutions count excluding S[j]
            y = (j >= 1) ? table[i][j-1] : 0;

            // total count
            table[i][j] = x + y;
        }
    }
```

```
    }

    return table[n][m-1];
}
```

The time complexity of the above solution for the coin change problem is $O(m \cdot n)$.

Brute-force algorithms

A brute-force algorithm consists of checking. For instance we have a text between 0 and n-m, whether an occurrence of a text pattern starts there or not. Then, after each attempt, it shifts the pattern by exactly one position to the right.

The brute-force algorithm requires no preprocessing phase, and a constant extra space in addition to the pattern and the text because we don't care about whitespace. During the searching phase, the text character comparisons can be done in any order. The time complexity of this searching phase is $O(m \cdot n)$ (when searching for am-1 b in an for instance). The expected number of text character comparisons is 2n. The brute-force algorithm requires n-1 multiplications. The recursive algorithm for the same problem, based on the observation that an = an/2 * an/2 requires $\Theta(\log(n))$ operations.

Brute-force search and sort

A sequential search in an unordered array and simple sorts—selection sort and bubble sort, for instance—are brute-force algorithms. In sequential search, the algorithm simply compares successive elements of a given list with a given search key until either a match is found or the list is exhausted without finding a match.

The complexity of a sequential search algorithm is $\Theta(n)$ in the worst possible case and $\Theta(1)$ in the best possible case, depending on where the desired element is situated.

In a selection sort, the entire given list of n elements is scanned to find its smallest element and replace it with the first element. Thus, the smallest element is moved to its final position in the sorted list. Then, the list is scanned again, starting with the second element, in order to find the smallest element among the $n - 1$ and exchange it with the second element. The second smallest element is put in its final position in the sorted list. After $n-1$ passes, the list is sorted.

The basic operation of a selection sort is the comparison A[j] < A[min]. The complexity of the algorithm is $\Theta(n2)$ and the number of key swaps is $\Theta(n)$. Bubble sort is another application of a brute-force algorithm. In the algorithm, adjacent elements of the list are compared and are exchanged if they are out of order.

The basic operation of the bubble sort is comparison A[j+1] < A[j] then swap A[j] and A[j+1]. The number of key comparisons is the same for all arrays of size n, and is $\Theta(n2)$. However, the number of key swaps depends on the input and in the worst case is $\Theta(n2)$. The preceding implementation of bubble sort can be slightly improved if we stop the execution of the algorithm when a pass through the list makes no exchanges (indicating that the list has been sorted). Thus, in the best case, the complexity will be $\Theta(n)$, and will be $\Theta(n2)$ in the worst case.

Strengths and weaknesses of brute-force algorithms

The strengths of using a brute-force approach are as follows:

- It has wide applicability and is known for its simplicity
- It yields reasonable algorithms for some important problems, such as searching, string matching, and matrix multiplication
- It yields standard algorithms for simple computational tasks, such as sum and product of n numbers, and finding the maximum or minimum in a list

The weaknesses of the brute-force approach are as follows:

- It rarely yields efficient algorithms
- Some brute-force algorithms are unacceptably slow
- It is neither as constructive nor as creative as some other design techniques

Randomized algorithms

A **randomized algorithm** is a technique that uses a source of randomness as part of its logic. It is typically used to reduce either the running time, or time complexity; or the memory used, or space complexity, in a standard algorithm. The algorithm works by generating a random number within a specified range of numbers and making decisions based on the value.

The algorithm could help in a situation of doubt by flipping a coin or a drawing a card from a deck in order to make a decision. Similarly, this kind of algorithm could help speed up a brute-force process by randomly sampling the input in order to obtain a solution that may not be optimal, but would be good enough for the specified purposes.

The algorithm is one that receives, in addition to its input data, a stream of random bits that it can use for the purpose of making random choices. Even for a fixed input, different runs of a randomized algorithm may give different results; thus it is inevitable that a description of the properties of a randomized algorithm will involve probabilistic statements:

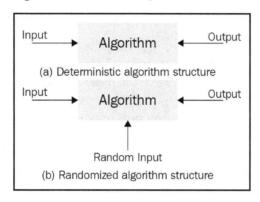

For example, even when the input is fixed, the execution time of a randomized algorithm is a random variable. Isolated examples of randomized algorithms can be traced back to the very early days of computer science, but the central importance of the concept became generally recognized only about 15 years ago. Among the key early influences was the randomized primality test developed by Solovay and Strassen. Randomized algorithms are used when presented with a time or memory constraint, and an average case solution is an acceptable output. Due to the potential erroneous output of the algorithm, an algorithm known as *amplification* is used in order to boost the probability of correctness by sacrificing runtime. Amplification works by repeating the randomized algorithm several times with different random subsamples of the input and comparing their results. It is common for randomized algorithms to amplify just parts of the process, as too much amplification may increase the running time beyond the given constraints.

Randomized algorithms for tasks such as sorting and selection gather information about the distribution of their input data by drawing random samples. For certain problems, it is useful to randomize the order in which the input data is considered; in such cases, one can show that, for every fixed array of input data, almost all orderings of the data lead to acceptable performance, even though some orderings may cause the algorithm to fail. In a similar way, randomized divide and conquer algorithms are often based on random partitioning of the input. Practically speaking, computers cannot generate completely random numbers, so randomized algorithms in computer science are approximated using a pseudorandom number generator in place of a true source of random number, such as the drawing of a card.

By now, it is recognized that, in a wide range of applications, randomization is an extremely important tool for the construction of algorithms. There are two principal types of advantages that randomized algorithms often have. First, often the execution time or space requirement of a randomized algorithm is smaller than that of the best deterministic algorithm that we know of for the same problem. But even more strikingly, if we look at the various randomized algorithms that have been invented. We find that invariably they are extremely simple to understand and to implement; often, the introduction of randomization suffices to convert a simple and naive deterministic algorithm with worst-case behavior into a randomized algorithm that performs well with high probability on every possible input.

Random algorithm classification

Randomized algorithms can be classified in two categories; they are:

- **Las Vegas**: These algorithms always produce correct or optimum result. The time complexity of this algorithms is based on a random value and time complexity is evaluated as the expected value. For example, randomized quicksort always sorts an input array and expected worst-case time complexity of quicksort is $O(N \ Log \ N)$.
- **Monte Carlo**: These algorithms produce correct or optimum result with some probability. These algorithms have deterministic running time and it is generally easier to find out the worst-case time complexity. For example, this implementation of Karger's algorithm produces minimum cut with probability greater than or equal to $1/n2$ (n is number of vertices) and has a worst-case time complexity of O (E). Another example is the Fermet method for primality testing.

Random number generators

Since our algorithms require random numbers, we must have a method to generate them. Actually, true randomness is virtually impossible to do on a computer, since these numbers will depend on the algorithm, and thus cannot possibly be random. Generally, it suffices to produce pseudorandom numbers, which are numbers that appear to be random. Random numbers have many known statistical properties; pseudorandom numbers satisfy most of these properties. Surprisingly, this is much easier said than done.

Suppose we only need to flip a coin; thus, we must generate a 0 (for heads) or 1 (for tails) randomly. One way to do this is to examine the system clock. The clock might record time as an integer that counts the number of seconds since some starting time. We could then use the lowest bit. The problem is that this does not work well if a sequence of random numbers is needed. One second is a long time, and the clock might not change at all while the program is running. Even if the time was recorded in units of microseconds, if the program was running by itself, the sequence of numbers that would be generated would be far from random, since the time between calls to the generator would be essentially identical on every program invocation.

We see, then, that what is really needed is a sequence of random numbers. These numbers should appear independent. If a coin is flipped and heads appear, the next coin flip should still be equally likely to come up heads or tails. The simplest method to generate random numbers is the linear congruential generator, which are x_1, x_2, ...

Here is the implementation of the Random class:

```
static const int A = 1;
static const int M = 10;

class Random
{
    private:
        int state;

    public:
        explicit Random(int initialValue = 1);

        int randomInt();
        double random0_1();
    int randomInt(int low, int high);
};

Random::Random(int initialValue)
```

```
    {
        if(initialValue < 0)
        initialValue += M;

        state = initialValue;

        if(state == 0)
            state = 1;
    }

    int Random::randomInt( )
    {
      return state = (A * state) % M;
    }

    double Random::random0_1( )
    {
      return static_cast<double>(randomInt()) / M;
    }

    int main()
    {
        return 0;
    }
```

Applications of randomized algorithms

We will now work on writing a program to generate **CAPTCHA** to verify the user. A **CAPTCHA (Completely Automated Public Turing test to tell Computers and Humans Apart)** is a test to determine whether the user is human or not. So, the task is to generate unique CAPTCHA every time and to tell whether the user is human or not by asking user to enter the same CAPTCHA as generated automatically and checking the user input with the generated CAPTCHA.

The set of characters to generate CAPTCHA are stored in a character array chrs[] that contains (a-z, A-Z, 0-9), therefore size of chrs[] is 62.

To generate a unique CAPTCHA every time, a random number is generated using rand() function(rand()%62), which generates a random number between 0 to 61. The generated random number is taken as index to the character array. chrs[] thus generates a new character of captcha[] and this loop runs n (length of CAPTCHA) times to generate CAPTCHA of given length.

Here is the implementation of C++ code for generating a CAPTCHA:

```cpp
string GenerateCaptcha(int n)
{
    time_t t;

    srand((unsigned) time(&t)); //all characters

    char * chrs = "abcdefghijklmnopqrstuvwxyzABCDEFGHI"
        "JKLMNOPQRSTUVWXYZ0123456789";

    // Generate n characters from above set and
    // add these characters to captcha.
    string captcha = "";

    while(--n)
        captcha.push_back(chrs[rand() % 62]);

    return captcha;
}
```

Backtracking algorithms

The last algorithm design technique we will examine is **backtracking**. As the name suggests, we backtrack to find the solution. We start with one possible move out of many available moves and try to solve the problem; if we are able to solve the problem with the selected move then we will print the solution, else we will backtrack and select some other move and try to solve it. If none of the moves work out, we will claim that there is no solution for the problem. In many cases, a backtracking algorithm amounts to a clever implementation of exhaustive search, with generally unfavorable performance. This is not always the case, however, and even so, in some cases, the savings over a brute-force exhaustive search can be significant.

The pseudocode, a notation resembling a simplified programming language, for this algorithm is as follows:

```
Pick a starting point.
while(Problem is not solved)
    For each path from the starting point.
        check if selected path is safe, if yes select it
        and make recursive call to rest of the problem

        If recursive calls returns true,
            then return true.
        else
            undo the current move and return false.
    End For

If none of the move works out, return false, NO SOLUTON.
```

Performance is, of course, relative; an $O(N^2)$ algorithm for sorting is pretty bad, but an $O(N^5)$ algorithm for the traveling salesman (or any NP-complete) problem would be a landmark result.

Arranging furniture in a new house

A practical example of a backtracking algorithm is the problem of arranging furniture in a new house. There are many possibilities to try, but typically only a few are actually considered. Starting with no arrangement, each piece of furniture is placed in some part of the room. If all the furniture is placed and the owner is happy, then the algorithm terminates. If we reach a point where all subsequent placement of furniture is undesirable, we have to undo the last step and try an alternative. Of course, this might force another undo and so forth. If we find that we undo all possible first steps, then there is no placement of furniture that is satisfactory. Otherwise, we eventually terminate with a satisfactory arrangement.

Notice that, although this algorithm is essentially brute force, it does not try all possibilities directly. For instance, arrangements that consider placing the sofa in the kitchen are never tried. Many other bad arrangements are discarded early because an undesirable subset of the arrangement is detected. The elimination of a large group of possibilities in one step is known as **pruning**.

Playing tic-tac-toe

Tic-tac-toe is a draw if both sides play optimally. By performing a careful case-by-case analysis, it is not a difficult matter to construct an algorithm that never loses and always wins when presented the opportunity. This can be done, because certain positions are known traps and can be handled by a lookup table. Other strategies, such as taking the center square when it is available, make the analysis simpler. If this is done, then by using a table we can always choose a move based only on the current position. The more general strategy is to use an evaluation function to quantify the *goodness* of a position. A position that is a win for a computer might get the value of +1; a draw could get 0; and a position that the computer has lost would get a −1. A position for which this assignment can be determined by examining the board is known as a **terminal position**. If a position is not terminal, the value of the position is determined by recursively assuming optimal play by both sides. This is known as a *minimax strategy*, because one player (the human) is trying to minimize the value of the position, while the other player (the computer) is trying to maximize it.

A successor position of P is any position, Ps, that is reachable from P by playing one move. If the computer is to move when in some position, P, it recursively evaluates the value of all the successor positions. The computer chooses the move with the largest value; this is the value of P. To evaluate any successor position, Ps, all of Ps's successors are recursively evaluated, and the smallest value is chosen. This smallest value represents the most favorable reply for the human player.

The most costly computation is the case where the computer is asked to pick the opening move. Since at this stage the game is a forced draw, the computer selects square 1. For more complex games, such as checkers and chess, it is obviously infeasible to search all the way to the terminal nodes. In this case, we have to stop the search after a certain depth of recursion is reached. The nodes where the recursion is stopped become terminal nodes. These terminal nodes are evaluated with a function that estimates the value of the position. For instance, in a chess program, the evaluation function measures such variables as the relative amount and strength of pieces and positional factors. The evaluation function is crucial for success, because the computer's move selection is based on maximizing this function. The best computer chess programs have surprisingly sophisticated evaluation functions.

The basic method to increase the look-ahead factor in game programs is to come up with methods that evaluate fewer nodes without losing any information. One method that we have already seen is to use a table to keep track of all positions that have been evaluated. For instance, in the course of searching for the first move, the program will examine the positions. If the values of the positions are saved, the second occurrence of a position need not be recomputed; it essentially becomes a terminal position. The data structure that records this is known as a **transposition table**; it is almost always implemented by hashing. In many cases, this can save considerable computation. For instance, in a chess end game, where there are relatively few pieces, the time savings can allow a search to go several levels deeper. Probably the most significant improvement one can obtain in general is known as **α–β pruning**.

Summary

In this chapter, we have discussed real-life applications of algorithms. We can solve a coin-change problem using the greedy algorithm. We can improve matrix multiplication time performance using the divide-and-conquer algorithm.

By using dynamic programming, we can improve the time complexity of Fibonacci number by removing the recursion. Also, we can see that selection sort and bubble sort, which we had discussed in a previous chapter, are brute-force algorithms.

Also, we have found that using a randomized algorithm could help in a situation of doubt, such as flipping a coin or drawing a card from a deck in order to make a decision.

Finally, we used a backtracking algorithm to arrange furniture in a new house or to play a tic-tac-toe.

QA section

- What is the best algorithm we can use to solve change-coin problems?
- Why is Strassen's algorithm better in multiplying a matrix?
- What is a simple example of backtracking algorithm?
- What algorithm do we use to generate CAPTCHA?

Further reading

For further reading, please visit the following links:

- https://www.geeksforgeeks.org/greedy-algorithm-to-find-minimum-number-of-coins/
- https://www.uscurrency.gov/denominations
- https://www.immihelp.com/newcomer/usa-currency-coins.html
- https://www.geeksforgeeks.org/greedy-algorithms-set-3-huffman-coding/
- https://www.geeksforgeeks.org/strassens-matrix-multiplication/
- https://www.geeksforgeeks.org/randomized-algorithms/

Other Books You May Enjoy

If you enjoyed this book, you may be interested in these other books by Packt:

C++ High Performance
Viktor Sehr, Björn Andrist

ISBN: 978-1-78712-095-2

- Benefits of modern C++ constructs and techniques
- Identify hardware bottlenecks, such as CPU cache misses, to boost performance
- Write specialized data structures for performance-critical code
- Use modern metaprogramming techniques to reduce runtime calculations
- Achieve efficient memory management using custom memory allocators
- Reduce boilerplate code using reflection techniques
- Reap the benefits of lock-free concurrent programming
- Perform under-the-hood optimizations with preserved readability using proxy objects
- Gain insights into subtle optimizations used by STL algorithms
- Utilize the Range V3 library for expressive C++ code
- Parallelize your code over CPU and GPU, without compromising readability

Mastering the C++17 STL
Arthur O'Dwyer

ISBN: 978-1-78712-682-4

- Make your own iterator types, allocators, and thread pools.
- Master every standard container and every standard algorithm.
- Improve your code by replacing new/delete with smart pointers.
- Understand the difference between monomorphic algorithms, polymorphic algorithms, and generic algorithms.
- Learn the meaning and applications of vocabulary type, product type and sum type.

Leave a review - let other readers know what you think

Please share your thoughts on this book with others by leaving a review on the site that you bought it from. If you purchased the book from Amazon, please leave us an honest review on this book's Amazon page. This is vital so that other potential readers can see and use your unbiased opinion to make purchasing decisions, we can understand what our customers think about our products, and our authors can see your feedback on the title that they have worked with Packt to create. It will only take a few minutes of your time, but is valuable to other potential customers, our authors, and Packt. Thank you!

Index

G

getline() 183
Greedy algorithms
  about 274
  coin-changing problem, solving 274, 276
  Huffman coding algorithm, applying 276, 279, 281

H

hash function 248
hash tables
  about 248
  collision handling 250
  data type, constructing 248
  data, storing in 249
  technical requirement 247
HashTable ADT
  applying, linear probing technique used 266
  applying, separate chaining technique used 256
Huffman coding algorithm
  applying 276, 280, 281
Huffman tree
  building 276

I

insertion sort 130, 132, 133, 135
integrated development environment (IDE)
  code development experience, enhancing 10
interface 32
interpolation search
  about 166
  applying 168
  developing 166

J

jump search algorithm
  about 169
  applying 171
  developing 170

K

keyword 37

L

Last In First Out (LIFO) 100
linear probing technique
  used, for applying HashTable ADT 266, 269
linear search algorithm
  about 158
  developing 158
  implementing 159
linked list
  about 69
  applying, with STL 91
List ADT
  building 56
  consuming 61
  index, searching from selected item 59
  item, fetching 58
  item, inserting into List class 58
  item, removing from List class 60
list
  about 56
  applying, with STL 91
loop statement 17, 20, 22

M

merge sort 135, 139, 141

N

node 63, 66, 68

O

one-dimensional array 56
open addressing technique
  double hashing 260
  implementing 259
  Insert() operation, developing 262
  IsEmpty() operation, developing 265
  linear probing 259
  linear probing technique, used for applying HashTable ADT 266
  PrintHashTable() operation, developing 266
  quadratic probing 260
  Remove() operation, developing 264
  Search() operation, developing 263

P

palindrome
  detecting 186
partitioning 141
pattern 201
pattern searching 201, 204
pivot 141
pop_back() 183
power set 196
predecessor
  about 218
  searching, of key in BST 220
pruning 296
push_back() 183

Q

Queue ADT
  building 109
  consuming 113
  element, inserting 111
  element, removing 112
  value, obtaining 110
quick sort algorithm 141, 143, 144

R

radix sort algorithm 150, 152, 154
rbegin() 183
recursive method 47
Regular Expression (RegEx) 201
rend() 183
randomized algorithm
  about 290, 292
  applications 294
  Las Vegas 292
  Monte Carlo 292
  random number generators 293
  random algorithm classification 292

S

selection sort 127, 128
separate chaining technique
  about 250
  hash key, generating 251

  implementing 250
  Insert() operation, developing 252
  IsEmpty() operation, developing 255
  Remove() operation, developing 254
  Search() operation, developing 253
  used, for applying HashTable ADT 256, 258
Singly Linked List
  building 69
  index, obtaining of selected item 74
  item, fetching in LinkedList class 70
  item, inserting in LinkedList class 71
  item, removing from LinkedList class 75
  LinkedList ADT, consuming 78
size() 183
skewed left 211
skewed right BST 211
Stack ADT
  building 100
  consuming 104
  example 105, 108
  item value, fetching 101
  popping 103
  pushing 102
Standard Template Library (STL)
  about 7, 40, 183
  used, for applying LinkedList 91
  used, for applying List 91
std list 94
std vector 91
string
  about 182
  constructing, as character array 182
  std string, using 183
sublist search algorithm
  about 175
  developing 175
  performing 177
subsequence string
  about 195
  checking 198
  subsequences, generating from string 196, 198
successor
  searching, in BST 218

CPSIA information can be obtained
at www.ICGtesting.com
Printed in the USA
LVHW101712210220
647795LV00006B/275